CULTURE IN ACTION

CULTURE IN ACTION

*Family Life, Emotion, and
Male Dominance in
Banaras, India*

Steve Derné

State University of New York Press

Published by
State University of New York Press, Albany

© 1995 State University of New York

For information, address the State University of New York Press,
State University Plaza, Albany, NY 12246

Production by Christine Lynch
Marketing by Dana E. Yanulavich

Library of Congress Cataloging-in-Publication Data

Derné, Steve, 1960-
    Cultures in action : family life, emotion, and male dominance in
    Banaras, India / Steve Derné.
        p.   cm.
    Includes bibliographical references and index.
    ISBN 0-7914-2425-1 (alk. paper). — ISBN 0-7914-2426-X (pbk. :
alk. paper)
    1. Family—India. 2. Marriage—India. 3. Marriage—Religious
aspects—Hinduism. I. Title.
HQ670.D46 1995
306.8′0954—dc20   94-18314
                                                                 CIP

10 9 8 7 6 5 4 3 2 1

CONTENTS

PREFACE

I interviewed North Indian Hindu men about women, marriage, and family to develop an understanding of how culture works. My analysis of these interviews suggests that one way of solving the tricky problem of how culture constrains is to focus on commonsense understandings of human motivation. By highlighting Hindu men's commonsense understanding that people are motivated by social pressures, I suggest that such understandings constrain individuals and affect their emotions, social life, and social institutions. While focusing on cultural constraint, I also consider how individuals manipulate cultural ideas to advance their own interests.

Cultural Constraint and Innovation

The dominant perspective in the social sciences has been that culture is shared and constraining (Stromberg 1986: 5). This book evaluates the power of this perspective. In what way is culture shared within a particular social group? Are some aspects of culture more shared than others? In what ways do different aspects of culture constrain the individual? How do individuals use a common culture to accomplish diverse goals?

I develop an approach to culture that focuses on how commonsense understandings constrain individuals and shape social life, by emphasizing three theoretical tools.

The Hindu men I interviewed largely—although not wholly—share an informal commonsense understanding of what motivates individual action. This distinctive *social framework for understanding action* is different from the dominant framework of American men. Unlike white, middle-class American men, who usually see actions as depending on the choices of autonomous individuals (Bellah *et al.* 1985; Varenne 1977), Hindu men understand individual actions as determined by the social group to which the individual belongs. While American men believe an individual's self-control can prevent antisocial action, Hindu men fundamentally distrust any individual action unrestrained by caste and family. A focus on how social frameworks for understanding action constrain individuals is an important contribution of this book.

Individuals use cultural ideas to invest actions with meaning. Because meaning does not inhere in cultural symbols themselves, I focus on *culture work*. A study of culture work considers how individuals manipulate cultural components to attribute meaning to action. My study of culture work asks the following questions: How do social frameworks for understanding action influence the culture work that people do? How does social position influence the ability to do culture work? What resources enhance the ability to successfully perform culture work?

Finally, following Ann Swidler (1986), I find it helpful to consider *strategies of action*. Individuals use particular strategies of action when embarking on unconventional actions that depart from their routine patterns of action. How do social frameworks for understanding action limit the strategies of action which individuals can use? Are people constrained by the strategies of action available in their cultural repertoire?

COMPARATIVE SOCIOLOGY

In anthropology, there has been an increasing interest in ethnopsychology—indigenous understandings of the psyche, mental processes, and human motivation (Lutz 1988; White and Kirkpatrick 1985; Heelas and Lock 1981). Sociologists, too, have a long tradition of focusing on understanding social action from the point of view of the social actor (see Derné 1994a: 268-270). Berger and Luckmann (1966: 15) argue, for instance, that the "sociology of knowledge" must focus on "what people 'know' as 'reality' in their everyday" lives because these commonsense notions constitute "the fabric of meanings without which no society could exist."

Frameworks for understanding action are an important part of any body of commonsense knowledge. All people, after all, need some way of understanding human motivation. This book focuses on the links between ethnopsychological understandings and other parts of social life by pursuing the following sorts of questions: Do ethnopsychological beliefs about human motivation shape emotions and psyche? Does Hindu men's framework for understanding action influence their family life? How does family structure shape implicit knowledge? Do frameworks for understanding action shape systems of social control or the nature of social movements?

INDIA

I am also trying to reveal something new about Indian Hindu men. My concern with indigenous understandings of the relationship between person and society has been of central concern in South Asian studies. While scholars have long recognized that Indians de-emphasize individual volition, few have focused, as I have, on how Indians see action as shaped by their social group (Roland 1988; Kakar [1978] 1981). Fewer still have recognized that Indians are frequently active agents who pursue their own private goals (Mines 1988; Béteille 1986). In contrast to scholars who focus on how Indians see individuals as guided by hierarchy (Dumont [1966] 1980), the abstract laws of *dharma* (Shweder 1991) or the diverse physical substances they encounter (Marriott 1989; Daniel 1984), I emphasize that while most Indians usually see themselves as guided by social pressures, some also follow their individual desires: They marry for love, separate from their families, and break caste rules and kinship ideology.

Why have some scholars found that Indians de-emphasize individual choices, while others have emphasized that Indians also sometimes follow their individual desires? Are ethnopsychological understandings contradictory and shifting? By answering these questions, I develop a fresh understanding of how Indians view the world, while suggesting that ethnopsychological understandings are usually complex and inconsistent.

GENDER INEQUALITY

I did not ask men about their family lives in order to examine implicit knowledge. This concern emerged from my analysis of the interviews. Rather, I hoped that by talking with men about their motives and desires, I might better understand how culture bolsters gender inequality, a theme I still pursue in this book.

Women's subordination in Indian society is bolstered by an oppressive gender ideology. In this book, I argue that a focus on the culture of the powerful is central to understanding the social construction of gender. I pursue the following sorts of questions: How do men use a gender ideology in their own interests? How is a particular gender ideology maintained as the dominant one? How do women respond to the dominant gender ideology? I argue that cultural ideas operate to benefit social groups that construct them, and suggest that ethnopsychologies may not be shared by both dominant men and subordinate women.

Hindu Gender Culture

Having outlined my main areas of concern, let me briefly describe the gender culture I am examining to get at these concerns. My purpose in doing this in the preface is to introduce the reader to the cultural terrain of Indian families, and to the four clusters of ideas and norms I examine in this book. For the moment, I will leave aside the question of how shared these ideas are.

First, most Hindu men say that they prefer to live in *joint families*. Most say that the ideal state of affairs is one in which parents live under one roof and share a common hearth with their sons, daughters-in-law, and grandchildren.

Second, most Hindu men prefer *arranged marriages*. Parents almost always arrange the marriages of their sons and daughters, often without giving the bride and groom even one chance to meet before the marriage. The men I interviewed use the English phrase "love marriage" to refer to marriages in which a bride and groom choose each other without parental input. Love marriages are uncommon and most men consider them dangerous and improper.

Third, Hindu men continue to *restrict women's activities outside the home*. Anthropologists report that in village India, men sometimes do not allow their wives and mature daughters to go outside the house at all. While most of the men I interviewed allow their wives to go outside the home in certain circumstances, all men restrict the time that their female relatives can spend outside the home and carefully monitor the demeanor and actions of women while they are outside the home.

Finally, Hindu men continue to *restrict contact between husband and wife*. Ethnographies report that the norm in many villages is for a husband and wife to avoid each other as much as possible during the day. While most of the urban men I interviewed do not require such strict limitations, most men still embrace some restrictions on interaction between husband and wife. Commonly, for instance, men consider it improper to speak with their wives in front of their parents.

Acknowledgments

In India, I was capably assisted by a number of talented research assistants and scholars. Nagendra Gandhi, Parvez Khan, and A. Ramchandra Pandit assisted me with arranging and conducting interviews. Awadesh Kumar Mishra, Nagendra Gandhi, and A. Ramchandra Pandit assisted me in translating the interviews into English. My Hindi interview schedule was improved by the comments of Virendra Singh.

Among those who provided practical support in India, I would like to thank Virabhadra Mishra, the *mahant* [head] of the Sankat Mochan Temple, Robert Thomas Wilson, Bhipul Charkraborty, Todd Nachowitz, and Nandu Lal Sahani. R.K. Nehru, Sharda Nayak, and O.P. Bhardwaj of the United States Educational Foundation in India helped in important ways. Joseph Alter, Purnima Bose, Cezary Galewicz, Jan Heiderer, Tony Heiderer, Nancy Kozor-Niggli, Philip Lutgendorf, Thomas Niggli, Reiko Ohnuma, Joseph Schaller, Karen Stetson, and Robert Thomas Wilson, among others, provided both intellectual stimulation and friendship, while they pursued their own research.

The United States Department of Education supported this research with a succession of Foreign Language and Area Studies fellowships to study Hindi, and with a Fulbright-Hays grant that funded the research itself. I would like to thank Nancy Plunkett and Mary Byrnes, capable grant administrators at the University of California, Berkeley.

It would be difficult to overstate the usefulness of the comments I received on drafts of this work from Arlie Hochschild and Ann Swidler, both of whom continually pressed me to think harder and to clarify my thoughts. Each of them contributed both substantially and editorially, and each suggested some of the nice turns of phrases I use in this book. Gerald Berreman, Kenneth Bock, and Hervé Varenne also read the whole manuscript at its dissertation stage, and made many important and useful comments. Mattison Mines's comments on a revised manuscript helped me turn it from a dissertation into a book. Others who commented on portions of the manuscript at some stage include André Béteille, Carol Copp, Claude Fischer, Morris Freilich, Lisa Jadwin, Grant Jones, Deniz Kandiyoti, Pauline Kolenda, Stanley Kurtz, Stanley Lieberson, Philip Lutgendorf, Catherine Lutz, McKim Marriott, Carol Mukhopadhyay, Charles Nuckolls, Bruce Pray, Lakhi Sabaratnam, Susan Seymour, Richard Shweder, and Margaret Trawick. I have especially benefitted from the comments of a number of anonymous readers.

I presented portions of this work in colloquia at the University of California, Berkeley, the University of Chicago, Colorado College, Cornell University, Davidson College, Florida International University, Hobart and William Smith Colleges, Indiana University, the University of Kentucky, Loyola University of Chicago, Nazareth College, the University of North Carolina at Charlotte, Occidental College, the University of Puget Sound, Rutgers University, SUNY—Geneseo, the Southern Illinois University at Carbondale, Temple University, the University of Vermont, Vassar College, and Wheaton College. I also presented portions of this work at various meetings of the Society for Cross-Cultural Research, the American Anthropological Association, the Association for Asian Studies, the American Sociological Association, the Pacific Sociological Association, the Eastern Sociological Society, and the Southeastern, New York, and Mid-Atlantic Regions of the Association for Asian Studies. The comments I received in those settings were also helpful.

I must also briefly mention the support I received for 1991 research on male filmgoers in Dehra Dun, India, that I discuss in chapter 5. Bharat Krishnamurthy assisted me in preparing the interview schedule and in translating scenes from *Maine Pyar Kiya*. Narender Sethi and Vimal Thakur assisted me in conducting and translating the interviews. The American Institute of Indian Studies funded the work with a senior research fellowship. The University of North Carolina-Charlotte and Hobart and William Smith Colleges assisted me in paying the administrative fee to the AIIS. Davidson College supported the study of Hindi films by providing funds for research assistance and the purchase of videotapes of Hindi films.

The fact that this book refers to my subsequent research reflects the fact that the process of turning this dissertation into a book was a long one. I am grateful for the encouragement offered by Lisa Jadwin, Jonathan Reider, Margaret Trawick, Peter Stromberg, Mattison Mines, Lawrence Cohen, Eugene Irschick, Eviatar Zerubavel, Magali Larson, Allan Grimshaw, Diane Harriford, Patricia Roos, Charles Nuckolls, Arlie Hochschild, Ann Swidler, Gerald Berreman, and Grant Jones.

Some portions of this book are recasting of materials already published in the form of articles. I am grateful to the American Anthropological Association for permission to reprint portions of "Beyond Institutional and Impulsive Conceptions of Self," *Ethos* vol. 20; to Peter Lang Publishing for permission to reprint portions of "Hindu Men's 'Languages' of Social Pressure and Individualism," *International Journal of Indian Studies* vol. 2; and to JAI Press for permission to reprint portions of "Hindu Men Talk About Controlling Women" *Sociological Perspectives* vol. 37, and "Structural Realities, Persistent Dilemmas, and the Construction of Emotional Paradigms," *Social Perspectives on Emotion*, vol. 2. Portions of chapters 3 and 7 were originally published in *Contributions to Indian Sociology*, vol. 26, no. 2. Copyright © Institute of Economic Growth, Delhi 1992—all rights reserved. Reproduced with the permission of the copyright-holder and the publishers, Sage, Publications India Pvt. Ltd., New Delhi.

A NOTE ON TRANSLITERATION AND PRONUNCIATIONS

I have used standard transliterating practices with a few exceptions. I have written as "sh" both the retroflex sibiliant (ṣ) and the palatal sibilant (ś). I have written the "c" as "ch," and the "ch," as "chh." I hope that this gives the non Hindi-speaker a better sense of how words are pronounced.

I have not transliterated proper names or film titles but have used common Anglicizations.

The vowels ā, ī, and ū are long and have approximately the same pronunciation as the vowels in the English words father, machine, and rule respectively. The vowels a, i, and u are short, and equivalent to the vowels in the English words cut, bit, and too respectively. The diphthongs, "e," "ai," "o," and "au" are pronounced like the vowels in the English words paint, kite, pole, and cow respectively.

The "ṭ," "ṭh," "ḍ," and "ḍh" are retroflex, while the "t," "th," "d," and "dh," are dental. The "kh," "gh," "jh," "th," "dh," "ph," and "bh" are aspirated consonants.

My conventions are adapted from Eck 1983, Babb 1987, and Basham 1954.

1

Studying Gender Culture in a
North Indian City:
Beyond the Image of Culture
as Shared and Constraining

Until recently, the dominant perspective in the social sciences has been that culture is shared by members of society and is a constraining force. More and more, however, scholars are recognizing that cultural elements are not shared, but are contested and negotiated by individuals and social groups. All cultures, it turns out, contain a diversity of conflicting stories, symbols, and meanings, which culture-users interpret in a variety of ways. Everywhere, the cultural beliefs that any person knows vary. Even the shared knowledge of cultural components, moreover, may not lead to similar actions.[1]

As Peter Stromberg (1981: 545) points out, the rejection of the idea of culture as shared has proved difficult to reconcile with the idea that culture "exert[s] some regular influence on the behavior of group members." If culture is negotiated and contested, how does it constrain people and shape social life? The problem of recognizing both human agency and cultural constraint is one that is increasingly occupying the attention of social theorists (Giddens 1984; Archer 1988; Brubaker 1985; Schudson 1989). In this book, I offer one approach to recognizing culture's powerful causal significance while also accepting that individuals are not "cultural dopes" (Swidler 1986: 277), but are actively involved in negotiating and contesting cultural norms and meanings.

I emphasize that individuals manipulate the available cultural repertoire for their own purposes, to invest meaning in their own diverse actions. Some of the men I interviewed marry for love, separate from their parents' households, and reject customary limitations on interactions with their wives. But I suggest that the culturally constructed understandings of motivation that I focus on nevertheless constrain even individuals who act unconventionally. Such frameworks for understanding action constrain individuals, and shape psyche and social life.

I went to India in November 1986 to uncover and analyze how one group of Indian men used their gender culture in diverse ways. Because I was interested in variations in the cultural ideas within a particular social group, I focused on men of common caste and class, interviewing 49 upper-middle-class, upper-caste men living in Bānaras, North India, over the course of the next year. I hoped to analyze how men share cultural ideas about gender, why they embrace these ideas, and how they use their common culture to pursue diverse goals.

THE PLACE

Banāras[2] is an important pilgrimage city of about one million people (Government of India 1985: 109). So sacred to Hindus that it is visited by millions of pilgrims each year (Eck 1983), Banāras bustles with business on its narrow streets and lanes. Even away from the city center, overcrowded buildings cluster tightly together separated only by narrow lanes.[3] The downtown streets are sometimes so crowded with bicycles, scooters, cycle rickshaws, autorickshaws, pedestrians, livestock, and the occasional bus that it is physically impossible to move even on foot (see also Lutgendorf 1987: 71).

Few will fail to be struck by the beauty of the city or its religious significance. The views along the great river Gangā (or Ganges) are magnificent and etched into the consciousness of many Indians. Bathing in the river is an important religious act, which Hindus come from all over India to perform. Recitations of religious texts broadcast over loud speakers in many of the city's temples pierce the morning calm, and Banāras's many great festivals and fairs give the city a special air (Eck 1983; Kumar 1988; Lutgendorf 1990).

Seventy-five percent of Banāras's residents are Hindus and nearly 25% are Muslims (Government of India 1971a: 16-17). Occasionally, as happened on a couple of occasions during my stay there, relations are tense between the two religious groups.[4] Thirteen percent of the population is made up of the scheduled (or untouchable) castes (Government of India 1971a: 16-17)—a percentage a bit lower than that of India as a whole (Mahar 1972: xxix).

As in many other parts of North India (Miller 1981), men outnumber women. In Banāras, there are only 84 women for every 100 men (Government of India 1985: 109). While the percentage of Banāras residents who are literate is increasing, literacy is still fairly low—32% overall, and women's literacy in Banāras is still one-third that of men (Government of India 1971b: 2-3).

THE PEOPLE

CLASS

The men I interviewed are upper-middle-class. Most of their families own such prized consumer items as televisions and motor scooters, and a few have telephone connections. Some of them give as much as

200,000 rupees dowry (about $15,000 in 1987) when their daughters marry. None of them, however, is upper-class. None owns an automobile or has been abroad.

OCCUPATION

Because I was interested in discovering variations within a particular group, I focused on a few occupations. I started by interviewing merchants, but expanded my net by interviewing some men who work in banks and post offices. Six of the 49 men I interviewed work in white-collar service, but nearly 40% had worked in white-collar service at some time, or had close relatives (fathers, sons, brothers) who did so.

WIVES' WORK

According to the census, only 3% of Banāras women are employed outside the home (compared with the 46% employment rate for men) (Government of India 1985: 742-743). While the census undercounts women who work in the informal economy as maids, vegetable vendors, and agricultural laborers (Standing 1991: 44), most upper-middle-class men probably do not allow their wives to work outside the home unless they are well-educated and can get jobs that pay well.[5] Since employed women are usually from families at the highest as well as at the lowest income levels (Standing 1991:29), it is not too surprising that none of the wives of the men I interviewed work outside the home. Still, a handful of the men I interviewed have *bhābhīs* [older brothers' wives] who work outside the home, and a few more say that they will allow their wives to work when their responsibilities for raising children diminish.

EDUCATION

The men I interviewed are literate and well-educated. Slightly more than half of those younger than 45 years of age have at least some college education, and roughly a quarter of those under 45 have completed high school. While none of the men over 45 attended college, more than a third are high school-educated.

CASTE

The men I interviewed are privileged by the caste system. All are caste Hindus, and all but four are of the twice-born castes.[6] Twenty are Brāhmaṇs, who are at the pinnacle of the caste system. Seventeen are

Vaishyas and eight are Kshatriyas, the other two twice-born *varṇa*. I also interviewed four Shūdras, all of whom are *ahīr*s, an upwardly mobile sanskritizing caste.[7] (*Ahīr*s are not untouchables.)

The Brāhmaṇs, Kshatriyas, and Vaishyas I interviewed are of various *jātī*s.[8] In order to identify each respondent's caste, I have given each member of each *varṇa* caste grouping a shared surname. Some, but not a majority, of the respondents actually had this surname. I have given all Brāhmaṇ respondents the surname Mishra, all Vaishya respondents the surname Gupta, all Kshatriya respondents the surname Singh, and all *ahīr* respondents the surname Yadav.

MEN'S POSITIONS IN JOINT FAMILIES

Most of the men I interviewed live in joint families. Eighty percent live in households with more than one married couple and about half live in households with three or more married couples. While joint-family living is more typical in the Banāras region than in other places in India (Kolenda 1987: 243), most Indians spend much of their lives in families with more than one married couple (Kolenda 1967: 386; Kakar 1981: 114; Rao and Rao 1982: 130-134). As I will describe in chapter 3, most men see joint-family living as providing emotional satisfaction and economic security.

The men I interviewed range from 20 to 75 years of age,[9] and represent various positions in joint and nuclear families. I interviewed 10 unmarried men, 21 men who live with their wives as junior members of joint families, 6 married men who head nuclear families, and 12 men who head joint families.[10] All 6 of the men who head nuclear families are over 35, and all had lived with their wives in joint families for much of their early married life. This range represents the cycle of a typical joint family. After spending the first years of married life in joint households, most men separate from their parents or brothers to spend some years in a nuclear family as their children grow. These men's families become joint once again when their own sons marry, bringing daughters-in-law into a household.

THE INTERVIEWS

I usually approached men at their place of business during the period of "rest" of early afternoon. Men's small shops are often gathering places for friends to share tea, *pān* [a betel leaf, spice, and lime-paste preparation], conversations, and laughter, especially during regular lulls of business, like early afternoon. These conversations were only occasionally interrupted when a shopkeeper needed to see to a customer.

I usually approached men when they were alone during times like early afternoon when business is slow.[11] I initially chatted with them about their family situations and about arranged marriages. We sometimes discussed the changing status of women, which is often debated in modern India. During these talks, men often had a child bring tea to share with me, and offered me *pān*. Men typically commented on the rarity of meeting a foreigner who was interested enough in Hindu culture to have learned Hindi, which they often insisted (exaggerating, I think) that I spoke very well. Eventually, I explained my position as a scholar and suggested that I would be interested in interviewing them to learn about their own ideas about joint-family living, arranged marriages, interactions with family members inside the home, and issues concerning women's position in India.

I conducted interviews in Hindi (the language spoken in Banāras) in men's shops, in their homes, and in my own home. The rate of refusals was extremely low (less than 15%), and with only a few exceptions, the people I interviewed enjoyed the experience.[12] Few men showed any reluctance to having the interview taped, and the presence of a research assistant did not seem inhibiting.[13]

One of my first dozen interviews was with Gopal Mishra. Gopal, 29, runs his family's small print shop, which is located in the crowded center of Banāras. His business prints business cards, wedding invitations, and the like. Gopal is an eldest son and lives nearby with his parents, wife, young child, and unmarried brothers and sisters. Like most, Gopal says that living in a joint family provides "happiness [*sukh*]" and financial security.

Gopal's shop is reminiscent of the print-shop described in R.K. Narayan's (1962) *Maneater of Malgudi*. In a tiny room in the front of the dark print shop is a large, wooden sitting platform on one wall, and several chairs against the facing wall. Friends, relatives, and customers often fill these sitting places. Gopal's father visits the shop regularly as do relatives who come to Banāras from surrounding villages. Tea and *pān* are often shared among friends. As is the case in nearly all of the business houses in which I conducted interviews, the room is decorated with a variety of pictures brought from the bazaar. Gopal's shop displays pictures of Shiva, Hanuman, Saraswati, Lakshmi and Durga, as well as a black and white photograph of Mahatma Gandhi.

I spoke with Gopal several times before I formally interviewed him. On the cold January afternoon in 1987 on which I conducted the interview, Gopal was wearing a blue *dhotī*, a shirt and sweater, and had wrapped a scarf around his head. Gopal has a lively face, and his laughter is engaging. Gopal sent for sugary milk tea from a nearby shop to warm us up several times during this initial interview. My research assistant sat on the wooden sitting platform near the door, smoking *bīḍī*s and gradually was forgotten for most of the interview, although he did ask a number of perceptive questions near the end.

As in each interview, I began by telling Gopal that I was interested in his own ideas, not those of society and not the common ideas. I base my conclusions on taped interviews with 49 respondents like Gopal. In the structured, but still open-ended interview, Gopal told me about the advantages and disadvantages he found in joint-family living, and about his attitude toward arranged marriages and love marriages. He told me what he thought about women going outside the home, and about his own relationships with his wife and other family members within a joint family. Wherever possible, I asked Gopal to tell me about his own experiences with marriage, with joint-family living, and with a wife and sisters who sometimes moved about outside the home.[14]

Gopal spoke with enthusiasm, and sometimes with passion. He usually spoke with conviction, although he was also unsure of himself when discussing some topics. Like many, he commented that he tried to answer all of my questions and to open up his heart. The interview lasted for an hour, but we talked for another two hours after the interview, as I answered Gopal's questions about America. On another day, I interviewed Gopal's father, Lakanlal Mishra, and I returned 5 months later during the hot season to interview Gopal about wedding ceremonies, honor, and the epic Rāmāyaṇa—follow-up interviews I conducted with each of my married Brāhmaṇ respondents who lived with their parents as junior members of a joint family.

FINDING VARIATION

Interviews with 49 men of different ages and living in different situations in joint and nuclear families reveal variations in their ideas about women, families, and marriages. Consideration of these variations is an important part of this book. Which men are more likely to reject dominant cultural ideas? What culture work are they forced to do when they reject these ideas? Why is there more consensus about some ideas than about others?

Variations in ideas about what constitutes proper husband-wife relationships proved fairly common. While most men believe, like Gopal, that "too many contacts" between husband and wife are "very harmful for the joint family," many others insist, instead, that any limitation on contacts between husband and wife would be "unfathomable," to use the words of one married 47-year-old. Men are more likely to share ideas about the desirability of joint-family living, women remaining inside the home, and arranged marriages. Gopal, for instance, takes the stance that a love marriage could never succeed "because everyone will see it as a love marriage." Yet, an occasional man expressed his disagreement with these cultural norms as well. One married 25-year-old says, for instance, that arranged marriages only cause a "big mental heat in the heart of men."

SHARED MEANINGS

In addition to learning about these variations, and about the culture work men do to bolster and to reject dominant cultural ideas, I slowly recognized a largely shared vocabulary centering on a concern with honor. Gopal Mishra hints at this concern with honor when he comments that a love marriage faces difficulty because "everyone will see it as a love marriage." This concern with honor, with how others see action, is a manifestation of an understanding of human motivation and social control, which is different from the dominant understanding of middle-class American men, and which I only learned about gradually. The shared vocabulary focusing on honor and tradition suggests men's implicit distrust of individual actions which are not controlled by larger social groups.

One way I came to recognize the importance of this collectivist framework for understanding action was through my own interactions in the neighborhood I shared with slightly more than half of the men I interviewed. Instances that were originally bewildering alerted me to the existence of such an understanding shared by my respondents but not by me. I was surprised when a near-stranger approached me on the street to complain about the behavior of the blind musician who unlocked the front gate of the building where I lived. It seemed to me that the person should approach the blind man directly. It also seemed strange to me when neighbors warned me of the improper dishonoring behavior of other neighbors, insisting, for instance, that I should not speak with a young man who had been thrown out of his parents' house for fighting with his wife. But I gradually learned that this sort of gossip reflects a particular understanding of the relationship between the individual and society, an understanding which holds that the individual must be everywhere controlled by larger social groups. It is this distinctive understanding that I came to focus on as an important element of culture that constrains individuals.

STUDYING CULTURE

Culture is the machinery which individuals use, as Clifford Geertz ([1966] 1973b: 363) puts it, "to orient themselves in a world otherwise opaque," to make sense of actions they see around them. As C. Wright Mills ([1959] 1963) argues, culture is the "lens" through which people see the world.

CULTURAL COMPONENTS

Culture is an apparatus for understanding, which includes two important elements. First, culture includes the cultural components of what Ann Swidler (1986) calls a tool kit. These cultural components include values, tales, and key symbols. They include the meanings found in cultural products like movies, religious performances, and works of literature.

Individuals often know cultural components without embracing them; they regard some as authoritative guides to action and others as meaningless entertainment; and they may interpret existing values or stories in diverse ways.[15] They know, moreover, that even their most cherished practices are culturally constructed. For instance, the men I interviewed hold firmly to the belief that marriages should be arranged by the parents of the bride and groom, but they also believe that among certain groups in India love marriages are common. They know that in the United States, marriages are not arranged by the parents of the bride and groom. While they insist that it is right and proper for marriages to be arranged, they know that the practice of arranging marriages is not part of the natural world, but is a distinctive part of Hindu culture.

Most critiques of the conception of culture as shared and constraining have focused on cultural components like values, norms, symbols, and cautionary stories. My focus is instead on commonsense, but nonetheless, cultural understandings of human motivation.

COMMONSENSE CULTURAL UNDERSTANDINGS

A second aspect of culture consists of people's implicit, commonsense understandings about what determines individual actions, what constitutes individuals, and what controls individuals' anti-social impulses. People attach meanings to events not merely through the tool kit of cultural components but through these implicit commonsense understandings of the world.[16] Such understandings are what Mary Douglas (1982b:1) calls the "perceptual controls" through which "anything whatsoever that is perceived at all must pass."

As Douglas (1982b:1) recognizes, these perceptual controls are not "a private affair." Instead, the processes of perception by which only some things are admitted into consciousness are "largely cultural."[17] Some, like anthropologist David Schneider (1976: 202-3), see such commonsense understandings as the most central part of culture: "Where norms tell the actor how to play the scene, culture tells the actor how the scene is set and what it all means."

Although both the cultural components of a tool kit and informal commonsense understandings are cultural constructions, people usually do not self-consciously recognize informal commonsense understandings of self and human motivation as social products. When individuals are aware of these commonsense understandings, they tend to regard them not as cultural constructions, but as simply the way things are, as something anyone in his or her right mind should know.[18]

Catherine Lutz (1988: 83) refers to the sorts of "cultural constructions of particular persons" and of "human nature" that I am discussing as "ethnopsychological knowledge systems." Anthropologists have developed a productive research tradition examining ethnopsychology—indigenous understandings of psychological functioning—while sociologists continue to study indigenous understandings of the individual's relationship to larger communities.[19] My focus on commonsense conceptualizations of human motivation is part of these traditions of research. I bring the focus on ethnopsychology to bear on important causal questions in anthropology and sociology: Are commonsense understandings widely shared? How do they constrain individuals? How do they shape social life?

I focus attention on *social frameworks for understanding action*—commonsense understandings of why people act the way they do. Swidler (1986: 276) argues that in the Protestant West action is "assumed to depend on the choices of individual persons" (see also Bellah *et al.* 1985; Varenne 1977; chapter 7). Even "collective action," she says, is "understood to rest on the choices of individual actors." Most of the Hindu men I interviewed understand individual actions not as the result of individual choices but as a simple reflection of the group—family, caste, or religion—to which the individual belongs. They see action as driven by social pressures.

I argue that frameworks for understanding action are a particularly constraining element of culture, which limit the strategies individuals can use, even when they act unconventionally. The constraining power of social frameworks for understanding action is greater (although its dictates less precise) than the constraint of any cultural component.

METHODOLOGY: INTERVIEWING 49 MEN

A FOCUS ON MEN

My methodological choices have both important advantages and significant limitations. I decided not to systematically interview women in the families of the men I interviewed because of my theoretical focus and because I took seriously my respondents' statements that speaking with their wives would harm their families' honor.[20] In chapter 6, I examine women's responses to the gender culture that oppresses them by considering ethnographies done by female anthropologists and the journalism of Indian feminists. Since I did not interview women in the community I studied, however, my work remains limited by its focus on men. While I know, for instance, why men say that they restrict their wives' movements outside the home, I can't know for sure how upper-caste, upper-middle-class Banārasī women feel about these restrictions, Do they embrace them? Do they enforce them? Do they resent them? Do they buck them?

But my focus on men's perspective of gender issues has its own advantages, as well. Rather than examining variations between men and women, I focus on analyzing how men use a common culture in diverse ways. Moreover, as I show in the next chapter, my focus on men allowed me to see how men's perceptions of their own gender interests drive their interactions. Only by talking with men in a private setting could I expect to begin to understand men's conscious interests and desires.

RELIANCE ON INTERVIEWS

Second, I chose to base this book more on interviews than on participant observation. While I did observe interactions in several homes, my work is limited by its reliance on what men told me. Just as participant observation may not accurately reveal the inner thoughts and feelings of individuals, interviews may not accurately reveal how people act in their daily lives. Still, one reason for confidence in my findings is the

broad consistency between what men told me about family life and conclusions based on more ethnographic fieldwork. A more important problem is that focusing on interviews may obscure the larger context in
which people live their lives. The men I interviewed may focus on
restricting their wives to the home precisely because some women are
challenging the restrictions that have been placed on them. My focus on
individual men gives inadequate attention, then, to how men are
responding to larger changes in India today.

Private, personal interviews are nonetheless a useful methodology
for studying the commonsense understandings, emotions, and subtle
rebellions that I focus on. First, much of my work analyzes men's
unselfconscious use of emotion words and their taken-for-granted understandings of human motivation. This analysis focuses not on men's
overt points about marriage, family, and gender, but rather on the
assumptions they make in talking about emotions and why people act
the way they do. While it would be desirable to study men's naturalistic
talk in their day-to-day lives to confirm my findings, the implicit
assumptions about human motivation and emotions that I analyze are
probably equally apparent in interview situations.

Second, private interviews may be the only way to reveal some of
the critical stances men take toward dominant cultural norms—especially in a context where honor demands outward conformity. For
instance, some of the men I interviewed say that, while they have to try
to maintain the appearance of acting according to established norms,
they are actually working to subvert social rules. While people's public
actions and statements in their day-to-day life may be driven by the
need to cultivate public approval, then, private interviews allow people
to talk about hidden motives and strategies for attaining their goals.

Third, interviewing people is a particularly useful way of understanding people's motives. Only by using private interviews could I
gain access to men's conscious reasons for restricting women to the
home. The fact that I am a male outsider may have encouraged men to
be particularly frank about their sometimes sexist motives. Because I am
an outsider, men didn't need to concern themselves with maintaining
their honorable place within their community by offering acceptable
explanations of their motivations.[21] While they talked about honor, they
also talked of the self-interested reasons they have for restricting
women. Furthermore, my insider status as a man may have encouraged
men to discuss their sexist views openly. Nita Kumar (1992) reports
that to interview male informants in Banāras, she had to present herself
as a sister, public worker, or writer. While this was not a disadvantage
for Kumar's (1988) study of popular culture, men would probably hes-

itate to discuss their interest in subjugating women to a woman whom they saw in these roles. In-depth interviews with a male outsider, then, may be one of the best ways to reveal men's self-interested motivations.[22]

QUESTIONS OF REPRESENTATIVENESS

How representative are the men I interviewed? The ethnopsychology and gender culture of the men I interviewed are likely to be common among upper-middle-class, upper-caste male Hindu merchants living in North Indian cities in the Hindi-speaking region. It is possible, moreover, that the ideas of the men I studied are fairly widespread. As I show in chapters 2 and 3, the ethnopsychology and gender culture I describe are broadly consistent with the descriptions of others who have investigated these topics among urban and rural men in other parts of India. While the ideas of the men I interviewed may be broadly similar to other upper-caste, upper-middle-class Hindu men in India, these ideas should not be attributed to women, lower-caste Hindus, Muslims, poor Indians, South Indians, or villagers. Indeed, there is good evidence that women and lower-caste Hindus may have quite different orientations (see chapter 3).

OUTLINE

In the next chapter I suggest how cultural ideas may be a tool of the powerful by examining how the men I interviewed construct gender culture to bolster male dominance. In chapter 3, I explore men's "first language," which holds that individuals are driven by social pressures. In chapter 4, I examine how this framework for understanding action affects Hindu men's psyche, including their emotions.

While the collectivist framework for understanding action is important, it is not the only understanding which Hindu men can access. In chapter 5, I examine Hindu men's "second languages" which emphasize the individual. In chapter 6, I consider the range of stances women and men take to the reality of social pressure. While many men and some women are true believers who think they should be guided by social pressures, many others try to escape the consequences of dishonor. In chapter 7, I focus on the culture work that men do when they buck social pressure by marrying for love, separating from their families, or becoming close to their wives. My discussion of men's and women's dissatisfactions with and rebellions against gender culture suggests that

the emphasis on social guidance is often challenged by Indians themselves. In chapter 8, I consider why some men break social norms, while
others conform.

In chapter 9, I examine how joint-family living, the collectivist
framework for understanding action, and men's emotion culture mutually constitute each other. In chapter 10, I consider how the collectivist
framework for understanding action shapes social movements and social
institutions, and draw general conclusions about how a focus on frameworks for understanding action improves our understanding of cultural
constraint.

2

Making Gender Culture:
Men Talk About Controlling Women

One reason that 35-year-old R.P. Mishra embraces joint-family living, arranged marriages, and restrictions on women's movements outside the home is that he believes these practices insure that Indian wives will faithfully obey their husbands, and diligently cook and clean within the home. R.P., who lives with his parents and his wife and children, says that if a husband and wife live separately from the joint family "both will always be fighting" about "who will go outside and who will look after the children." College-educated and working in a white-collar service job, R.P. recognizes that in today's "very advanced society [English]" women often work outside the home alongside men. R.P. says that women who can get the right kind of work should work outside, but he also insists that, because the husband is superior to his wife, he must always be her boss [*mālik*][1]: "For a wife to work, the husband must give permission." When R.P.'s wife interrupts the interview to serve us tea, she jokes that she is demonstrating the benefits of an Indian marriage. Using English, R.P. agrees: "I have spoken," he says, "and the tea has become ready."

Feminist scholars have shown that Hindu gender ideologies bolster male power and subjugate women.[2] In this chapter, I show that one reason men embrace arranged marriages, joint-family living, restrictions on women's movements outside the home, and limitations on interactions between husbands and wives is that they believe these practices help maintain male privilege by making women docile, obedient servants in their husbands' families.

Too often, scholars' emphasis on how social structural factors shape gender culture neglects the agency of individuals. Sharma (1978) argues, for instance, that women's subordinate economic position generates Hindu gender ideology; Douglas (1966, 124-5) argues that ideas about women are an expression of upper-caste groups' need to protect their boundaries (see also Ganesh 1989); and psychoanalytically oriented scholars argue that Indian family structure shapes gender culture (Kakar 1981; Obeyesekere 1984; Carstairs 1957). Yet, a focus on structural characteristics of societies should not obscure the interests of social actors (Homans 1964: 810). Structures don't act; people do (Collins 1987: 195). Gender culture is constituted by the talk and other social practices of common people. While these practices are constrained by

larger structures, it is vital to understand how gender culture is constituted and reconstituted through interaction at the micro-level.

Some scholars have devoted attention to how women influence
Hindu gender culture. As they encounter gender culture, women use it,
and find that it assists or impedes them as they try to achieve their
objectives.[3] In chapter 6, I review studies which suggest that women
take diverse stances toward gender culture, some of which bolster it
and some of which contest it. First, some studies suggest that some
women embrace dominant gender ideologies. These studies suggest
that some women support restrictions on women, believing that these
restrictions provide protection, honor, and security.[4] Second, some studies suggest that some women reinforce gender norms as they struggle to
advance their security in their families. To protect her authority in a
joint family, an older woman may try to limit her daughter-in-law's
influence by demanding that her son limit his attachment to his wife,
reconstituting limits between husbands and wives.[5] To cultivate an ally
in her family, a young wife may try to become close to her husband by
acting docile and obedient, reconstituting the ideology that makes
women subservient to men (see chapter 6; Bennett 1983: 176). Third,
some studies suggest that some women feel isolated and subordinated by
the restrictions they face, but may be unable to do anything about their
situation.[6] Finally, some studies suggest that some women openly subvert gender expectations. For instance, Hindu women's songs often take
a critical stance toward the dominant gender culture (Raheja and Gold
1994), and some women actively challenge the restricted role imposed
upon them.[7]

At the end of this chapter, I briefly consider how women's interests
may drive some women into a "bargain with patriarchy" (Kandiyoti
1988) that unwittingly contributes to the maintenance of Hindu gender
categories, but my main aim is to focus attention on how men confront
dominant ideas about gender.[8] Embracing the feminist argument that
women's subordinate position is imposed by men,[9] I describe here how
men are active agents who bolster Hindu gender culture in order to support their own dominance.

JOINT-FAMILY LIVING AND ARRANGED MARRIAGES AS A WAY MEN CONTROL WIVES

Like urban and village Hindus throughout North India, the men I interviewed say that the ideal state of affairs is for a young man to live harmoniously under one roof with his wife, parents, and brothers.[10] As I

show in the next chapter, men who live in joint families feel comfortably guided by elders. But men also emphasize that by living in a joint family they feel confident that these same elders will control their wives.

Twenty-four-year-old Prem Singh earns a living by repairing radios, and operating a retail shop that sells light bulbs and parts for electric equipment like radios and fans. Prem likes to wear fashionable white clothes, and enjoys roaming [*ghūmnā*] through Banāras's narrow lanes. His marriage has just been arranged, and Prem says that after he marries he will continue to live with his parents so that he can support them:

> My parents have given me birth and until now they have looked after me. When I was born, I couldn't take care of myself. . . . The final stage will come and my parents will become old. Their bodies will become weak, and they will need to be fed and taken care of. Being young, both my wife and I will be able to serve my parents.

While serving his parents is his main motive, Prem also hopes that by living in a joint family he will be better able to control his wife. "If I live in a joint family," he says, "my wife will not be able to go anywhere alone."

Marital plans are also being made for Surjit Singh, a 33-year-old, who also says that he will continue to live with his parents and brothers after he marries. Surjit feels that the biggest difficulty of living separately is that one's wife will be vulnerable outside the home:

> [When a woman goes out], it is possible that a bad person may attack her with a look of doubt. Difficulties come up whenever she goes to the market. Because women are physically weak, someone might snatch money from her. This is the problem with living separately. In a joint family, women do not have to bother about these problems.

While both Surjit and Prem focus on protecting women from danger, both also emphasize how joint-family living effectively controls women. "If the marriage is through the parents and we live in a joint family," Surjit says, "the influence of [the wife's] father, [the husband's] father, and the whole joint family is on the woman. The woman is kept down [*dābnā*] a little from all sides."

Many men emphasize that such joint-family control keeps a woman from fighting with her husband. Ravi Mishra is an unmarried 24-year-old who operates a small store that sells cassettes of popular Hindi film music. Ravi, who intends to continue living with his older brother and *bhābhī* [older brother's wife] after he marries, says that if a young husband and wife live outside the joint family, their fighting "will never be tamed, but rather increases." By contrast, Ravi says that if husband and wife live with the husband's parents,

the parents come between them and hold down any fight that may
happen. Or for several days they may send their son outside or send the
girl back to her parents' house. Because of this, fighting [between husband and wife] happens rarely.

On several occasions during my stay in Banāras, neighbors told me of
families who had sent a young wife back to her parents' household to
bring her more firmly under the family's control (see also Minturn
1993: 315).

Men believe that such family pressures can only work to control a
wife if the marriage has been arranged by the couple's parents. An
arranged marriage allows the husband's parents to enlist the wife's parents to control their daughter. Vikas Mishra, 35, supports his mother,
wife and children, and younger brother and his family by operating an
electrical repair shop. One day that I visited Vikas, he was commiserat-
ing with a friend whose mother had died only nine days before. As they
smoked marijuana, they lamented that a family could run without a
father, but not without a mother. Vikas is very close to his mother, but
he wants his wife to be closely watched. Like Surjit Singh, Vikas Mishra
thinks that when marriages are arranged, a wife will live in a joint-family where she can be closely controlled:

> If a woman lives in her husband's family, she remains living under the
> society. She lives in the proper [kāydā] way; she does not run away;
> she does not go here and there; she will not do her own mind's work.
> She lives under pressure [dabāv]. If the [husband's] parents are there,
> and if she does any bad work, then they give her a lecture: "Daughter,
> don't do this thing!"

The framework for understanding action I will describe in the next
chapter is apparent in Vikas's statement: "Doing one's own mind's
work" is condemned; living under social pressure is praised. But Vikas,
like Ravi, Surjit, and Prem, uses this dominant first language of bowing
to social pressure to further his own interest in controlling his wife.

LIMITING INTERACTIONS BETWEEN HUSBAND AND WIFE

Hindu gender culture's insistence that interactions between husbands
and wives be limited restricts a young wife's influence in her husband's
family. The idea that the relationship between husband and wife must be
limited is part of the cultural landscape in Hindu India—everyone knows
about these limitations and believes that they were strictly followed in
some hazy past. K.K. Mishra is a married 30-year-old whose prosperous

shop has provided him with a comfortable home. A member of the Communist Party of India, which is in power in the neighboring state of West Bengal, K.K. nonetheless decorates his home with a picture of then Prime Minister, Rajiv Gandhi of the Congress (I) party. K.K., whose family includes his wife and children, mother, and younger brother and his family, says that, while today "contact [between husband and wife] remains limited,

> in the past, contact was very limited. Fifty years ago, the husband of a mother with four children could not look his wife in the face. Before, there was much shame in India. . . . The husband went to meet his wife fearfully at 11 o'clock at night and came back quickly in the morning. Because there was no electricity in the villages, the husband could not even see his wife's face at night. In the daytime, they had to stay apart. They did not like people to see them mixing with their wives. But now it has become very popular for people to go out with their wives.

Ramesh Mishra, a 35-year-old eldest son who married for love and who still lives with his parents and brothers, similarly contrasts present freedoms with past restrictions:

> Before, relations were very limited, but now it is slowly changing. Before, they could not talk between themselves, and could meet only at night. But now there is no such thing. We got married and have a separate room. We can talk at night and in the daytime, too. We can move around [ghūmnā]. Nobody is standing against you.

Men believe that limitations have long been an important part of Hindu culture, and they construct their relationships with their wives with this in mind.

Ramesh and K.K. emphasize the loosening of restrictions, but about two-thirds of the men I interviewed continue to believe that husband-wife interactions must be limited in some ways.[11] For example, while most men enjoy talking with their wives on many topics, only one-third say that there are no restrictions on conversations with their wives. One-third say that they never talk with their wives in front of their parents, and another third say that they cannot talk with their wives about every topic or that they did not talk with their wives in the early years of the marriage.[12] For instance, Dileep Singh, a 54-year-old heading a nuclear family, says that until his wife had given birth to his children, he felt "shame [sharm] to talk with her"—a state of affairs he regards as ordinary and normal. Rajesh Yadav, 27, similarly says that, while he cannot joke with his wife in front of his parents, he can ask her what she did that day or tell her to bring him tea. While Rajesh feels able to order his wife about, he is unwilling to openly discuss any problems she might be having.

As others have reported, the reason Hindus limit interactions between husband and wife is to prevent the blossoming of close ties between husband and wife that might threaten the harmony of the joint family.[13] Men fear that a wife may try to manipulate her husband, tempting him away from his obligations to his parents. About 60% of the men I interviewed say that if a husband spends too much time with his wife, he may neglect his obligations to his parents.[14] Twenty-one-year-old Tej Gupta believes, for instance, that

> there must be limitations [between husband and wife]. If the husband-wife relationship becomes too much, then the wife starts to say pinching words to the parents. The parents will not endure this. Then the parents will press on us and our own mind will move. Then it will happen that one can forget one's own mother and father.

Tej's father, Arjun, who is junior high school educated and heads a large joint family that includes his brothers and their wives and children, agrees: "If the husband gives too much time to his wife, then there will be a difference of opinion in the family because every family has one head and if you start to go in the line of the wife, then the family will not run." Both Tej and his father fear that closeness between husband and wife might give a wife too much power within a family.

By insisting that women be passive and silent in the presence of their husbands, men prevent young women from gaining power in their homes. A woman who becomes close to her husband might be able to convince him to talk to his mother about lessening her household burdens. As I show in subsequent chapters, men worry that a woman who is too close to her husband might even be able to convince him to break from the joint family. One reason that men continue to insist on restricted interactions between husbands and wives, then, is to limit a wife's ability to influence her husband.

NORMS THAT LIMIT YOUNG WIVES' INFLUENCE IN THEIR HUSBANDS' FAMILIES

Some men, like Ramesh Mishra, nonetheless develop close relationships with their wives (see chapter 5), but even these men insist on a range of norms that limit a wife's influence in her husband's family. Without exception, men say that it is a wife's duty to serve her husband's parents. Men expect young brides to take on the bulk of the cooking, freeing their mothers for enjoyable activities like doing *pūjā* [worship] or bathing in the Gangā. Thirty-year-old Deepak Mishra says, for instance, that, since his mother "has become old," his wife "lets her be completely free." Unmarried Ravi Mishra similarly says that the "wife who is youngest should serve the house's older respected people."

Men see themselves as superiors, who must mold their wives to live in their families. Anand Singh is a 47-year-old living with his wife and six older brothers and their families in a large joint family. A happy, white-haired man, Anand enjoys the Banāras lifestyle and often attends classical Indian music concerts after working long hours in his family's cloth shop. Anand likens the joint family to a "curved bottle" that is "thick" and "thin" in different places. He likens a woman to water that is poured in a bottle and molded to conform to it. It is the husband's responsibility, he says, "to mold one's wife according to his family. A woman should be molded to live within his family just as water flows into a bottle and occupies its place."[15] Prem Singh similarly focuses on how he will have to mold his wife-to-be to his family's routines:

> My wife will have to mold herself into my form. She has to make her daily routine as mine is. I will not have to make my routine to conform to her.

Jyothi Gupta, who also awaits a marriage that has just been set, similarly emphasizes that it will be his responsibility to teach his wife about proper behavior in his family: "If my wife gets up at 7 or 8 o'clock in the morning, I will make her understand that she should get up at 5 o'clock because of the situation here in the joint family. She will serve my mother by freeing her from housework."

While men often emphasize that they must teach their wives how to serve a husband's parents, they also expect their wives to be attentive to their every need.[16] Gopal Mishra's description of the ideal wife is typical:

> The most important quality of an ideal wife is that she obey her husband. She should do whatever the husband says.

Some men expect a wife to obey her husband's every whim. Twenty-seven-year-old Rajesh Yadav says, for instance, that

> the biggest thing for the ideal wife is that she accept whatever her husband wants. . . . She should always wear red clothes if that is what pleases him. If the husband wants her to wear jeans and T-shirt, then she should dress that way.

Such subservience pleases Rajesh. "It is the greatest thing," he says, "if a wife lives according to her husband's desires."

Most men, moreover, declare that a woman must never complain in her husband's household. Thirty-year-old Amrit Mishra says, for instance, that his wife "should not neglect anything" his parents say— "even if what [they] say is wrong." Prem Singh similarly believes that a wife should remain silent even if she has a real cause to complain:

> My wife should serve my parents as I do. If they tell her to do something, she should not complain. After listening to them, she should keep quiet and tolerate whatever they say because there is never any trouble if elders are obeyed. Some wives start to complain as soon as they come to their [husband's] house. The parents will tell them two things and they will tell their husbands four things. There are some wives, however, whose fathers-in-law and mothers-in-law may even beat them and they will not say anything. The woman who remains silent is the ideal wife.

Rajesh Yadav similarly says that

> even if there are difficulties [my wife] remains shy. . . . She will not say anything because she is in her *sasurāl* [father-in-law's house]. In Hindustan, shyness [*sharm*] and deference [*lihāj*] are women's status [*mān*] and prestige [*maryādā*]. Even if there are difficulties, the women of India will not say anything to anybody. In the *sasurāl*, whatever happens is right. Even if it is dirt, she understands it as gold. [This] is the most wonderful tradition.

These statements reflect men's general belief that people should be guided by their elders, but they also suggest that many men get pleasure out of limiting their wife's voice. For Rajesh, it is "wonderful" if his partner regards everything that happens in his family as gold "even if it is dirt."

While the ideal for most of the men I interviewed is for women to quietly endure, they know that some women try to convince a husband to leave his parents (see chapter 6). Because so many men value joint-family living, men often insist that a husband must not give attention to his wife's complaints. Amrit Mishra reasons, for instance, that "if we constantly listen to our wives' talk, the family will not manage to run very long." Deevender Mishra, a 37-year-old heading a household that includes his wife, aged mother, and unmarried siblings, comments that if a wife "complains against someone, the husband should not take too much notice of it *even if she is telling the truth*. If everything of the wife is accepted, there is only trouble in that."

Men contribute to the construction of a range of norms that limit a wife's influence in her husband's family. Contact between husband and wife must be limited, a wife must not complain in her husband's house-

hold, and she must obey everything her husband and his parents say.
Men embrace these norms partly because they want to protect the joint
family and believe, as Prem Singh puts it, that "there is no trouble if
elders' are obeyed." But many men reiterate and reenforce restrictions
limiting women's influence because of the personal pleasure they find in
having an obedient servant who takes care of their wants.

RESTRICTING WOMEN OUTSIDE THE HOME

Like men throughout North India, all of the men I interviewed restrict
their wives' time and demeanor outside the home.[17] Some men restrict
women less than others, and all admit that women can venture outside in
certain circumstances. But restrictions on women's movement outside
the home still remain the cornerstone of a gender culture that disadvantages women.

MARKETING AS AN EXAMPLE

Men's talk about who should do the house's marketing provides a good
illustration of the limitations men place on women outside the home.
Most men prefer that the bulk of marketing be done by men so that
women need not leave the home at all (see also Standing 1991: 75; Kishwar [1983] 1991: 190; Harlan 1992: 38). Twenty-eight-year-old Rajendra
Gupta echoes the sentiments of most, saying "we [men] bring all goods
into the house." Shom Mishra, a 46-year-old with two new daughters-in-
law, says that neither his wife nor his daughters-in-law ever have to go
outside because "the male caste does all the work—whether it be buying
vegetables or any odd jobs." More than three-quarters of the men I asked
say that men or children buy the family's vegetables,[18] and my own
observations of marketing in a neighborhood vegetable market confirms
that 85% of those doing marketing are men or children.

All men also admit that women must buy some goods. They often
say, for instance, that men would be embarrassed to purchase women's
clothes. But men insist that if a woman goes out, she must be accompanied by another family member. Rajendra Gupta admits that women
sometimes go outside, but he demands that "two of them go together.
For instance, my wife will go with my mother or with my younger
brother's wife." Forty-four-year-old Arjun Gupta also tries to bring
everything that women need into the house so that they don't have to go
outside at all. But if they must go, he says, they should "not go alone but
with their mother or their aunt [chāchī]."

Men also say that older women have greater freedom to move outside the home because over the years they have proved their loyalty to their husbands' families. One-quarter of the men I asked say that a woman does the house's marketing, but in all of these cases the woman who markets is old enough that she has at least one grandchild in the household. Ravi Mishra says that, while "young ones go outside very rarely, as women become old they go out more and more." Sunil Gupta, 35, emphasizes that the strictest restrictions are on young women, saying that his wife is only allowed to do *pūjā* [worship] inside the house because of her "young age."

Men also note that the usual restrictions can be eased if there is an emergency that affects the whole family. Sunil Gupta has a master's degree, and he runs the family's prosperous bangle shop which is located on the narrow alley that leads to Banāras's most famous temple. The youngest of four brothers living in a large joint family with his wife, children, brothers, and *bhābhī*s, Sunil says that

> my wife goes outside for buying small goods or children's clothes or for doing *pūjāpāth* [worship]. But she will not go alone, but taking someone along with her. If my mother-*jī*[19] is there, then she will go with my mother. If not, then with someone else, like her *bhābhī* [elder brother's wife]. If there is no one, then she will go out with the children. But if she is alone and she is compelled to go, then she will go alone.

Anand Singh similarly says that "if there is compulsion and I am not here, and there is some accident, then she can go." What is important, Anand says, is that she not "intentionally try to go out alone. That is a different thing, and is wrong."

One reason that men find marketing acceptable for older women is because it is done for the benefit of her husband's family, rather than for the woman herself. Krishna Das Singh, a married 25-year-old, demands that his wife only go outside if it benefits the family as a whole:

> My wife can go outside, but not for a long time and not for purposeless things. If there is some work, if a child is ill, or some goods have to be brought from the market, she can go—but for the necessary things, not for useless things like roaming around [*ghūmnā-phīrnā*].

Chet Singh, a married 32-year-old who lives as a junior member of a large joint family, similarly criticizes women who go out for their own pleasure. Such women, he says, "have no concern with the society— they are spending time for their own self-interest, not the house's interest." Chet's reasoning reflects the collectivist framework for understanding action. He distrusts action which is for oneself, while praising

action that is for the benefit of the family. But it also reflects Chet's
desire that a wife be subordinate to her husband. It is telling that, while
men demand that women only go out to benefit the family, men themselves feel free, as I show below, to wander about aimlessly whenever
they like.

Men often emphasize that a woman must always be under the control of her husband. Shom Mishra is a 45-year-old head of household
whose sons have recently married. Shom is a religious man, and today
meditates daily after a hiatus of many years. Shom occasionally pub-
lishes articles in the local Hindi paper, enjoys talking philosophically for
hours, and sees himself as a literary person. For Shom, it is important
that a woman be closely controlled:

> She is your wife. She is your daughter-in-law. She should first take the
> advice of her family. Wives should be controlled and their behavior
> should be according to her *khāndān* [family lineage] and her family
> [*parivār*].

Men even say that a woman may go out for leisure activities like cinema
or roaming around if her husband gives permission. Like Shom, Lakanlal Mishra heads a joint family that includes a new daughter-in-law but
no grandchildren. Lakanlal embraces restrictions on women, but admits
that a husband may ease them if he wishes:

> It is the tradition of our place that women are not left independent.
> Women here are not free. They are under control. But they can go
> roaming around [*ghūmnā-phīrnā*] if it is my desire that she do so. If I
> give my permission, then she can go to the cinema—but not alone.
> She can travel somewhere for pilgrimage—but she goes on the desire
> of the husband. Even this is according to her age. If she is young, then
> she will not be allowed to go anywhere.

Consonant with the framework for understanding action I describe in the
next chapter, Lakanlal and Shom believe that a woman must be controlled by her family and by her husband. By recognizing that restrictions on a wife may be eased to fulfill a man's "desire," however,
Lakanlal also suggests that restrictions are based as much on men's
"desire" as on anything else.

RESTRICTIONS ON WOMEN'S DEMEANOR

Men also demand that women be appropriately modest whenever they
are outside the home. Like men throughout North India, the men I interviewed insist that their wives be shy, ashamed, and docile when they
venture out in public.[20] While men move freely through the streets,

alleys, and markets of Banāras, when women enter the public realm, they usually carefully drape their *sārī*s over their heads, making it difficult to even see their faces. Men regard veiling, which is known as using *ghūnghaṭ* [the veil], as an essential indication that women are acting appropriately modest.

Amrit Mishra, 30, has recently come to Banāras from a nearby village. He operates a small cloth shop that he has decorated with images of Hanuman and Lakshmi. Although he lives with his wife and parents in a small joint family, he still enjoys roaming around, and he sees movies often. Like most men, Amrit emphasizes the importance of women's public modesty and shyness:

> Shame [*lajjā*] and shyness [*sharm*] are the most important ornaments of Indian women. While thieves can steal gold or silver, shame [*lajjā*] and modesty [*shīltā*] can never be stolen. The most important ornament of the woman is her shame [*lajjā*], and the meaning of this is to use the veil.

Vinod Gupta, a 34-year-old married man living in a joint family, similarly extols the virtues of Indian women's shyness:

> The Indian woman is very humble [*vinamṛ*] and modest [*lājvant*] and she doesn't like to come out of the house freely in front of strangers. And our society also doesn't give permission for this.

Consonant with the framework for understanding action I describe in the next chapter, Vinod ties the imperative that a woman be bashful, modest, and shy to the importance of adhering to social pressures.

While men demand that women be modest, shy and inconspicuous in public, men like to roam, wander, and move around outside as recreation (see Kumar 1986, 1988; Sharma 1980a, 1980b). Most men say that *ghūmnā-phīrnā*, which I translate as "moving around" or "roaming," is among their favorite entertainments. Nita Kumar (1986: 44) describes how male Banārasīs "like to indulge in *ghūmnā-phīrnā*: to stroll in the *galīs* [narrow lanes], wander in the bazaars, hang around the *ghāṭs* [steps on the bank of the Ganga], visit the temples, [and] take in the ambience of the evening lights, crowds' bustle, and activity." But men deny these same pleasures to their wives. A retired Brāhmaṇ teacher laughed when I asked him if he ever roamed around with his wife, saying that he would have to leave her behind in a *galī*. Because of her shyness, he says proudly, she would never keep up with him. Limiting women's public activities to those which are useful for the house as a whole, men reserve the joys of aimless *ghūmnā-phīrnā* for themselves alone.

BOLSTERING MEN'S POWER

These restrictions on women outside the home contribute to women's subordinate position in India. They make it difficult for women to participate in public, political, and economic life.[21] Even when women have jobs outside the home, restrictions on their movement limit their economic opportunities. The refusal of government officers to send women to district jobs prevents women from getting experience which is vital for promotion (Liddle and Joshi 1986: 134). Male bosses often won't allow female engineers to do research work on site (Liddle and Joshi 1986: 136-7). Female accountants similarly find their opportunities limited by being refused permission to work late, do out-of-town audits, or work in certain areas of a city (Seghal 1985).

Men's Perception that Restricting Women Advances Their Own Interests

Why do men continue to restrict women's movements outside the home? Men confront an existing gender structure, seeing that in their own and most other households women do most of the domestic chores, and only rarely make substantial direct contributions to a family's income. They know that to maintain family prosperity, they must build family alliances (chapter 6), and that it is potentially dishonoring for women to move about freely outside the home. Certainly, for many men, the threat of dishonor is a constraint that leads them to insist that women of their families be restricted to the home (chapter 3; Derné 1994d). Still, the talk of many men is not driven by the structural realities they face, but by their understanding of their interests as men.

Twenty-eight-year-old Phoolchand Mishra has a B.Com. degree and worked as a journalist before opening a printing press. Phoolchand, whose father has some reputation as a local poet, prides himself on being an intellectual—a respected category among modern Indians. He loves living in Banāras, because it is a lively place with many movie theatres, *pān* shops, and good places for roaming around. For Phoolchand, the service his wife gives him is a great comfort:

> My wife remains at home doing all kinds of service, adorning the house, the door, and herself. She does household works so completely that when I come home and see the beauty I become very happy. [By contrast, if the woman works outside,] there is daily quarrel. The husband comes into the house and knows that his wife has gone outside to earn. The tired husband makes his own tea. He does everything by

his own hands. He even has to make his own tea! From this, his mental condition starts deteriorating and every form of corruption is born in
the mind.

For Phoolchand, like R.P. Mishra and many other men, having a stay-at-
home wife is part of the good life.

The emphasis men like Phoolchand place on a woman's domestic
duties is an important reason men embrace restrictions on women's
movements outside the home. When the men I interviewed describe
the qualities of the ideal wife, they almost always focus on domestic
responsibilities (see also Liddle and Joshi 1986: 150; Standing 1991:
81). Like most men, 30-year-old K.K. Mishra describes the ideal wife in
terms of her domestic duties: "It is enough if a woman cooks well, does
good sewing, and cleans the house well. These are the most important
qualities." Jyothi Gupta focuses on housework as the only important
quality he expects in his wife-to-be: "What qualities do I need? I think
she should do the housework. What else do I need?" Many men fear that
women's freedom of movement outside the home might threaten their
commitment to the domestic sphere. Some men say that limiting women
to the home bolsters their commitment to household work by limiting
women's mental horizons. Thirty-five-year-old Vikas Mishra demands
that his wife not even talk with anyone who visits his house, saying
that if she talks to other people, "her mind will expand." He insists that
she stay within the walls of his house, asking rhetorically, "if she likes it
outside, what work will she do inside the home?"

Some men insist that limiting women to the home keeps them from
fighting with their husbands. Phoolchand Mishra believes that "the mental condition of the thinking of women should be only up to a narrow
point of view." He praises his ancestral village where, he says, "women
are under so many restrictions that not even the sound of their foot-
steps, let alone their voices" are heard outside. Phoolchand speaks wistfully of village life where "it is as it should be. Wives do not fight
strongly with their husbands. When the husband is angry, his wife
remains silent." Anand Singh similarly says that "if a woman takes
even one step outside, her mind will go outside, too. But if she remains
in the house, then she remains controlled." Vinod Gupta, 34, seems to
genuinely love his wife, but he opposes women working outside the
home because

> when a woman earns something, she has the pride that 'I am also
> something.' For this reason she cannot give so much love [prem] and
> can not see things with the same eye with which she saw things before
> she started earning. Every earning wife has the pride that 'I earn. I
> feed myself. You do not feed me.' This is very wrong.

Vinod expresses the collectivist framework for understanding action
by suggesting that women's individuality must be subordinate to family
duties. But it is clear that Vinod imposes this imperative on women to
guarantee his own comfort and power within the family.

The men I interviewed guard their power over their wives by keeping them from going outside as much as they can. Some, like Phoolchand Mishra, fear that "today's women" "want to stand shoulder to
shoulder with men." For Phoolchand, such women challenge the pleasures he gets from having a wife who is always ready to serve him. A
main reason that men like Phoolchand forbid their wives from moving
freely outside the home is to bolster the male dominance they enjoy.

HONOR AND WOMEN'S SUBORDINATION

Like other cultural ideas surrounding Indian family life, men have also
constructed a focus on honor that advances their own interests as men.
Men claim that the threat of dishonor is only a modest restriction on
their own actions, while it tightly limits women's freedom. When men
talk about how they themselves might harm the family's honor, they
usually cite extreme, public crimes. Most commonly, men say that they
would harm their family's honor if they committed murder or theft,
became addicted to alcohol, or visited prostitutes.[22]

By contrast, when men discuss how women could harm the family's
honor, they emphasize innocent public behavior such as talking with
other men or going outside of the home too often, as well as a range of
private behavior such as causing enmity within the family by disobeying
one's husband or one's mother-in-law. More than half of the men who
describe specific actions that could harm the family's honor mention
women talking with other men and/or going outside the home too much.
More than 60% of men mention women's fighting within the home or
disobeying their husband's parents.[23] Only two men fail to mention at
least one of these reasons, and these two men cite failure to prepare tea
for the husband's guests as the source of dishonor!

A number of men explicitly contrast the extreme restrictions on
women with the mild restrictions on men. Phoolchand Mishra says, for
instance, that

> the caste of women [strī-jātī] is so vulnerable [komal] that any type of
> unlimited step in any field could destroy the honor [izzat] of the family.
> Whatever the social restrictions are, if she doesn't live according to
> them, the family's honor [izzat] will be finished. If she goes out on her
> own wish, people will point fingers at her over this. If she moves

around [*ghūmnā*] with a strange man, people will point fingers at her.
If she doesn't obey her elders, people will point fingers at her. If she
neglects whatever responsibilities she has toward her family or toward
her society or toward herself, then fingers will be pointed at her from
every side.

Phoolchand describes similar restrictions that are placed on his sister
who goes to a college in his neighborhood:

Although she goes to college, she has to return immediately afterwards. If she doesn't return right after college, then fingers can be
pointed at that girl because she is of the age when fingers are raised
against her.

Although Phoolchand says that there are "many problems in front of
men," he says that

for women, the decision [about whether one is acting appropriately] is
made immediately. People immediately decide whether she is good
or bad, but for men the decision is taken after some thinking.

Phoolchand confirms what my questioning of a range of men reveals—
that for women the range of actions which can cause the family dishonor are wider than for men.

Phoolchand's statements are consistent with the collectivist understanding of action I describe in the next chapter. Phoolchand vividly
visualizes the imperative that actions be consistent with social pressures, as he describes the fingers that point at women from all sides. But
fewer fingers are pointed in men's direction. The system of honor that
men have constructed bolsters men's interests. Men more easily control
their wives if they can appeal to the family's[24] honor in persuading them
to do as they are told. The cultural idea that a family's honor depends on
a range of women's actions is just another ace that husbands can play in
culture work aimed at controlling their wives.

EVERYDAY MICRO-INTERACTIONS THAT
BOLSTER MEN'S POWER

What are the processes by which gender culture is constructed? What
processes constitute the idea of women as vulnerable outside the home,
and dangerous interlopers in their husbands' families?

Theorists that focus on practice-based conceptions of the social
order argue that we need to focus on micro-mechanisms that can explain
the repetitive actions that make up the social structure.[25] These prac-

tice-based approaches hold, following Connell (1987: 17) and others, that "large scale structures of gender relations are constituted by practices" people engage in. The structure of gender inequality in Hindu society is not inevitable, but is socially constituted through the not always uncontested practices of individual Hindu men. I focus here on how the everyday talk of common men is part of the process that establishes and maintains the dominant gender ideology.

Men's everyday interactions with their sons, daughters, wives, friends, and parents reconstitute a wife's subordination to her husband. While it is difficult to know for sure if men's talk with an interviewer is repeated in their everyday talk, anthropologists report that women complain about men's concern about protecting them (Luschinsky 1962; Bennett 1983; Sharma 1980a; Liddle and Joshi 1986). Moreover, the talk about controlling women which I describe in this chapter was repeated again and again by nearly all of the men I interviewed. It is a discourse which men know well. This suggests that men's talk with me copies everyday talk about the importance of protecting and controlling their wives. My interviews indicate that men do not merely mimic dominant norms. They often know that these norms advance and maintain their own privileged position in the family.

The idea that a wife must obey everything in her husband's home is partly reconstituted, for instance, through the instructions fathers give their daughters when they marry. As soon as I started asking men what they tell their daughters before they leave their parents' houses, I realized that the question is so culturally salient that men always have a clear answer. Forty-four-year-old Arjun Gupta's description of what he told his daughter is typical:

> "You are going to your *sasurāl* [in-laws]. You should obey your mother-in-law and father-in-law. Don't give any type of disrespect. Listen to all things. Don't answer anybody's question in a bad way." But first of all in our place giving [any] answer [at all] is not respected as good.

Anand Singh, who, like most men, instructed his daughter to "serve her mother-in-law and father-in-law," warned his daughter of the dishonor of failing to act appropriately deferent. "You must," he told her,

> "adjust with that family in every way. No complaint should come to us that 'your girl is like this.' No one should complain to [us] that you are not obedient." The daughter is taught that "Daughter, live in the proper way. Serve your mother-in-law and father-in-law. Remain faithful with your husband. Never do any wrong things. No stigma [*lānchnā*] should come on us because someone says that our daughter is wrong." We teach [daughters] about these problems.

Seventy-six-year-old Devi Prasad Gupta similarly told his daughter to

> serve your mother-in-law and father-in-law. Do whatever work there is
> smoothly and in the right way. You should not have verbal disputes.
> You should follow their orders.

The fact that these instructions are so elaborated in Hindu culture suggests that the interactions in which they are repeated are common and
continually reconstitute the idea that a wife must always obey her husband and his parents.

If men's talk with me is any indication, women often must ask their
husbands whether they can go outside to purchase children's clothes or
other goods. Men often tell daughters to go straight to school and return
straight home. Family members often discuss who will chaperone a woman
who must go out for some shopping. These commonplace interactions
reconstitute the normal state of affairs in which women's movements outside the home are exceptional, restricted, and threatening to a family's
honor. One indication that discussions about chaperoning young wives
are common is the fact that a number of unmarried men view chaperoning
their *bhābhīs* [elder brothers' wives] as an important duty. Surjit Singh
says, for instance, that "guard[ing]" his *bhābhī* against troubles is his
"responsibility as *devar* [husband's younger brother]. [The *devar*] looks
after these things as do the elders." Surjit's comments suggest that this
duty is elaborated as an important one for unmarried male family members.

When men discuss the propriety of women's behavior, they similarly reconstitute the idea that women must be shy outside the home.
Men may criticize daughters-in-law for being too open and carefree
when outside the home (Sharma 1980a; Luschinsky 1962: 254-260).
A Nepali woman told Lynn Bennett (1983: 125), for instance, that if
"you are a woman then you are afraid to say anything because you
don't know what your husband or mother-in-law or father-in-law will
say." An Indian woman interviewed by Liddle and Joshi (1986: 184)
says that she is often criticized for working outside the home:

> You're always thought of as being complex and different. You're crit-
> icized for social mixing, for being "improper"—this criticism comes
> from women who don't work outside, and *from all men*. [Emphasis
> added.]

Men may even tease each other if their wives appear to be acting inappropriately. Sunil Gupta reports, for instance, that should his wife go to
her parents' house without asking,

> someone may see her going and coming on the road. He will come
> to me and ask, "Where has she gone?" I will have to reply that I do

not know. Then he will say, "see this man does not know whether
his wife is roaming in the market or has gone to the cinema."

Each of these interactions constructs the reality that a woman must be
appropriately limited outside the home or risk jeopardizing her family's honor.

What Indians call "eve-teasing," the common practice of teasing
and taunting women outside the home (Sharma 1980b: 219; Mandelbaum 1988: 91; Chadha 1986; Omvedt 1993: 79; Mankekar 1993a,
1993b), also defines women as intruders in the public world. The men I
interviewed abhor eve-teasers as low-lifes who are a disgrace to India.
Still, eve-teasing as a common practice that is extensively covered in
Indian newspapers helps constitute both the idea that women are never
safe outside the home, and the idea that women who roam about shame-
lessly without a guardian deserve to be ill-treated.

Finally, the consequences of bringing dishonor on a family may
also be publicly discussed. Veena Das (1976a: 15-16) describes, for
instance, how a news report of a group of brothers who killed their sister to prevent her from marrying outside the community was widely
discussed within an urban Punjabi kinship network. While many in this
network were horrified and repelled, others thought that "the brothers
had to sacrifice their own selves in killing their beloved sister."
Although the "moral judgment" of her informants varied, all "agreed
that the sister had been killed to save the honor of the family." Despite
this disagreement, interactions considering the appropriate punishment
for the young woman constitute her actions as dishonorable and worthy
of punishment.[26]

The gender culture that advances men's interests is constituted
through men's common interactions with their wives, sons, daughters,
daughters-in-law, and male acquaintances. One reason that men continually revalorize the importance of a husband's control of his wife
and of limiting women's movements outside the home is that men realize that they benefit from these cultural norms. They enjoy having a
wife who cooks for them, cleans for them, and makes tea for them when
they arrive home. They enjoy the power they hold over their wives'
every move. They recognize that easing restrictions on women outside
the home might threaten their authority in the family.

While scholars often question whether men self-consciously pro-
pound gender ideologies to maintain their privileges (Chafetz 1990:18,
35; see also Scheff 1990:185), my interviews with Hindu men suggest
that men realize the advantages they gain by controlling women, and
that they consciously act and talk to maintain those advantages. Many

men recognize their personal interest in restricting women to the home, and reconstitute the collective arrangements that limit women's opportunities in interactions that define women as appropriately restricted.

WOMEN'S STRATEGIES AND THE CONSTRUCTION OF GENDER

While culture is a process of domination (Gramsci 1971), it is not uncontested. While those with power are often able to turn that raw power into cooked esteem (Ortner and Whitehead 1981), subordinates are sometimes able to challenge the dominant culture. Indeed, Indian women's practices also shape the gender order. As Kandiyoti (1988:275, 286) argues, however, women "strategize within a set of concrete constraints" that define "a patriarchal bargain"—the "set of rules and scripts regulating gender relations, to which both genders accommodate and acquiesce, yet which may nonetheless be contested, redefined, and renegotiated." As I will show in chapter 6, some women contest the image of women as docile and necessarily restricted to the home. Often, however, women's strategies for advancing their interests reinforce a gender culture propagated by men.

In pursuing their goal of power and security within the joint family, women often accommodate dominant ideas of what is appropriate behavior. As I will show in chapter 6, a young woman in a joint family often works to evade a mother-in-law's authority by fostering closeness with her husband. To gain her husband's love and trust, many women try to appear deferent and obedient, but in doing so they reinforce the gender culture which defines them as subservient in their husbands' homes.

Just as young wives may use adherence to conservative standards to accomplish their aim of getting close to their husbands, so an elder woman who benefits from her daughter-in-law's hard work in her household may use the dominant gender ideology to keep her son from becoming too close to his wife. A mother is often the one who demands the suppression of affection and contact between husband and wife (Carstairs 1957: 45; Luschinsky 1962: 341; Kakar [1978] 1981: 118-119). Mothers, moreover, sometimes try to limit a daughter-in-law's influence in a household by complaining that she threatens the family's honor with immodest behavior (Bennett 1983: 125; Das 1976a; Luschinsky 1962: 286, 398; Minturn 1993: 85, 312). One elder woman living in a village near where I did my fieldwork complained to Luschinsky (1962:429-430), for instance, that

> Young wives [have too much] influence [over] their husbands. . . .
> The wife of a young [head of household] may want something changed
> in the house, so she talks to her husband and he gets it done. . . . This is
> how some young women gain authority over their mothers-in-law.

Another elder woman in a Nepali village studied by Bennett (1983:194)
complained of a new bride who didn't show the proper respect by touch-
ing her mother-in-law's feet, "wonder[ing] what [the daughter-in-law
will] do to us later." These complaints reinforce a mother-in-law's
authority in the household, but in the process also reinforce the cultural
distrust of closeness between a young husband and wife.

Women who work to advance their individual interests within patriarchal families are sometimes forced into bargains with a patriarchal culture that reflects the interests of dominant men. Women are active agents
whose interactions contribute to the reconstitution of gender culture,
but that culture is still largely the result of men's efforts to dominate
women. The dominant cultural idea that women are appropriately
restricted to the home is a tool that powerful men use to maintain
women's subordinate position. While men's power is not always uncontested, hegemonic male interests often drive the interactions that shape
gender culture.

While dominant groups manipulate cultural components to advance
their own interests, culture is not simply a tool of the powerful. The
same men who enjoy restricting their wives often themselves feel constrained to be guided by family pressures. In the next chapter, I consider
Hindu men's focus on the importance of being guided by one's social
group. This understanding, while sometimes tempered, is often so much
a matter of common sense that it constrains many of the same men who
recognize their own interests when it comes to restricting their wives
within the home.

3

The Collectivist Framework for Understanding Action: Hindu Men's Focus on Social Pressures

Rajesh Yadav, 27, enjoys wearing stylish Westernized clothes, and looks forward to small excursions to nearby cities that relieve him from the long hours he works. When Rajesh's father suddenly fell ill ten years ago, Rajesh's marriage was hastily arranged and Rajesh became responsible for operating the paint shop his father started. Rajesh admits that he was pressured [*dabāv*] to marry in nervousness [*ghabarāhaṭ*], and he remains a bit dissatisfied with his ten-year-old marriage, which he describes as "so-so." Although Rajesh notices this personal cost of adherence to social pressure and now believes that a man should talk with a woman before marrying her, he nonetheless continues to focus on the importance of being guided by a respected social group. Rajesh believes that men who commit social crimes are driven by their membership in the wrong sorts of social groups: "Young men who belong to the type of society that loiters and becomes entangled in intoxications like *bhāng* and *charas* [two marijuana concoctions] are the ones who stand on the road and tease and taunt women." Rajesh feels that these men can only be stopped by social pressures: "If no one disgraces them, then their bad status [*astar*] will go even higher and they may start pulling off women's *sārīs* and picking people's pockets." For Rajesh, only a person "who has the fear [*ḍar*] of society—that my honor [*izzat*] will go—will never do that sort of thing."

Dileep Singh is a 54-year-old who left his parents' village to move to Banāras, where he now lives with his wife and young children. Although Dileep separated from his brothers to better support his own children, he still focuses on the importance of group control of the individual. Like Rajesh, Dileep believes that it is social fear that deters individuals from acting destructively:

> It is for the respect of society that people keep their character. If people don't see the society, then many people here will be bad. If one understands that the society is nothing, then one can do anything. Social fear [*samāj ke ḍar*] is the only thing that can educate people from doing wrong.

Like Rajesh, Dileep's folk notion of social control focuses on society directly controlling the individual.

Vinod Gupta is a 34-year-old high school graduate who lives with his wife, brothers, and their families in the building that is attached to his ready-made clothing shop. Although Vinod insisted that his father allow him to meet his wife before marrying her, Vinod, too, focuses on the importance of being guided by social pressures. Vinod emphasizes that individuals free of social restrictions will not be able to control their antisocial impulses:

> The social restrictions are there because it is man's nature to want to remain free, and where man is free there are only deformities upon deformities. Whenever a human being neglects the social restrictions and stays freely by himself, he will face calamities.

For Vinod, society prevents people from doing evil acts by dishonoring wayward individuals:

> A culprit must be dishonored by being forced to face disrespect [*tiraskār*], hatred [*ghṛanā*], and anger [*krodh*] everywhere in society. No one will sit and talk with him or share food with him. If this is not done, then there is the fear of the destruction of the society. If the culprit is not caught, then his terror will be let loose on every place. He becomes free of society and starts to dance like a devil. Therefore, every culprit's actions must be given results.

Vinod believes that the life of any individual who lives "separated from society" will be "full of darkness." "The life of a person who has separated from society," he says, "will be that of a fish without water."

Vinod, Dileep, and Rajesh recognize their individual desires as well. Vinod contested his father's wishes by insisting that he meet his bride before marrying her (chapter 7). Dileep separated from his brothers so that he could better provide for his children (chapter 7). While Rajesh has not rebelled against his parents, he laments the fact that he was pressured into marrying when his father fell ill. Still, although these men recognize their individual desires, they continue to focus most on the group control of the individual.

Like Vinod, Dileep, and Rajesh, most Hindu men talk about their family lives by using a language of understanding action which focuses on how people are rightly driven by social pressure. Most view a person's actions as a reflection of the larger social group—caste or family—to which the individual belongs, and they distrust individual actions undertaken independent of these larger social groups. While the statements of Vinod, Dileep, and Rajesh may appear to be just pompous moralizing, most men's talk reflects a similar, but usually only implicit, understanding of what guides family life. While unusually explicit, Vinod's, Dileep's, and Rajesh's statements suggest that the implicit understanding I am describing is an indigenous one, not one imposed by the sociologist.

How do men's assumptions and vocabulary reflect a collectivist framework for understanding action? How do men live by such frameworks in their own lives? Are frameworks for understanding action consistent, unified wholes which are widely shared? What is the place of such frameworks in the cultural apparatus?

JOINT-FAMILY LIVING: BEING GUIDED BY ELDERS

While Americans valorize the act of "leaving home" (Bellah *et al.* 1985; Varenne 1977), the Hindu men I interviewed want to live in a joint family, and often have difficulty understanding the American custom of leaving home. Several men were bewildered when they learned that I had, as they understood it, left my family and travelled to India. I sometimes explained that American sons and daughters often leave their parents' home on reaching the age of 18 to work or to attend school. On hearing this, Rajesh Yadav exclaimed that in India leaving home in that way "would be considered criminal. There would be objections from everyone—from one's parents, from the government, and from the society." Hindu men's attachment to the joint family indicates their fundamental distrust of the individual acting separately from larger social groups. The men I interviewed prefer to see their own actions as guided by a joint family, and they rely on the family to control their own behavior and the behavior of their wives and other family members.[1]

EMOTIONAL ATTACHMENT

Men living in various positions within their joint families regard living harmoniously with one's parents and brothers, or one's sons and daughters-in-law as one of life's greatest pleasures. Tej Gupta, 21, is an eldest son who lives with his parents, brothers and sisters, and three uncles and their families. A college graduate who expects to be married soon, Tej operates a small flour mill on the outskirts of Banāras near the Banāras Hindu University. When I interview Tej, he is covered with flour, but he has a bright smile. He wears fashionable glasses and has a dark red *ṭīkā* on his forehead. Tej, who respects his father so much that he insisted that I interview him, gets emotional satisfaction from joint-family living:

> The biggest difficulty [of living separately] is that one has left one's parents! There is great pleasure [*ānand*] in living in a family with my parents. In our home, food is cooked and eaten together. If anyone has any trouble, they bear it together.

Surjit Singh, an unmarried man living with his parents, two older brothers, and their wives and children, similarly says that "the joint family is the best place for us. It provides a close mutual relationship with cooperation and convenience in all things."

Married men who live with their wives and parents in joint families also, almost without exception, profess the pleasures of harmonious joint-family living. Raj Kumar Singh is a recently married man of 23, living with his wife, parents, and two older brothers and their families. A college graduate, Raj enjoys listening to cricket matches on the radios he sells in his shop. A youngest son who has long enjoyed interactions with his elder brothers' wives, Raj enjoys interacting with his brothers in a family headed by his father: "We live together, laughing and talking. Every brother shares each other's pains and sorrows." Vinod Gupta similarly says that

> when we compromise and cooperate, the joint family gives man a very happy life. As much love [pyār] as one gets in the joint family one will not get living separately. What security one gets in that, one will never get living alone. The feeling of insecurity is very much among those that live separately.

In the next chapter, I consider how this focus on love as directed toward many members of a joint family, rather than toward one's wife and children alone, is related to men's collectivist understanding of action.

Heads-of-household, too, value life in a joint family. Sureshwar Mishra is the mālik [head] of a joint household that includes his wife, three of his five sons, their wives, and his grandchildren. Sureshwar, too, says that he likes living in a joint family because "everyone's love [prem] remains together." Living alone is self-evidently undesirable for Sureshwar. In living separately, he says, "one does one's actions for oneself separately! One will not be able to manage to work together. This is the badness in living separately."

The feeling that one is pleasing one's elders is also an important emotional satisfaction of joint-family living. After commenting on how everyone in the joint family bears each other's troubles, Tej Gupta adds that he is satisfied with joint-family living because his parents are "happy to see us living together." A common refrain is that as parents served their sons when they were unable to serve themselves, so sons must serve their parents in their old age (see chapter 2). Similarly, 45-year-old Shom Mishra enjoys seeing his sons prosper while they continue living under one roof with him. Parents, he says, "always have happy imaginations about our sons and their children," adding that he is satisfied to see his sons living happily together with wives he himself chose for them.

MUTUAL SUPPORT

Men often say that they rely on other family members for support. For instance, men see the division of labor between women of a large joint family as preferable to wives performing all tasks in separate households. A man's mother might organize household tasks, while his wife sews clothes, a younger brother's wife cooks a meal, and an elder brother's wife takes the children to school. Men find such arrangements convenient in comparison to the burden of having one woman do all such tasks. Men who live in joint families also say that they benefit from the ability to pool money for large expenses, like weddings, and from the economy of operating the single stove that is required for joint-family living.

Men often focus on the availability of family members to help out if a husband or wife falls ill. Sureshwar Mishra's son, Deepak, studied to get an M.A. in literature, and earns his living by operating a photography studio. Like two of his four brothers, Deepak continues to live with his parents, and he is happy with this arrangement:

> If I am living separately and my wife falls sick, then there is no one to cook for us. Making clothes and sending the children to school is a problem. But in the joint family, there is no such trouble. If my wife is sick, then my *bhābhī* [elder brother's wife] cooks the food, my mother makes the clothes for the children, and my younger brother's wife prepares the children for school.

Krishna Das Singh, a 25-year-old living with his wife, parents, and older brother's family, describes the help that a healthy brother can offer a sick brother:

> Today, my brother may have food and money when I have none. We can both live from what he earns. If my brother does not have these things, then I can feed him, just as he feeds me. If I am ill and cannot walk around, then brother can look after me and show me to the doctor. When I become well again, I can show him to the doctor [should he become sick]."

Rather than focusing on supporting oneself, men emphasize the importance of helping (and being helped by) others in the family.

THE PREFERENCE FOR BEING DIRECTED BY ELDERS

Perhaps the most interesting reason men give for living in joint families is their preference for being directed by elders, a preference that suggests the importance men place on social guidance. Newly married Kumar

Yadav, who is an eldest son living with his parents in a joint family, runs a milk shop that he decorates with images of Hanuman and photographs of wrestlers. A strong handsome man with a moustache and a tough smile, Kumar, who majored in sociology at Banaras Hindu University, reports that he relies on his father's guidance for even the smallest tasks:

> I wouldn't even do the smallest bit of work without asking father. If the work will be spoiled [because he can't be asked], let it get spoiled. We don't act according to our own mind without asking. We only do the types of work that he tells us to do.

Phoolchand Mishra similarly says that he must always obey his father's orders—even when he disagrees with them:

> Father's opinions are given the main importance. [All problems are] solved in the way he says. This is our mental state [man:sthithi]. Even if [what we say] is good, if he doesn't like it, we must accept whatever advice he gives.

Indeed, men often rely on parents to provide guidance about what occupational and educational opportunities they should pursue (Roland 1988: 98-100; Béteille 1991: 16-17; Seymour 1980: 150, 1992; Bassa 1978: 335).

GROUP CONTROL IN JOINT FAMILIES

Men often see family guidance as necessary to control wayward family members. They commonly say that whenever there are any tensions in a family, male family members join together and bring the pressure of the group to bear on the individual responsible. Tej Gupta's 44-year-old father, Arjun, heads a large joint family that includes his brothers and their families. The day I interview Arjun he is wearing a plain *dhotī*, having just done *pūjā* on the roof. A pleasant, happy man, Arjun lives in a crowded family. Men, women, and children often crowd around the television in a room decorated with bazaar posters of Hindu deities, magazine clippings of cricket stars, soap advertisements, family photos, and pictures of freedom fighters. Arjun admits that there are sometimes tensions in his family, but says that

> when any tensions arise, we sit together, think, and solve the problem. . . . If my younger brother did something wrong, then all four brothers say to him, "You are doing wrong." This has a mental effect [*mānsik asar*] on him [and] . . . he comes again to his place.

Although idealized, Arjun's description of how the joint family works is a common expression of the idea that only group pressure controls the individual.

Some men even see the presence of elders as necessary to check their own antisocial impulses. As Prem Singh, 24, anxiously awaits his marriage, he continues to distrust his sexual urges. He believes that no young man can "control himself when it comes to matters of sex." Prem says that unless young men such as himself are controlled by their families, they cannot help but "run behind the back of girls" and lose themselves in the "intoxication of sex." Prem laments his own sexual urges as destructive to his "power of thinking and understanding" and he is thankful his family checks these urges. He says that because he lives with his parents he has "the emotional calculation that my parents are above me. There is somebody to guide me and I am under somebody." As I show in the next chapter, the collectivist framework for understanding action leads many men to focus on how this sort of social fear insures that they won't go astray.

UNEASINESS ABOUT ACTING ON ONE'S OWN

The preference for being directed by respected elders in a joint family sometimes leads men to feel uneasy when forced to make independent decisions. Twenty-six-year-old Ashok Mishra fears that living separately would have disastrous consequences:

> If one lives outside a joint family, one will face many difficulties. One will have to tolerate very much in society. Today's men are unable to tolerate these things. If a person lives alone he will either do bad things or he will commit suicide. But living jointly, one can pass one's life.

Some men describe how uncomfortable they were when they first had to act on their own. Anil Gupta, 76, has operated a tobacco and *pān* shop for many years. He continues to live with one of his sons in a quiet house in close proximity to the residences of his other sons. He has a white beard, and lively, bright eyes. He loves to talk about his activities in the independence movement. Anil is an only child whose mother died when he was an infant, leaving him with just his father and grandmother. Anil felt intensely uneasy when his father and grandmother died:

> I became completely helpless. Even for an ordinary thing, I had to act according to my own mind! Because I didn't have any relatives, there was no one to advise me. I did whatever came into my mind with whatever results! The situation was very terrible because when I looked around my neighborhood I saw that someone had two brothers, someone else had three brothers and some others had four brothers. Then, this came into my heart: "How unfortunate I am because I don't have anyone!"

Having focused on being directed by his father, Anil felt ill-equipped to use his own judgment when his father died. He sees "whatever came into [his] mind" as guiding his actions, and he is wary of these thoughts as unpredictable and haphazard. The common (Kakar [1978] 1981: 20-1; Roland 1988: 103) unease men feel at being separated from their joint family indicates their focus on being guided by elders rather than internal judgment.

ARRANGING MARRIAGES:
THE DISTRUST OF INDIVIDUAL CHOICE

An example of men's focus on being guided by their families is the fact that nearly all men believe that the choice of a spouse is best decided by parents, rather than by the individuals concerned. The practice of arranging marriages reflects the distrust of individual decisions which are not directed by one's family. In both village and urban India, the overwhelming majority of upper-caste Hindu marriages are arranged by the bride's and groom's parents. Most young Hindu men, moreover, agree that the main responsibility for choosing their bride should rest with their parents.[2]

Of the 40 married men I interviewed, only one married for love. Only four others had a chance to meet their brides prior to the marriage, although many more were able to see a photograph of their bride prior to the wedding. Only one man had more than a brief perfunctory meeting with his bride-to-be. Usually, parents give the boy just enough time for a glance at his bride's face, and in all cases, elder family members strictly chaperon the meeting of a prospective bride and groom.

Many (22/49) men mention that experience makes parents better equipped than their children to choose a proper mate (see also Vatuk 1972: 88; Roland 1988). Narayan Singh, 32, sells teas and sweets at a shop located on the outskirts of Banāras. Unlike his brother who has separated from the family, Narayan continues to live with his parents, along with his wife and children. Narayan is convinced that

> whatever marriage the parents arrange is good. When one does by one's own way, the marriage is half-baked [kachchā]. The parents have travelled the world and know all about it. They have experience from before. I do not have the knowledge which they have gained.

Tej Gupta, who at 21 thinks that his father, Arjun, will arrange his marriage soon, similarly says that the advantage of arranged marriages is that

the parents have passed their time. They have lived through these
things. They will arrange the marriage with the proper girl because
they come from that position. They have the experience of marriage.

Men feel more comfortable relying on their parents' judgments than
on their own. This reliance on parental experience reflects men's emphasis on family guidance. Unlike middle-class American men, who focus
on making their own way, Hindu men emphasize that they follow
received authority.

THE PROSPECT OF LOSING PARENTAL SUPPORT

More than two-thirds (32/49) of the men I interviewed spontaneously
mention that pressures from parents and society doom love marriages to
fail. As I show below, men regard the dishonor of marrying against
one's parents' wishes as having real, harmful consequences. Hindu men
have a deep respect for the power of social pressure and feel uneasy
about living without the guidance of family and society.

Men often assume that those who marry for love jeopardize life in a
joint family. Kumar Yadav says, for instance, that the biggest disadvantage of marrying for love is that then one "cannot live in the joint
family." Thirty-two-year-old Ramchandra Mishra similarly says that
those who marry for love "will be thrown out and won't have any contact with their families." Even those who do not assume that separation is inevitable are wary of the loss of respect that they believe they
would suffer if they married for love. Unmarried 26-year-old Jyothi
Gupta believes, for instance, that if he were to marry with his own inclination, "no one in my house would ever respect my talk."

About 40% (20/49) of the men I interviewed spontaneously mention
loss of parental support as a problem for those who marry for love.
Because so many Indian men in their twenties rely on their parents for
financial support, jeopardizing their relationship with their parents by
marrying for love is often a real loss. Phoolchand Mishra values his
close relationship with his father and is thankful that his father supports him:

> Now, you are seeing what kind of friendship I have with my father.
> [The relationship] is good because I married according to my parents'
> liking. If I had gone according to my own mind, he would feel hurt and
> would not take any interest in solving my problems.

Phoolchand counts on his family to assist him:

> If the marriage is by the family's desire, then the family cooperates
> [with the couple] in every way. There is a social link and if any prob-

lem or dispute arises, then both families come together and set it right. There is much convenience in this. If the marriage happens by the liking of the family, a big form of society is always ready to cooperate in every way.

By contrast, Phoolchand says that if a boy and girl marry for love, the family "becomes indifferent [*udāsīn*]" to the boy and "sees him with a hateful [*ghranā*] look." Because of this "anger," they "separate" the son, "abandoning him to himself." Phoolchand, like many others, values the helpful guidance of family and regards being abandoned to live on one's own as a horribly frightening possibility.

I know of several cases of a family ostracizing a son who married for love, but it is difficult to know how common such cases are. What is certain is that most men believe that marrying for love inevitably leads to being boycotted by one's parents. Lakanlal Mishra, the *mālik* of a small joint family, regards it as a "tradition of India that if I make my own marriage, the family members will hate [*ghranā karnā*; *nafrat karnā*] me." K.K. Mishra, a young household head, believes that the "father and family members walk out" on the son who marries for love, leaving him to "struggle alone."

Many men believe, moreover, that the whole society ostracizes those who make love marriages. Dileep Singh says that it is not only the boy's parents and brothers who will reject him: "No one," he says "will drink water touched by him. He will have to live separately from society." K.K. Mishra says that by accepting an arranged marriage people "get cooperation and sympathy from all society." For K.K., one can only succeed by following society's rules:

> When you arrange your marriage for yourself, you don't get cooperation from anyone. Man is a social animal. If he disregards everybody, then how can he rise up?

These men share an understanding that the individual needs to follow social rules to prosper. They see people who have been "abandoned to themselves" as facing the most horrible fate of all—the fate of losing social support.

RELYING ON ONE'S SOCIAL GROUP AS A GUIDE

Men sometimes explicitly emphasize that one must always act in accordance with one's social group. Thirty-two-year-old Ramchandra Mishra says, for instance, that he embraces arranged marriages because

> We have to move under whatever is the family's society. We cannot go outside our society. Whatever customs are there in the society of Brāhmaṇs, we move according to those customs.

Rajesh Yadav similarly says that he restricts his wife and daughters to the home because "society does not understand it as good" if a woman is outside the home. "Because I am living in society," he says, "it is therefore not good for me."

Men often do not evaluate their caste's or society's customs as right in some ultimate way, but feel simply that established customs must be followed whatever they may be. Sunil Gupta comments that women go outside the home more now than they did in his youth, but refuses to consider whether the times of his youth or modern times are right, saying only that

> whatever situation is moving right now is right. . . . It doesn't mean that because my father wore a *dhotī* that I should wear a *dhotī*, too. By moving according to the demands of the times, you maintain your honor [*izzat*] and reputation [*pratishṭhā*] in society.

Thirty-five-year-old R.P. Mishra similarly solves the "problem of understanding what is right" by answering the question "what is the time saying?" For R.P. and Sunil, like most men, the most important thing is to follow the social demands of the day.

MORAL VOCABULARIES: HONOR AND TRADITION

I was first alerted to men's focus on being guided by their social groups by a shared vocabulary focusing on honor and tradition that men use repeatedly to justify joint-family living, arranged marriages, and restrictions on women outside the home (see also Roland 1988: 242-3; Mandelbaum 1988). By declaring that they act honorably or that tradition is motivating their actions, men assert that their actions are not the result of individual inclination, but are simply the actions that are appropriate for any member of their social group. While men recognize that male dominance is bolstered by living in joint families and restricting women to the home, they usually focus on honor and tradition to explain their actions.

TRADITION, HONOR, AND JOINT-FAMILY LIVING

Sometimes men justify joint-family living by emphasizing the importance of following tradition. Sunil Gupta says, for instance, that he likes

living in a joint family because "this tradition of joint-family living has
been running from the beginning." For other men, it is honor that is on
their minds. College-educated Ashok Mishra is a 26-year-old living in a
small joint family with his parents, wife, small child, and brother's family. Ashok aspired to be a high school teacher like his father, but eventually decided that he could make more money by running a blanket
store, which his father set up for him at an important downtown cross-
ing. Ashok emphasizes that

> by living in the joint family, man's honor [*izzat*] will always remain.
> Man's esteem [*mān*] will never be damaged. [When the joint family is
> strong], people know to which *khāndān* [family lineage] a man
> belongs.

Deepak Mishra, too, sees honor in joint-family living. Deepak feels
"very bad" that two of his brothers live separately. He frets that "people
think we have become weak. If all five brothers live together, then all
people are afraid of them and no one dares to stand up to them." Deepak
emphasizes the point by clenching his five fingers into a fist to highlight
the strength of five brothers living together.

TRADITION, HONOR, AND ARRANGED MARRIAGES

Two-thirds (33/49) of the men I interviewed mention tradition as one
reason that they prefer arranged marriages. Fifty-four-year-old Nathuram Mishra says, for instance, that he embraces arranged marriages
because they are in accord with the "tradition of our *khāndān* [family
lineage]." Ashok Mishra puts it this way:

> This tradition [of arranged marriages] is the Hindustani tradition. It
> has been running from many years ago. It is right and good. . . . As
> long as there are Hindustani people in the real sense, the tradition will
> run. Nobody will finish it. . . . We should not do what our forefather's
> *khāndān* has not done.

Phoolchand Mishra believes that by following tradition, a person always
achieves good results:

> Marrying by one's own wishes cannot take place according to our
> *dharma* [religion]. The rules of *dharma* are so proved that one knows
> there will be little corruption if the marriage is arranged by one's fam-
> ily. . . . *Dharma* has made rules that you should live in a certain way,
> you should talk in a certain way, and your lifestyle should be in a cer-
> tain way. From following these rules there is very little chance of cor-
> ruption.

Arjun Gupta, whose son Tej will marry soon, simply states that "meeting the girl before the marriage is very bad according to Hindu law. The biggest advantage I am getting from marrying according to the parents' wishes is that it is our Hindu law."

Nearly half (24/49) of the men I interviewed mention a loss of honor as one of the chief disadvantages of love marriages. Ramlal Mishra is a 30-year-old college graduate who lives with his wife, children, and parents in a joint household. During the ten hours a day that he works six days a week, he often enjoys chatting with friends in his spotless cloth shop, which is decorated with a prominently placed image of Ram's monkey-lieutenant, Hanuman. Ramlal is a happy man, who enjoys playing music with his wife and his father, who taught him to play the sitar. Ramlal regards love marriages as very dishonoring:

> Society will look at a [love marriage] with bad eyes [burā nigāh]. We don't accept it as a marriage, whether it is passed in the courts or not. Even if it is a legal marriage, in the Hindu society it is seen with a very hateful [ghraṇā] look. [People say] "no marriage has taken place. They are living without marriage." We see it as fallen.

For Ramlal, public opinion is what brands behavior dishonorable. Ramlal's conviction that love marriages are dishonorable is based on his assessment that "society" sees love marriages "with bad eyes."

HONOR, TRADITION, AND RESTRICTIONS ON WOMEN OUTSIDE THE HOME

While men restrict women to the home to bolster their own privilege and comfort, they also continually mention the importance of following tradition and maintaining their honor as reasons for restricting women's movements outside the home. Many (19/49) men regard it as traditional that men do the bulk of the work in the public sphere. Twenty-year-old Shobnath Gupta says, for instance, that women remain inside the home because it "is an old tradition that has been running for a long time. Therefore, people have accepted it even to the present day." Phoolchand Mishra similarly emphasizes religious tradition: "The religious texts [dharma sūtra] have fixed the areas of work for women and for men. Those determined routines are so definite that their example should be followed."

About half (24/49) of the men I interviewed mention the need to protect a family's honor as a reason that they restrict women's movements outside the home. For many, a wife's contacts with men outside the home threatens the family's reputation. Rajendra Gupta, a 28-year-old college graduate who lives in a joint family with his wife, parents, and younger brother and his family, emphasizes that the joint family doesn't restrict him in any way. Yet, because of his concern with protecting the family honor, Rajendra doesn't grant women the same freedom:

> To talk with any other male is harmful to our prestige [*pratishṭhā*]. If my wife starts to talk with you and another person sees it, then it harms our social prestige [English phrase].

Nandu Gupta also cites the demands of honor to explain restrictions on women:

> [If my wife] has any wrong relationship with anyone, it is very dishonorable [*beizzatī*] for the whole family. Therefore, we keep them under control. We don't let them go anywhere alone. If it happens like this, it is a very shameful [*sharmī*] thing for the whole family from the father on down.

I describe above Phoolchand Mishra's conviction that the whole family's honor depends on the propriety of women's actions. Phoolchand's concern that people will point fingers at women who go outside the home shows that honor primarily involves adherence to social pressures. A woman, he says, must live according to the social restrictions "whatever they may be."[3]

Men present their family actions as based on received authority and a consideration of what others will think. They say that they must live in joint families, embrace arranged marriages, and limit women's actions outside the home to maintain tradition and family honor. Men proudly wear honor as a badge which indicates that they live according to the dictates of larger social groups.

COMMON NIGHTMARES OF PEOPLE OUTSIDE GROUP CONTROL

The importance men place on people being guided by their families is so great that they are wary of individuals outside of such control. Men are especially concerned that nonrelatives will act inappropriately if they lack family guidance—a concern apparent in the statements of Rajesh Yadav, Dileep Singh, and Vinod Gupta that open this chapter. Men seem to especially distrust women who are not supervised by their families. Prem Singh says, for instance, that

> today's environment is such that 60% of the girls in colleges are hunted by their own bad thoughts during their study time. The bad thoughts are that "I am free. I have no restrictions. I am not under somebody."

Prem's focus on the "bad thoughts" which "hunt" a person who is left unsupervised suggests that the social group, rather than an internalized conscience, is the best guarantor of social control.

Men's distrust of relationships between individuals that exist on an equal footing outside the hierarchical control of larger groups is most strongly evident in the common idea that love marriages inevitably fail. Two-thirds (32/49) of the men I interviewed mention that most love marriages fail. Commonly, men believe that such marriages fail because the relationship of husband and wife might be an equal relationship that is not controlled by social pressures.[4]

Narayan Singh believes, for instance, that love marriages break because the husband and wife understand each other as equals:

> Slowly a gap is born in their love [*prem*] *because they remain equal to each other.* Because they see themselves as equals, they start to fight amongst themselves. Mostly, both understand their rights as equal. Therefore, distance begins to be born and the marriage breaks.

Kumar Yadav says that, by contrast, family pressure insures that an arranged marriage will succeed:

> Love marriages often break. The thing is that neither one considers himself or herself less than the other one. They become stubborn. If they both are stubborn, then the marriage will spoil. One of them has to yield. But often this doesn't happen in love marriages. They have no pressure. There is no pressure from the family. Nor does the wife have the pressure of the husband. All these things lead to destruction.

As I emphasize in the next chapter, men see love as a dangerously powerful emotion unless it is clearly tempered by social fear. Men believe that the relationship between a man and a woman who marry for love will consist of friendship rather than the more stable, clear-cut, hierarchical relationship that they prefer. They have difficulty imagining how a marriage could succeed without the close control of family elders.

Men think that fear of dishonor is the only way of checking antisocial impulses, and they believe that those who marry for love don't care about their honor. They think that those who marry for love won't be able to control the fighting that naturally arises between husband and wife. These concerns are apparent in Deepak Mishra's description of an intercaste love marriage that occurred in his neighborhood. "After the marriage," Deepak says, "everyone boycotted them. No one from the boy's or the girl's family would even talk to them or let them enter their house." Although the boy and girl got along "for a few days," afterwards their fighting got out of control:

> Before the marriage, the boy said "I will give my life for you," and the
> girl said it as well. He said, "you are everything for me" and she said it,
> too. But after marrying they came to understand: "Oh, the romantic
> world has changed greatly." So, the boy and girl began to blame each
> other. The boy said, "you trapped me." The girl said, "you trapped
> me." The boy said, "this happened because of you." The girl replied,
> "what have I done? You have done it." They both started fighting and
> quarreling, and now the fight is moving with much strength. The boy
> beats the girl and they are on the verge of divorce.

The telling and retelling of stories like Deepak's help constitute and
reconstitute the cultural understanding that those who are not controlled
by appeals to their honor will never be controlled by anything. The
common belief that love marriages fail expresses the conviction that
equal relationships outside the pressures of a joint family are unstable
and dangerous.

Evaluating Others: A Focus on the Group

One reason men see parents' investigation of a prospective bride's qualities as exhaustive and effective is that they believe that parents will
focus on a woman's family to discover whether a bride is suitable.[5]
Sunil Gupta says, for instance that arranged marriages succeed because
the parents "look at the girl's *khāndān* [family lineage]. They look at the
origin of her family, and the family's whole life history." In particular,
men hope that parents will be concerned with whether a family is vegetarian or not. Thirty-year-old Ramlal Mishra emphasizes that

> the parents search about the *khāndān* of the girl and about the charac-
> ter of the whole family and about their way of eating and drinking.
> Vegetarian parents try to marry their son or daughter with a pure veg-
> etarian family. Parents watch these things, but the son would not. If the
> boy marries of his own liking, it is only for the purpose of sex. He
> only sees whether or not he likes the girl and he has no concern with
> whether she is a vegetarian or of our caste.

Like other men, both married and unmarried, Ramlal insists that parents
will not choose a "mistake girl" for their son. By contrast, a boy choosing his own bride might pick a "girl who is on the wrong path." Men
believe that parents conscientiously examine the girl's family, while an
immature boy would focus on the girl's beauty alone.

Men also focus on family background when they try to understand
the unconventional actions of others. Men usually regard the actions
of men who marry for love or who allow their wives to work outside the

home as a reflection of their caste or family, rather than the result of some unique inclination of the individual.[6] Ashok Mishra feels, for instance, that whether a boy should meet his bride before marrying her depends entirely on the family he lives in:

> In our *khāndān*, girls cannot be seen. But, every caste has their own customs and they do their children's marriages by their own customs. I am of the type of Brāhman family in which the girl cannot be shown.

Ashok does not discuss the propriety of arranged marriages in an abstract, general way, but instead sees how one marries as depending solely on the family to which the individual belongs.

Indeed, men commonly say that any marriage is proper if it is in accordance with one's society's rules. Seven of the men I interviewed mention that love marriages happen in educated society, and that for people in that society a love marriage would be workable. All but one of these men, moreover, do not aspire to be a member of an educated society and most of these men regard love marriages as undesirable. Fifty-four-year-old Nathuram Mishra says, for instance, that "educated people and people with jobs try to do love marriages and some can do them, but mostly those who are not educated and who believe in God, do not like this type of marriage."

Men similarly believe that the reason some women work outside the home is to be found in the nature of their social groups rather than in the inclinations of individual women. Most men realize that upper-class women, and poor women often work outside the home. Rajesh Yadav says, for instance, that women from educated societies can do anything outside the home: "If they are from advanced families, going and coming is a common thing. The advanced people like it if their wife works, but they will receive trouble from this." Amrit Mishra offers a similar explanation of why women from poorer families often work outside the home: "In Hindustan, there are many castes. In the poorer castes, both the husband and wife work." Men do not see some personal quality of a woman (or her husband) as an explanation of whether a woman will work outside the home. Instead, they evaluate the propriety of a woman working by considering the society to which she belongs. As Sureshwar Mishra puts it, "We don't want our women to work, but let whoever wants to allow them to work to do it."

A certain social framework for understanding action is apparent in the talk of the men I interviewed. Upper-caste Hindu men's common-sense understanding is that individual actions are driven by one's social group, and that individuals acting independent of their social group will act destructively. Most men see legitimate action as directed by elders in the family.

SOCIAL FRAMEWORKS FOR UNDERSTANDING ACTION

Implicit understandings are an important part of any cultural apparatus. Arguing that any society's cultural apparatus must fulfill diverse orientational requirements, Geertz ([1966] 1973b: 363) focuses on conceptualizations of the person. An understanding of what drives individual action, and of what prevents antisocial actions is just as important an orientational requirement (see Heelas 1981a; Lutz 1988). I use the term *social framework for understanding action* to describe the commonsense understanding of human motivation, and of what prevents people from acting destructively that is dominant within some social group.

INDIVIDUALIST AND COLLECTIVIST FRAMEWORKS FOR UNDERSTANDING ACTION

Solutions to the universal problem of how action is conceptualized vary from society to society, vary for subcultures within a society, and vary historically within any particular society (Heelas and Lock 1981; Lutz 1988). Specific conceptualizations of action are highly diverse. Actions can be understood, for instance, as driven by gods or spirits, by respect for elders, by spells cast by witches, by "substances" in the village soil, or by the self based on individual interests and desires.

Despite this diversity, two general types of understanding are fundamental (see Heelas 1981b). First, actions can be understood as driven by forces within the individual. Bellah *et al.*'s (1985) recent discussion of "languages"—distinct vocabularies attached to discourse—points to the individualistic understanding of action that is dominant among middle-class American men today. As Bellah *et al.* (1985: 81) argue, most Americans are limited by a "language of radical individual autonomy" and "cannot think about themselves or others except as arbitrary centers of volition." The American understanding, they argue, focuses on "the autonomous individual, presumed able to choose the roles he [or she] will play and the commitments he [or she] will make, not on the basis of higher truths, but according to the criterion of life-effectiveness as the individual judges it" (Bellah *et al.* 1985: 47; see also Swidler 1986: 276; Heelas 1981a: 4; Varenne 1977).

The second, contrasting understanding of what drives the actions of individuals focuses on forces external to the individual. These understandings focus on actions as driven predominately by external agencies. An example of this second type of understanding is the collectivist understanding of action which sees actions as driven by an individual's social group.

These divergent understandings of what drives action include a commonsense understanding of how social control works. Middle-class American men, who hold that the individual chooses his or her own actions, also focus on the individual in understanding how social control works. For American men, the individual's self control is what prevents antisocial acts (Bellah *et al.* 1985). By contrast, Hindu men, who see actions as driven by the individual's social group, hold that only group pressure can prevent the individual from acting destructively.

These commonsense understandings of what drives action and of how social control works also imply an understanding of what should drive action. Those who appear to American men to be driven by group pressure discredit themselves as lacking normal individual initiative. Those who appear to Hindu men to be choosing actions independent of their social group discredit themselves as selfish and foolishly independent. Since American men see destructive acts as prevented by the individual's self control, those who appear too influenced by group pressure appear dangerously vulnerable to being pressured into committing horrible acts. Since Hindu men see antisocial acts as prevented by the person's social group, those who appear too influenced by their own particular desires may seem vulnerable to acting destructively.

A COMMONSENSE UNDERSTANDING

The social framework for understanding action is a commonsense description of the world. Common sense, as Swidler (1986: 279) puts it, is the set of cultural assumptions so unselfconsciously held that they seem a "natural, transparent, undeniable part of the structure of the world." Religion rests its case on revelation, and science on method, but for common sense, as Geertz (1975: 75) argues, "the world is its authority." Following Geertz, Thomas Scheff (1990: 138) describes systems of commonsense knowledge as "made up of whatever the members of a group take to be self-evident, of what is taken for granted, of what goes without saying and, in fact, had better not be said or talked about."

While people recognize most cultural components, including some of their deepest values, as socially constructed, people regard their understanding of action as simply a description of the natural order, as something anyone in their right mind should know. While an outsider can comment on them, an insider usually cannot (Scheff 1990: 138; Geertz 1975). Scheff (1990: 141) argues that while human beings "have the capacity for instant reflexive awareness about many things, one's own system of common sense is not one of them."

Because it is informal and unsystematized, commonsense knowledge is intractably diverse (Geertz 1975: 90; Scheff 1990: 140; Swidler 1986). Individuals use commonsense understandings in an adhoc fashion to support a diversity of concrete acts. Because it is flexible, unsystematic, and usually left unsaid, commonsense knowledge is rarely directly challenged, making it relatively stable.

MERELY WAYS OF UNDERSTANDING ACTION

These different cultural understandings of what drives action should not be confused with actual differences in what influences the actions of individuals. In all societies, both forces external to the individual and forces within the individual have an objective influence on individual actions. What varies cross-culturally is whether one understanding or the other is culturally elaborated (and, thus, whether group control or individual volition is more easily recognized). Social frameworks for understanding action are not ways of acting, then, but ways of understanding or perceiving actions. Social groups have an important influence on actions of middle-class American men even though they are unlikely to recognize that influence. In their accounts of their own success, for instance, middle-class American men emphasize their own individual effort, ignoring the contributions of family and neighbors, which are often just as essential (Varenne 1977: 28-29; Bellah *et al*. 1985: 82). At a more general level, the imperative that Americans be self-reliant and make decisions on their own is itself not chosen by the individual but is a social imperative (Varenne 1977: 47-8; Dumont [1966] 1980: 9-10; Bellah *et al*. 1985). Similarly, individual interests play an important part in driving the actions of individual Hindu men even though they may see even their most self-interested actions as directed by the received authority of caste and family. An individualistic understanding of action, then, does not imply greater individual autonomy, just as a collectivist understanding does not imply stronger group control. Culture is not behavior, and indigenous ethnopsychologies are not a completely accurate description of psychological motivations (see Ewing 1991: 132-134).

PRACTICES AND THE *SOCIAL* FRAMEWORK FOR UNDERSTANDING ACTION

The framework for understanding action is "social" in two ways. First, the framework is social in that it is largely shared by people within a particular social group. Most, although not all, people hold it as their personal orientation. Second, the understanding is not individually invented, but is received through the individual's interactions with others.[8] In particular, the framework is made compelling by social practices in which people act on the dominant understanding of action. Here, I follow social constructionist traditions which argue that people understand the world the way they do because they have participated in social practices that presuppose those understandings.

Hindu men who distrust actions independent of the individual's social group act in ways that tell others that independent actions render a person untrustworthy. Because many men see individuals acting outside of social controls as dangerous, they believe such individuals must be dishonored. Vinod Gupta warns, for instance, that those who act dishonorably must be "forced to face disrespect, hatred and anger everywhere in society."

An important expression of the understanding that social control rests with the group is tattling—the reporting of untoward actions to those responsible for controlling them, rather than to the individual perpetrator. I describe above how Sunil Gupta reports that if his wife went outside the home without asking, a person who saw her on the road would surely come up to him to ask him where she was going. Neighbors and acquaintances often report untoward behavior to fathers and husbands in order to bring the pressure of the joint family to bear on a wayward individual. Deepak Mishra says that when someone acts dishonorably "the person is not [criticized] directly. Someone else is told— either a friend or a relative." During my stay in Banāras, neighbors sometimes came to me to tattle about the improper behavior of other foreigners living in the city whom I knew barely, if at all. This surprised me but I later came to see that this was the way the social control of the group is brought to bear on the individual.

If tattling does not bring an individual in line he or she may be boycotted. Almost all of my respondents identify the primary consequence of dishonor as being boycotted [bahishkār]. Ramlal Mishra says that if a person is boycotted

> every type of relationship is severed. Family, friends, and everyone else separate him from themselves. They refuse to mix with him. They refuse to eat with him, drink with him, sit with him, or talk with him.

Lakanlal Mishra similarly describes being boycotted as the main consequence of dishonor. If one acts dishonorably, he says, "no one will keep company with him or stand by him." Earlier in this chapter I note Deepak Mishra's description of the boycott faced by a neighbor who married for love. Deepak thinks that this boycott is putting so much pressure on the husband and wife that they are on the verge of divorce.

During my one-year stay in a Banāras neighborhood I witnessed several instances of individuals being boycotted and heard of many others. On one occasion, I had given a couple of *roṭīs* [the staple bread] to a young man who had came to me hungry and in dirty tattered clothes. After he left my home, several neighbors hurried to tell me I should not associate with this person. "You must know he has been expelled from his father's house!" one of them exclaimed. Examples of such boycotts are much discussed. Many respondents told me of men who were boycotted by their families for marrying against parental opposition. One man whom I knew quite well was totally boycotted by his family for marrying outside of his caste. His brothers and parents severed all ties with him, refusing to even speak with him.

In my own day-to-day interactions, I found that people felt honored when I offered them food and drink. Amrit Mishra, a 30-year-old eldest son living with his parents, wife, and younger brothers, told me, for instance, that I honored him by offering him things to eat and drink when he came to my house for an interview: "When you come to my place, I will give you honor just as having come to your place you go running and fetch two glasses of water and bring biscuits to eat." By way of contrast, Amrit says that if his character were bad, I would dishonor him by not offering him anything:

> If my character is bad and I go to you place, then you would not kindly give me water to drink. Nor would you let me sit with you with honor. Rather, you would want that I should leave your house as soon as possible.

Honor is known by the willingness of others to associate themselves with a person. Dishonor is reflected in the unwillingness of others to do so.

Boycotting individuals and tattling on them are practices that express the understanding that individuals acting outside of their social group's guidance are dangerous. People boycott those who act dishonorably not only to bring the dishonored individual under the control of the society, but also because they fear coming into contact with a dangerous person who is outside family control. Deepak Mishra told me, for instance, that the reason he would report dishonorable behavior to a person's elders rather than to the individual himself is because the offender "might fight or quarrel" or "beat you up." Ramlal Mishra similarly says that people are not told directly that their behavior is bad because "enmity [*dushmanī*] might develop." Those who don't care about their honor, then, are assumed to be dangerous.

Men also fear being seen associating with people who act dishonorably (see also Dumont [1966] 1980: 179). Because so many Indians evaluate individuals by focusing on who their friends and relations are, it is dangerous indeed to associate with those who are dishonored. The social practice of dishonoring those who act separately from their social group results directly from the commonsense understanding that individuals are evaluated based on who they associate with and that individuals acting outside of their social group are dangerous.

Boycotting and tattling, in turn, help constitute the understanding that the individual who acts outside of his or her social group is dangerous. These oft-discussed and at least occasionally seen social practices convey to everyone that a particular framework for understanding action is dominant, that people act on this framework, and that to appear to act in ways inconsistent with this framework has social consequences.

SECOND LANGUAGES:
THE COMPLEXITY OF ETHNOPSYCHOLOGY

I have described two fundamental understandings—an individualistic understanding that sees action as chosen by the individual, and a collectivist understanding that sees action as driven by the individual's social group. But all individuals have the experience, even if vaguely understood, both of being able to determine what they do in the world and of being controlled and nourished by family and society. Because of this, all ethnopsychological understandings are complemented by a range of second languages that give voice to the opposite pole of human experience (see Bellah *et al.* 1985; Bailey 1991: 214-215).[9] Sometimes these languages are primary for some groups in society. Sometimes they exist simply to discredit people who act in ways counter to the dominant framework. But often they valorize an understanding at odds with the dominant framework for understanding action. While important, second languages are less elaborated, less familiar, and less legitimate than the dominant first language.

"LANGUAGES" OF DOMINATED GROUPS

Important groups in both the United States and India do not embrace the dominant framework for understanding as their primary orientation. American women, for instance, think much more in terms of relationships to others than in terms of the isolated individual that dominates the thought of American men (Gilligan 1982; Bellah *et al.* 1985: 111). African-Americans, recognizing how their life-chances are limited by forces outside themselves, are more likely to emphasize collective strategies for advancement than are European-Americans who focus more on individual volition (Weis 1985; Stack 1974). While members of the American middle-class focus on success through individual initiative, members of the American working-class may focus more on advancement through adherence to external authority (Carnoy and Levine 1985).

Similarly, some groups in India do not embrace the understanding of action that dominates among upper-caste Hindu men. Lower-caste people may have an individualistic rather than collectivist understanding of the world (see Appadurai 1986: 751-2; Khare 1984; but also see Moffatt 1979). As has long been recognized, lower-caste people do not see the social roles that constrain them as a legitimate part of the social order but as something imposed by the efforts of the powerful (Berreman 1971; Mencher 1974). Similarly, while upper-caste Indian men try to advance their position by strengthening their family, Indian women, often isolated and subjugated in their husbands' households, may try to advance their own position by persuading their husbands or sons to separate from the joint family, breaking up the larger groups that men prefer to hold together (see chapter 6; Bennett 1983).

DOMINANT GROUPS' SECOND LANGUAGES

While one understanding of action tends to be dominant among a social group, other conflicting ways of understanding action coexist in any society. While middle-class American men's framework for understanding action focuses on individual volition, this focus is sometimes tempered by recognition of the human experience of being sustained and nourished by family and society. While the first language of the American middle-class focuses on the individual, there are also, as Bellah *et al.* (1985) argue, second languages which center on the Biblical and republican traditions and which allow for a discourse based on shared commitments to communities. Critics of American culture similarly argue that the refusal to extend rights to colonial people or minority groups represents a second language that implicitly rejects the idea that all individuals have the same right to shape their own destiny (Béteille [1979] 1983: 34; Harding 1988).

Similarly, because total passivity or powerlessness runs counter to the human experience of being able to act in the world (Heelas 1981b: 47), various second languages recognizing the importance of the individual complement the dominant Indian first language that sees action as driven

by forces external to the individual. While in considering family matters
most of the men I interviewed focus most of the time on social pressures
as driving actions, various other conflicting understandings, or subtexts,
complement this dominant focus.[10] Hindu men often use a second language that recognizes individual volition when they think about political
goals, religious strivings, certain family relations, and sensuous desires, to
note several examples. I explore these second languages in chapter 5.

OTHER ACCOUNTS OF INDIAN COMMONSENSE THINKING

I have so far skirted a discussion of other accounts of Indian commonsense thinking. A long tradition of research holds that Indians de-emphasize individual autonomy. Some scholars focus, as I do, on how Indians
see themselves as guided by their caste and family (Kakar [1978] 1981;
Roland 1988), but most neglect how Indians see themselves as driven by
such guidance. McKim Marriott (1976, 1989) argues that Indians see
people as influenced by the physical substances the person comes into
contact with, Richard Shweder (1991) focuses on how Indians see themselves as guided by the demands of *dharma*, and Louis Dumont ([1966]
1980) focuses on how Indians stress "the society as a whole, as collective Man." The commonsense understandings of motivation that Marriott, Shweder, and Dumont describe do not focus on social pressure.
But they are still part of a class of understandings that focus on how
action is driven by forces outside the individual.

MARRIOTT'S FOCUS ON PHYSICAL SUBSTANCES

Marriott devotes substantial attention to describing indigenous Hindu
ethno-theories of what constitutes the self and what drives the actions of
individuals. Marriott (1976: 110-111) argues that, while Westerners see
individuals as autonomous, consistent bundles of volition who control
their own destiny, Indians do not think of persons as "'individual', that
is, indivisible, bounded units," but rather focus on how the person is
made up of diverse substances, which are unstable and subject to many
influences. He argues that Indians see the "world's inhabitants" as "generated by, and constituted of, more or less malleable substance that is
continually moving in and out of them and also moving, like other features of the hydrosphere, under the variable influences of heat, gravity,
currents and wind" (Marriott 1989: 18).

Marriott bases his argument largely on classical Sanskrit texts, but
ethnographic evidence supports his argument as well (Marriott 1989: 33,

see especially Daniel 1984; Barnett 1976; Trawick 1990: 133-4). E. Valentine Daniel (1984:79) describes, for instance, how the South Indian villagers he studied see "the quality of the soil substance" of the village as "ultimately mixed with the bodily substance of" the villagers, influencing their actions. Daniel (1984: 84) argues that villagers see people who live in a certain place as influenced not by "association with the people" of the place but by the personality of the soil.

SHWEDER'S FOCUS ON OBJECTIVE LAWS OF DHARMA

Of the works that have focused on how Indians see action as properly driven by self-evident *dharmik* social duties, Richard Shweder's ambitious investigation of moral reasoning in Bhubaneshwar has been influential. Shweder (Shweder and Miller 1985: 41) sees the Western moral code as "rights-based": Westerners understand the social order as "built up out of self-interested individuals in pursuit of their wants and preferences." In rights-based societies, Shweder (Shweder and Miller 1985: 53) argues, the individual "is fundamental and real and the passions, tastes and preferences of the individual and his or her liberty to pursue them" are "salient." By contrast, the moral code in India is "duty-based." In India, "it is the organization of social roles that is fundamental and real and role-based obligations" are "salient" (Shweder and Miller 1985: 53; see also Shweder, Mahapatra and Miller 1987: 20-1). Shweder (Shweder and Much 1987: 227) argues that his informants see correct behavior as "completely independent" not just of the person's own opinion but of "group opinion," as well. He reports that his informants see *dharma* "not as a social norm" but as "an independently existing and objective reality, somewhat like the law of physics" (Shweder and Much 1987: 230).[11]

METHOD AND FINDING

Shweder and Marriott report that Indians do not see action as properly chosen by the individual. But Shweder reports that Indians see themselves as obeying the objective demands of *dharma*, while Daniel (1984) and Marriott (1976: 112) report that Indians see actions as determined by the "circulations and combinations of particles of substance code [that] are continuously occurring." I found, by contrast, that Hindu men see actions as driven by social pressures and group opinions. What explains our different interpretations?

Some of our findings may be due to regional differences. I interviewed urban Hindi-speakers with secular jobs in North India. Daniel

(1984) did research with South Indian, Tamil-speaking villagers, while Shweder interviewed East Indian Oriya-speakers. It is not surprising that there are substantial variations among the billion people living in South Asia. Indeed, it is notable that even according to these accounts, the understandings of South Indian Tamil-speaking villagers, urban East Indian Oriya-speakers, and urban North Indian Hindi-speakers all de-emphasize individual volition (despite the different ways that they do so).

I think, however, that our different interpretations may also be due to the type of data we gathered. While Marriott (1989: 32) and Dumont ([1966] 1980] rely on classical Sanskrit texts—commentaries by indigenous intellectual elites—I focus on common people's commonsense understandings about family issues.[12] While Shweder uses Kohlberg interviews that create a religious context by focusing on moral reasoning about hypothetical situations, I created a context that revealed the implicit knowledge people apply to their own decisions in their families. The understandings I discuss are neither the understandings presented in classic texts nor the understandings people use when thinking about religion. Rather, they are the understandings that Hindu men use in explaining their day-to-day family life. In short, instead of relying on texts or ideology, I have taken what F.G. Bailey (1991: 213) calls the "agency point of view" (see also Mines 1988: 569.)

Roland (1988: 64), who did psychoanalytic therapy with urban, educated Indian patients, demonstrates the usefulness of in-depth, confidential discussions with Indians, and reached conclusions similar to my own. Roland found that "beneath the observance of an overt etiquette of deference, loyalty, and subordination, Indians keep a very private self" which he found to be very accessible "in a psychoanalytic relationship . . . where the Indian patient feels that the therapist is empathic and receptive, and where strict confidentiality of communication is assured." In these situations, "Indians tend to reveal their inner life more openly, and even to be more in touch with it, than most American patients." My impression is that the interviews I conducted worked in a similar way: Indian men enjoyed presenting the private inner self that is an important part of their psychological makeup (Roland 1988: 227) in interviews which were enjoyed as a time outside of the strict hierarchical structures in which they live most of their lives.

While a series of psychoanalytic sessions are much better at getting to know people than brief interviews, our methods are nonetheless similar, and it is not surprising that Roland, who also interviewed urban and educated Indians, reached conclusions similar to my own. Roland (1988: 155) found that Indians have a "radar sensitivity" that alerts them to what is expected in any group or situation. Roland (1988: 252-3) argues that Indians are constantly sensitive to "what is expected of them, acutely aware of how others are reacting to them. How one's behavior will be regarded by others . . . [is] always of the most central concern."

There is no doubt that Indians can draw on the understandings that Marriott and Shweder describe. Indeed, these understandings are apparent in some of what I have described in this chapter. When men emphasize that marriages should be arranged between vegetarian families, they do so partly because of their belief that physical substances influence people. Some men, notably Phoolchand Mishra, say that they follow the tradition of arranged marriages because of *dharmik* religious law. If questioned about it, many Indian men would say that their focus on being guided by their parents is neither arbitrary nor conformist, but is based on their conviction that their parents have the experience to guide them wisely. But in their day-to-day thinking about family matters the indigenous understanding of most Hindu men focuses most of the time on being guided by social pressures rather than *dharma* or particles of substance-code.

It seems likely that Indians rely on these different understandings in different contexts and to explain different arenas of experience. Indians may speak of physical substances when they discuss Ayurvedic medicine and diet (see, for instance, Alter 1992). As Shweder's (1991) research suggests, they may speak of the laws of *dharma* when they consider hypothetical situations. My research shows that in their commonsense thinking about family life, Indian men's main understanding is that people should be guided by social pressures. It is striking, moreover, that all of these understandings contrast with the American focus on the individual in their emphasis on how people are driven by forces external to them.

Much of the rest of the book explores how the collectivist framework for understanding action shapes and constrains Hindu men. If men focus on being guided by social pressures, how do they nonetheless buck these pressures? How do men balance the first language of social pressures with second languages of individual choice? If men can act on their own, in what way are they still constrained by the collectivist framework for understanding action? Before taking up these questions, however, I proceed in the next chapter to consider how the focus on social pressure shapes Hindu men's psyche, emotions, and conceptions of self.

4

Culture and Psyche:
Emotions, Conscience,
and Self-Conceptions

Several men who consent enthusiastically to having their marriages arranged don't believe that an arranged marriage will ever make them happy. Surjit Singh is a 33-year-old unmarried college graduate who lives with his parents in a large joint family. Surjit assists his parents in working their ready-made clothing shop in the vibrant downtown of Banāras. Surjit feels "unfortunate" that he remains unmarried at 33, seeing the age of 25 as the "golden chance" to wed while one's "body and intellect are very solid." Surjit says that he will marry soon, and he looks forward to the day that his parents arrange his marriage. Yet, Surjit believes that an arranged marriage will deny him the love he desires:

> To marry for love is a marriage in the true sense [sahī māne me], and to marry according to one's parents' wishes is not successful in any true sense [sahī māne me]. The inner self [antrang atmā] will never be happy. The arranged marriage is like some hackneyed [ghisāpiṭā] thing that is unable to achieve its end. Hindustani men do not live the way man should live in the true sense [sahī māne me]. In love [English], even if we get one day's success, then our whole life is meaningful [sārthak]. But Hindustanis live their whole lives, but they don't experience even one day's bliss [ānand] in a real sense.

Surjit's focus on love as "meaningful" anticipates the second languages of individual desires that I discuss in the next chapter. What I want to emphasize in this context is that Surjit is comfortable having his marriage arranged, even though he thinks such a marriage will never make his "inner self" happy. This lack of discomfort is difficult to comprehend if the focus is on individual choices. But because for Hindu men it is being guided by social pressures that is most essential, Surjit feels little discomfort acting in a way that he is convinced will never bring him personal happiness.

Surjit's emotions, sense of self, and conscience are all rooted in his conviction that the individual must be guided by social pressures. Surjit's lack of cognitive dissonance at embracing an arranged marriage that he is sure will not bring him personal happiness suggests that Surjit finds his most true self in obeying his parents. His emphasis on obeying parental dictates suggests that Surjit gives priority to his feelings for parents and family, rather than feelings for any woman he may marry.

Surjit's conscience seems, moreover, to demand being guided by others rather than by an inner voice.

Psychoanalysts, sociologists, and anthropologists are increasingly examining how emotions, self-conceptions, conscience, and cognitive dissonance vary from place to place and from person to person.[1] Richard Shweder (1990, cited in 1991: 73) argues that this focus has led to the emergence of a new discipline, cultural psychology, which charts how "cultural traditions and social practices regulate, express, and transform the human psyche, resulting less in psychic unity for humankind than in ethnic divergences in mind, self, and emotion." How do cultural under- standings of human motivation shape the psyche? In particular, how does the collectivist framework for understanding action shape the self- conceptions, consciences, and emotions of Hindu men?[2]

SELF-CONCEPTIONS[3]

A person's conception of his or her real self is a subjectively-held sense a person has of who he or she really is (Turner 1976: 1012). Men who embrace the collectivist framework for understanding action as their personal orientation find their true selves in being guided by social pres- sures. Since this framework de-emphasizes individual desires, those who embrace it usually do not regard consistency between actions and inner desires as an essential element of an authentic self. Thus, Surjit Singh's sense of self is not threatened by marrying according to his parents wishes, despite his conviction that an arranged marriage will not bring him inner happiness.

Neither is Krishna Das Singh discomforted by the discontinuity between his individual desires and socially demanded action. Krishna, 25, runs a dilapidated luggage store. He has completed his high school years but failed to graduate—something which is not discrediting for many Indians. Like Surjit, Krishna has access to second languages that allow him to see that he is unhappy with the wife his parents chose for him. Despite disliking his wife, however, Krishna says that he com- fortably acts out his role as husband:

> Whatever I have got I have passed with her and have fulfilled my roles according to my capacity. I don't act as if I don't like my wife. I do everything for her when it comes to food, drink, and clothing. Although I don't like her, I fully play the role of my responsibilities. Everybody thinks that I like my wife but I don't like her.

Krishna does not feel conflicted or tormented because of the incon- gruity between his actions and his inner feelings. He focuses instead on the fundamental importance of bowing to social pressure. For Krishna, too, it is continuity between actions and social pressures that is important for an authentic self.

All humans face social pressures and recognize individual desires. Middle-class American men, most of whom focus on how action should be directed by the autonomous individual, give preference to individual desires, while Hindu men focus most on bowing to social pressure. The cultural framework that makes family pressures visible and exemplary leads many Hindu men to see consistency between individual actions and social demands as the most essential element of an authentic self. What causes men to feel cognitive dissonance (Festinger 1957) is actions that are inconsistent with the demands of social pressures (Derné 1992a: 274-277).

CONSCIENCE[4]

Rather than carrying social standards around inside themselves, Hindu men sometimes discard these standards once they leave the watchful eyes of family and neighbors. As Sudhir Kakar ([1978] 1981: 135) observes, "infringements of moral standards [are] likely in situations 'when no one is looking.'"

The men I interviewed describe such infringements as both likely and unimpeachable as long as violations are not observed by neighbors. Thus, some men regard drinking as dishonorable, but only if it is done publicly. Thirty-year-old Amrit Mishra says, for instance, that

> if you drink whiskey it's not a good thing—meaning people consider this inferior. They don't see it with the look of honor [izzat]. Yet, many honorable people [izzatdārs] drink even though it is considered a low thing in the eyes of society. They drink, but only a little bit in their house. You can drink for the sake of entertainment. But you can't drink whiskey and roll on the street, talking nonsense and shouting abuses. Then, people will not see you with the look of honor [izzat]. [Emphasis added.]

The collectivist framework of understanding is clear in Amrit's statement: How "the eyes of society" view something determines whether it is right or wrong. Because of this focus, Amrit is unconcerned with actions that are not publicly observable. As I show in chapter 8, men similarly see fighting among women of a family as dishonorable—but only if such fighting is loud enough to be heard by an outsider.

Men usually assume that public pressure is what prompts conformity. R.P. Mishra, 35, says that even a respected priest of a local temple violates Hindu norms while travelling abroad:

> You know Pandit-ji. He is very respected and pure. We know his
> nature is good because he lives nearby and we can see him. But if he
> goes to America, *since the people of this place will not see him*, he will
> certainly drink wine and beer. [Emphasis added.]

R.P. assumes that Pandit-ji is guided not by abstract principles, but by
the people who are observing and judging his actions. Like many other
men, R.P. conceives of social pressures rather than inner conviction as
driving individual actions.

How does Hindu men's conscience work if men see social pressure as prompting conformity? Kakar ([1978] 1981: 135) argues that
Indians have a weak superego and are actually shaped by social pressures:

> Much of the individual behavior . . . that in westerners is regulated . . .
> by the demands of the superego, is taken care of in Indians by a com-
> munal conscience. . . . In contrast with the western superego, the com-
> munal conscience is a social rather than an individual formation: it is
> not "inside" the psyche. . . . [I]nstead of having one internal sentinel an
> Indian relies on many external "watchmen" to patrol his activities. . . .
> (Kakar [1978] 1981: 135, emphasis deleted.)

Other psychoanalysts rightly argue, however, that Indian men have an
internalized superego, but one that focuses most on adhering to social
pressures, rather than abstract principles. Alan Roland (1988: 271)
argues, for instance, that

> the Indian conscience is profoundly internalized, but into psychic struc-
> tures that develop and function significantly differently from those of
> Westerners. . . . [Indians'] radar sensitivity to the cues and norms of a
> given situation and others' reactions . . . [are] deeply internalized into
> psychic structures and an inner representational world.

Indians violate moral standards when no one is looking not because
Indians have no superego and must be controlled by others, but because
the conscience of many men demands only that they be guided by and
aware of the reactions of others.

EMOTIONS

It is increasingly recognized that emotions are not biological univer-
sals but are culturally and socially shaped.[5] Thomas Scheff (1990), Randall Collins (1990), and Arlie Hochschild (1983) focus attention on
how class and gender affect emotional experience. Steven Gordan
(1990), Peter Stearns (1989), and Francesca Cancian (1987) have

explored how emotion culture shifts historically in response to structural changes in family and economy. Catherine Lutz (1988), Margaret Trawick (1990), Owen Lynch (1990b), and others have focused on how emotions vary cross-culturally. As Shweder (1991:7) puts it, "human infants come into the world possessing a complex emotional keyboard; yet as they become Eskimo, Balinese, or Oriya only some keys get played."

My consideration of the unselfconscious way the men I interviewed talk about emotions suggests that the collectivist framework for understanding action shapes Hindu men's emotional life. Although I asked only one interview question that included an emotion word, men nevertheless often talked about emotions to frame their discussions of family life.[6] Because Hindu men focus on how action is rightly guided by social pressures, they regard social fear—fear that is prompted by loving respect for authority—as an exemplary emotion. Men are sensitive to social fear and easily recognize it. Because Hindu men distrust individual desires, most are wary of exclusive love as a dangerous emotion that might blind people to social pressures. While men are alert to the pulls of love, they are so aware of its dangers that they usually try to limit the power of love's attraction.

SOCIAL FEAR AS AN EXEMPLARY EMOTION

Catherine Lutz's (1988) description of the ethnopsychology and emotion culture of the Micronesian Ifaluk people shares some similarities with the Hindu ethnopsychology and emotion culture I am describing. Like Hindu men, the Ifaluk regard "the sources of behavior" as "multiple and interpersonal" rather than "to be found exclusively in" an "independent or central part of the self" (Lutz 1988: 88). Like Hindu men, the Ifaluk see the person "as first and foremost a social creature and only secondarily and in a limited way, an autonomous individual" (Lutz 1988: 81). Lutz found that the Ifaluk, consequently, see fear as a moral emotion: "To the Ifaluk way of thinking, fear is what keeps people good. The person who fears the justifiable anger of others is one who carefully watches her own behavior's 'social wake,' always attentive to the risk of rocking another's boat" (Lutz 1988: 201). Fear is moral because it indicates that people are guided—as mature, normal people should be—by pressures from others.

Hindu men similarly regard social fear as an exemplary, moral emotion that is the foundation of good behavior.[7] I use the English "fear" to translate the Hindi *ḍar*, but *ḍar* also implies respect and love for authorities in a joint family.[8] I open the last chapter by noting that Dileep Singh and Rajesh Yadav believe people are only educated from doing wrong by "social fear [*samāj ke ḍar*]."[9] Men often refer to social fear as what keeps people's individual desires in check. Gopal Mishra's father, Lakanlal, helps run the family's print shop, but spends more time these days socializing with relatives who visit from nearby villages. Lakanlal believes that "common people live happily jointly." But he emphasizes that social fear is what keeps people in line:

> Here, the social ties are so great that people act according to what they see in society. Common families, common societies, with the fear [ḍar] of society do not make love marriages.

Other men sometimes comment that fear is what makes marriages work. Sureshwar Mishra says, for instance, that, while love marriages will never last long, arranged marriages "run because of the fear [ḍar] of public shame [lok lajjā]."

People make similar references to the importance of fear in maintaining cooperative life in a joint family. Nathuram Mishra, 54, heads a large joint family that includes many sons, daughters-in-law, and grandchildren. While I was interviewing Nathuram in an upstairs room that is attached to the family's grain shop, two women made chapātīs [the staple bread cakes] in a ground floor room, and several men lounged on chārpāīs [cots] in the courtyard. Nathuram, who wears a cap, dhotī, and black jacket, is talkative and congenial. He loves to talk about Rām līlā performances in Banāras, and he insisted on playing me audio tapes of his favorite performances.[10] For Nathuram, social fear is essential in keeping his large family together. The family remains united, he says, because "all of the family members fear [bhaybhīt] to do something bad to each other. They yield [mānanā] to each other, love [paraspar prem rahanā] each other, and fear [ḍarnā; bhaybhīt rahanā] each other."[11] Prem Singh's explanation of how his antisocial impulses are checked by his "emotional calculation" that his parents are above him (chapter 3) similarly suggests the importance of social fear in Indian families.

How is this elaboration of social fear as a moral, mature emotion linked to the understanding that action is driven by social pressures? In a world where adherence to social pressures is seen as of greatest importance in assuring harmony, fear becomes exemplary, because it is seen as the emotion that prompts correct behavior. It is exemplary to be always fearful of negative evaluation of others. Indian men easily recognize fear, and point to their fear to indicate that they are harmless and will not act inappropriately.

CONCEPTIONS OF LOVE

How does Hindu men's focus on how individuals ought to be driven by social pressure influence their conceptions of love?[12] Unlike Americans who focus on individual personality characteristics to understand behavior, Hindu men (like the Ifaluk [Lutz 1988: 102-3]) focus on generic human responses to situations (Shweder and Miller 1985). Where little emphasis is placed on the individual's own personal traits, the idea of love for a special, unique person makes little sense (see also Kurtz 1992: 254). Ann Swidler (forthcoming) shows that American conceptions of romantic love focus on a feeling for a unique other person of equal status.[13] By contrast, within Indian families, love that does not threaten includes the following components. First, love is based on a duty owed in a relationship, not on special qualities of the beloved individual. Second, love is not exclusive, but extends toward many in a family. Third, love between equals or between husband and wife is potentially volatile if it is not tempered by social fear.

When I asked husbands to tell me about their wives' special qualities, the most common response was to state that she "has no special qualities."[14] Deepak Mishra says that his love for his wife is based on the duty he owes her as his wife, rather than on her specialness:

> If my child is beautiful or ugly, I will love [*pyār*] him. It should also be this way with the wife. Whether the wife is good or bad, after the marriage she is a member of the family and for the sake of the relationship we certainly love [*mohabbat*] her—however she is to look at.

For Deepak, love is owed in a situation, rather than directed toward someone independently worthy of affection. While Americans see themselves as choosing whom to love (Varenne 1977; Bellah *et al.* 1985: 89), for Hindu men, love is a duty.

Because Indian men de-emphasize the individual, love is not for an exclusive individual, but is owed to many in a family. Vikas Mishra says, for instance, that the "culture" of India emphasizes that there must be a "tie [*bandhan*] with everybody—with brother, sister, mother, and wife." Men often describe the pleasures of joint-family living by focusing on what Tej Gupta calls the "love [*prem*]" one gets "from every member of the family." *Mālik* Sureshwar Mishra says that he likes living in a joint family because "the love of everyone remains together [*sab kā prem eksāth rahanā*]." R.L. Yadav, a young man staying with relatives in Banāras to attend the university, comments that he enjoys getting "love [*sneh*] from" everyone he lives with—his *nānī* [maternal grandmother] and *māmā*s and *māmī*s [maternal uncles and aunts]. "I get such love [*prem*]," he concludes, "that everything is good."[15]

Men commonly emphasize that a woman's love should not be directed toward her husband alone but should be directed toward many in her family. Anand Singh says, for instance, that a wife should "live in love [*pyār-mohabbat se rahanā*] with her husband, mother-in-law and father-in-law, and with other people, too." Anand says that his wife must care not only for their own children, but for his brothers' and *bhābhīs*' children as well. "If they cry, she should take them in her lap and love [*pyār*] them." Deepak Mishra similarly describes how the ideal wife should spread loving attention throughout the household:

> She should behave equally with everyone. It is not that she should obey [*mānanā*] her husband greatly and neglect her mother-in-law and father-in-law. Nor should she serve [*sevā*] her mother-in-law and father-in-law and neglect her husband. Rather, she should adjust [English word] to all equally [*barābar se*]. The biggest quality of the ideal wife is that she should establish harmony [*sāmanjasy*] in every relationship.

Similar descriptions are voiced by many others. Sunil Gupta says, for instance, that the ideal wife "should see everyone in one way. There should not be any small differences for anyone." Ravi Mishra says that a wife should "love [*prem karnā*] everyone [*sab*] in the house."

In contrast to the exemplary love which extends toward many, men see love as dangerous if it becomes too focused on one individual or aspect of life. Ravi Mishra says, for instance, that one must love [*prem*] god [*bhagvān*], one's work, and one's wife. He says that "from the love [*prem*] with god, the world runs; from the love [*prem*] with the shop, the stomach runs; and from the love [*prem*] with the woman, the family runs." Ravi goes on to note that if the husband places too much love on his wife, family members will be "angry. They will say 'he is passing most of the time with the wife.' Then his mind will not attach on the daily bread."

For Hindu men, the danger is that an exclusive love which is not balanced with love for other family members will get out of hand. Phoolchand Mishra gets at this point in a roundabout way as he focuses on how an overemphasis on sexual attraction is dangerous:

> If the husband and wife love [*chāhat*][16] each other because of sex, then they may neglect their elders. But if the reason for the deepness of their relationship is not the sexual relationship, then it is less possible to have this type of corruption of neglecting elders because the *mentality of human beings doesn't remain restricted to one place. It keeps reflecting everywhere.* [Emphasis added.]

For Phoolchand, "love [*chāhat*] should be for everyone—not for some special person." Phoolchand's interpretation of Hindi film love stories similarly emphasizes the imperative that love should be directed toward society as well as toward one's spouse. Phoolchand says that heroes and heroines in Hindi films are exemplary because their love [*chāhat*] for each other does not minimize their love [*chāhat*] for the whole society. Their feelings [*bhāvnā*] are not limited to each other. The hero likes the society as much as he likes the heroine.

By contrast, a Hindi film villain is evil because he "likes the heroine's fleshy beauty alone. He has no concern for the beauty of society." For Phoolchand, then, a person's love is dangerous when it becomes too focused on one person, instead of extending to everyone in a family.

Phoolchand goes on to say that loving one's wife more than others is not good for the family, and that love for a wife should not be based on a special characteristic:

> The husband who has more love [*chāhat*] for his wife than for his family is wrong inside. This love [*chāhat*] is not stable. It may break. This love [*chāhat*] is maintained due to a special thing. If that special thing finishes, the love [*chāhat*] itself will be over.

Such "love [*chāhat*]," for Phoolchand, "is not love [*chāhat*] at all." For Phoolchand, love should not be based on a special characteristic, and should extend toward many in a joint household. While American notions of love focus on a feeling directed toward a unique, special other person, Indian men's notions of exemplary love focus on a feeling directed toward numerous people in the family who may not have any special characteristics but toward whom one owes love because of a role obligation.

LOVE AS A DANGEROUSLY INDIVIDUALISTIC EMOTION

There is, then, a view of exemplary love between husband and wife which is consistent with the collectivist framework for understanding action. This view holds that love is safe if it is neither exclusive nor built on special characteristics of the person.

But most men emphasize the dangers of love between husband and wife. In particular, men insist that love must always be bounded by social fear. Men see love as a dangerously individualistic emotion that might tempt men away from the benevolent guidance of social pressure from a wise family. My findings, like those of other ethnographers,[17] indicate that Hindu men often see love as a dangerously wild, powerful, and unpredictable emotion that can blind a person to family obligations.

Men often see sex, and sometimes love, as something that automatically happens when men and women come together. They see love as natural, unstoppable and dangerous. Ramlal Mishra enjoys seeing Hindi films, but he worries that "if boys and girls are together seeing the world and the bad films, sex automatically arises in them. They will go in the wrong way and go astray." Bhipul Gupta, 62, often enjoys conversation and laughter with his wife, but he fears that if unmarried boys and girls

> have contact and talk, then jokes automatically happen. Love [English word] itself originates! They go further ahead and become one. When they become one, both will be in trouble.

Bhipul, like several others, offered this maxim: "love is not done; it happens [*prem kiyā nahī jātā hai, ho jātā hai*]." The prohibition on boys and girls even speaking with one another after a certain age reflects men's conviction that individual self control can not be counted on to prevent sex between men and women.[18]

Many men say that restrictions on women are necessary to prevent their own sexual urges from overpowering them. Raj Kumar Singh is delighted with his marriage, and enjoys talking with his wife about their childhoods. Yet, Raj is thankful that unrelated women never tempt him from the path of propriety. "The shame [*sharm-lajjā*] of women is good," he says. "If women walk around uncovered, my mind will spoil." Phoolchand Mishra is similarly wary of the desire he would feel if he came into contact with an unveiled woman: "The advantage of veiling [*ghūnghaṭ*] is that my mind's corruptions [*vikṛatīyā*] are over as soon as they arise." The unmarried Prem Singh is similarly concerned that "whenever sex comes to man, he will lose his power of thinking and understanding. Few people," he says, "will be able to control themselves in that period." Prem is wary of being blinded by love:

> Because I have joy [*umang*] within me, I am not sure if I can control myself. I may become entangled with the love [English word] of somebody. If I meet a girl and love [English word] happens between us, I cannot stop meeting her. I will meet her.

For Prem, the "hobby of sex" threatens to be addicting:

> The man who will lose himself in sex can forget the roles he has to play as in any intoxication. If you drink wine and you've got 100 rupees, then you will go straight to the wine shop, whether there is food in the house or not. The same process runs with the worshipper of sex. His mind will not be peaceful because he will always be entangled in women.

Like many men, Prem doubts that individuals can control their sexual urges. He and others worry that love may blind men to their responsibilities toward their families.

Men often say that unmarried persons who are charmed by love are unable to choose an acceptable spouse for themselves. Sunil Gupta thinks that parents carefully investigate a potential spouse's family history, but he cautions that boys who choose their own spouse "marry due to emotion [*bhāvnā*]. Boys don't get complete understanding." Anil Gupta similarly reasons that

> with age, the experience increases a little bit. The youngsters only see the girl's color.[19] What else can they see and understand? The person who is a bit older examines the nature of the girl's *khāndān* [family lineage].

Many men emphasize that, while parents thoroughly consider the girl's family, young men are likely be blinded, as 28-year-old Rajendra Gupta puts it, by the "charm of sex."

Men fear that married men who love their wives too much might not be appropriately guided by elders in the joint family. Sureshwar Mishra, a 60-year-old head of a joint family that still includes three of his five married sons, believes, for instance, that

> if there is too much relationship and she says to jump in a well, then I will have to jump in a well. But if the relationship remains limited what she says will not happen and what I want will happen. If the relationship is too close and the wife says 'go to a different house,' then the husband goes, leaving the family members [*gharvālle*] to go to hell without any concern.

Kumar Yadav says that, if a husband and wife don't keep their relationship limited, they come to consider themselves "great [*mahān*]. They become careless and forget their duties toward their families." Kumar's emphasis on how the individual must not take priority over the group reflects the collectivist orientation he shares with most men.

Sometimes men focus on how love for one's wife can lead a husband to neglect the imperative of being fearful. Ravi Mishra says, for instance, that if the love between husband and wife is not limited, "the couple will not remain fearful [*dar*] of the parents." About two-thirds of the men I interviewed believe that interactions between husbands and wives must be limited,[20] and most of these men believe that too much love between husband and wife might threaten the harmony of the joint family.[21]

Cautionary tales about love marriage hold that love is so intoxicating that it can never be the basis of marriage (see also Sharma 1980: 40; Kolenda 1993: 112). Phoolchand Mishra says that love marriages fall apart because the "love [*prem*] is built before marriage." From the height of their love, he says, they have "daze and fear" and may fall as they try to maintain that height. By contrast, in a familial marriage, people are unknown to each other from the beginning. Because of this, their love [*prem*] is built afterward. The ladder of love [*prem*] proceeds ahead. In the love marriage, the ladder of love [*prem*] has proceeded too high.

Raj Kumar Singh similarly believes that the love between husband and wife would necessarily diminish after a love marriage:

If we marry for love after liking each other from childhood, then the attachment [*lagāv*][22] becomes less. It does not grow. As much as one lives apart from each other, the attachment [*lagāv*] grows. If you like each other from childhood, there will be no such attachment [*lagāv*], but only fighting and quarrelling.

While Americans believe that love is the essential basis for marriage (Bellah *et al.* 1985: 89; Swidler forthcoming), Hindu men believe that love between husband and wife can develop only after marrying.

As I show in the last chapter, cautionary tales about love marriage portray equal relationships as always dangerous unless tempered by social fear. Narayan Singh says, for instance, that a husband and wife who marry for love continually quarrel because "they see themselves as equals." Kumar Yadav says that the problem in love marriages is that neither the husband nor the wife "considers himself less than the other one." Rajesh Yadav similarly reasons that

the family tie does not remain for very long because the boy and girl don't understand themselves as lower than anybody else. If any talk or friction happens between them, the boy will want to be superior to the girl and the girl will want to be superior to the boy. The result will either be divorce or tension. She may say to you, "I have to go shopping" and you reply that you have no time. She will replay "OK, you have no time, I am going alone." Then one feels hurt.

Vinod Gupta says that in arranged marriages "the wife is a wife for the husband," while in love marriages the wife is "a friend." Vinod, Kumar, Rajesh, Narayan, and other men see equal relationships between husband and wife as impossible to maintain. They can only lead, as Vinod puts it, to "endless fighting."

These cautionary tales about the dangers of love marriages indicate the dangers of love when it is not tempered by social pressure, highlighting the distinction men make between exemplary social fear and dangerous love. Men say that the love they believe drives love marriages tears a marriage apart because it is not subordinate to social fear. They hope that in arranged marriages, social pressures in a family tame the love between husband and wife, forcing the wife to yield to her husband. Kumar Yadav reasons, for instance, that love marriages lead to destruction because the husband and wife "feel no pressure." In arranged marriages, as Surjit Singh reasons, "the woman is kept down a little from all sides." Men imagine that since love marriages give love primacy and lack family pressures, they can only end in failure.[23]

Because men emphasize social guidance, they have an elaborated notion of social fear as an exemplary emotion. Because they de-emphasize individual characteristics, they see love as based on a duty rather than on the specialness of the beloved. Because they de-emphasize the singular person, they demand that love be extended toward many in a family. Because men distrust individual desires, moreover, they often see love as a dangerous emotion that might tempt people away from joint-family guidance. Men's elaborate understanding of love makes them alert to the charm of their wives. But because they emphasize social fear and the goodness of love that extends toward many in the family, men often try to limit love that pulls them toward their wives. The dominant understanding of which emotions are exemplary and which emotions are dangerous is consistent, then, with Hindu men's collectivist framework for understanding action. In chapter 9, I explore how this emotion culture is also rooted in persistent dilemmas associated with joint-family living.

HINDU MEN'S USE OF EMOTIONAL PARADIGMS

Catherine Lutz (1988:10) argues that "each emotion word evokes in the listener of shared cultural background some variant of an elaborate 'scenario' or scene."[24] Men associate typical chains of events with particular emotions. Thus, for Hindu men, social fear prompts moral, correct behavior, while love for a special other threatens to tempt individuals from family responsibilities. These emotional paradigms sensitize men to some aspects of an emotion rather than others. While people often interpret their own experiences as different from cultural models (Averill 1985; Swidler forthcoming), emotional paradigms provide a "guide" indicating what is relevant to take notice of.

Hindu men are familiar with the richly elaborated paradigm of love as exemplary if duty-based, tempered by social fear, and directed toward many in the family, and as dangerous if exclusive, egalitarian and more powerful than family pressures. Men find it easy to recognize the benefits of social fear and the dangers of love. The first impulse of many men who feel a pull of love toward their wives is to check the emotion by limiting their contact with their wives or emphasizing their connections to their brothers and parents. Because their emotion culture emphasizes the benevolent aspect of social fear and the dangerous aspect of love, men often have difficulty seeing that social fear may prompt over-conformity, while love for one's wife might rightly prompt a husband to be sure that his wife is fairly treated in his family.

Emotion culture shapes emotions by providing a lens through which feelings are understood. But culture does not totally control emotional experiences. I open this chapter by discussing how Surjit Singh sees love as one of the most meaningful things in life. Surjit nevertheless values his respected place in his family so much that he gives priority to family duties. But, as I show in the next chapter, many men recognize the benefits of unconstrained love and the costs of social fear, despite the dominant emotional paradigms. Yet, even these men are in dialogue with the dominant emotion culture. Even if they love their wives, most men are usually careful to fulfill the family obligations that are highly elaborated in their culture. They are often careful to explain to others that their close relationships with their wives have not led them to neglect their families. While many men embrace love, their concerns about love are still affected by the elaborate scene of a man who is so blinded by love that he neglects his parents.

5

Second Languages and Individual Desires

Nandu Gupta, a 35-year-old high school graduate who heads a nuclear family, operates a small luggage shop, which he decorates with images of various gods and goddesses. After Nandu's first wife died, he decided to remarry because he missed the satisfaction of a one-to-one relationship, which his relationships with his brothers could not provide:

> I used to feel uneasy when I went home at night. Whom did I have to talk to? None of my brothers were mixing with each other. None of us had a good relationship with each other. There should be someone to talk to, with whom I can share my joys and sorrows. Because there was no one, I decided to remarry.

After remarrying, Nandu continued to be dissatisfied living with his parents:

> Living in the joint family where four women live together, there are always quarrels, such as "She has no work; she is sitting and doing nothing." Because all these quarrels were happening daily, I was very unsettled. Furthermore, although I came home on time, I didn't get any special food. When the cooking is done for all, there is nothing special for me.

Partly because Nandu wished that his wife could treat him as a special person, he separated from his parents' household:

> I have [set up a separate household] so that I will be separated from all these problems. I have peace compared with what was happening before among the women. I have much peace and satisfaction.

Nandu's decisions are at odds with the framework for understanding action and emotion culture I describe in the last two chapters. Nandu gives priority to a one-on-one relationship with his wife, rather than his relationships with his brothers. Rather than de-emphasizing his particular needs, Nandu wants to be treated as a special person. Nandu recognizes his individual desires and acts on them, leaving his brothers and parents to attain the "peace and satisfaction" of being away from family pressures.

Yet, the first language of social pressures is so strong that even Nandu continues to idealize a situation in which he and his brothers are guided by his father: "I wish that my brothers and I would go home at night after doing our business, and put our problems in front of our father and take advice from him. But these things are not in my brothers." Nandu continues to hope that one day he will reconcile with his brothers:

> Tensions happen, but it always becomes right again. If there is ever any fighting between brothers, it ends the next day. Anger [gussā] comes, but it cools down after one or two days and brothers meet again. Even if tensions rise up, they do not last forever.

Nandu also continues to feel the imperatives of family duty, and he emphasizes that he continues to fulfill his obligations to his parents: "I have to look after my father and mother. My wife also has to serve my parents." Nandu even emphasizes that he continues to be guided by his father about important decisions. He insists that his father is "the mālik. Above me is my father-jī. He is the one who directs the family. We are all under him." Although this is not literally true, the first language of group control is so strong that Nandu still feels uncomfortable presenting himself as living outside the control of his father.[1] Nandu Gupta's individual desires temper his commitment to being guided by a social group, but they do not lead Nandu to abandon this commitment.

Nandu's decision to abandon the security of his parents' household is difficult to understand if Hindu men are cultural dopes, who follow their culture's norms without question. Nandu's emphasis on the peace and satisfaction he has gained by separating from his brothers, and his desire to be treated as a special person suggest that the focus on being guided by social pressures is complemented by second languages which emphasize the individual.

Because experiencing one's wants is as universal an experience as being nurtured by social groups (Heelas 1981b: 47), even men who give priority to group demands often sense their own contradictory desires to be free from social pressures. Prem Singh embraces the "emotional calculation" that his parents are above him, guiding and controlling him, but he nonetheless feels the desire to "run behind the back of girls" and lose himself in the "intoxication of sex." Surjit Singh accepts the group guidance of having his marriage arranged by his parents, but he nonetheless recognizes an "inner self" which suffers in the bargain. Rajesh Yadav and Krishna Das Singh married when their parents asked them to, but they both lament the personal unhappiness these marriages have brought them. Because having individual wants and feeling the benefits of social guidance are universal experiences, cultural systems tend to recognize both poles of human life.

A second reason that cultures are always divided is that a cultural emphasis on particular tendencies leads people to imagine opposed tendencies (Hewitt 1989). John Hewitt (1989: 72) argues that when culture emphasizes social duty,

> people will not only talk about it and devote their energies to it, but they will worry about its opposite, however they conceive it—as "self-ishness," as "sloth," or as "desire." They are likely to be anxious about whether they are doing their duty, daydream about being released from duty, . . . and be on the lookout to punish those who stray too far from its demands.

Rajesh Yadav, Dileep Singh, and Vinod Gupta are committed to being guided by social pressures, but all three also recognize that such pressures are necessary precisely because individuals are tempted by their own individual desires (chapter 3). Rajesh cautions that without group control, men will pull off women's *sārī*s and pick people's pockets; Dileep warns that without social pressures people will commit crimes; and Vinod insists that, since it is "man's nature to want to be free," social restrictions are necessary to prevent a person from terrorizing society and dancing "like a devil." The cautionary tales Narayan Singh, Kumar Yadav, and Rajesh Yadav tell about the dangers of love marriages similarly reflect an intense awareness that individual desires are a threat to group harmony. The very focus on the importance of being guided by social pressure leads Hindu men to imagine the opposite—destructive individuals who act based on their own selfish desires.[2]

Indeed, most men who talk of individual desires do so to discredit others by accusing them of having unacceptably selfish motives (see Heelas 1981a; Lutz 1988: 145, 167). Phoolchand Mishra says, for instance, that his brother separated from his parents because of "self-ishness," which Phoolchand condemns as a "corruption" (see also Kakar [1978] 1981: 121). Ravi Mishra criticizes his brother for "spending too much time with his wife," neglecting his family responsibilities (see also Das 1976a). Hindu women report that family members may criticize women with careers as "ambitious, self-centered, selfish" (Liddle and Joshi 1986: 183).

But Hindu men also have access to second languages which valorize the individual. These second languages complement the dominant Hindu focus on being guided by family pressures.[3] While less rich, familiar, and legitimate for most men than the dominant first language of group guidance, these languages are nonetheless also available as a way of understanding family life. Without the existence of a cultural under-standing of individual desires, how could Vinod Gupta insist that he meet his wife before marrying her (chapter 3)? Without these second languages how could Dileep Singh decide to separate from his parents to provide a better life for his own children (chapter 3)? How could Nandu Gupta decide to separate from his brothers so that his wife could cook special foods for him? In this chapter, my main focus is on men who recognize their individual desires in their family lives, but I begin by considering important second languages that celebrate the individual in the political and spiritual spheres of life.

INDIVIDUALISM IN POLITICAL AND RELIGIOUS LIFE

The political realm is one arena in which Indians valorize the individual. As André Béteille ([1979] 1983) notes, the Indian constitution includes provisions that make the individual an important bearer of rights and obligations. Mattison Mines and Vijayalakshmi Gourishankar (1990: 761) show that Indians perceive "leadership, achievement, and agency as valued features of individuality." They describe a South Indian Brahman monastic head who acts as a political agent to maintain his position, and who is recognized as a unique person worthy of public recognition. Mines and Gourishankar (1990: 784) conclude that Indians regard "individuality, achievement, and agency . . . as valued features of identity for anyone acting as a socially significant leader."

Powerful second languages also focus on the individual in the spiritual realm. While it has long been recognized that the tradition of religious renouncers in Indian society represents the possibility of the individual free of social hierarchies (Dumont [1966] 1980: 184-5), Roland (1988: 228, 240) has recently argued that common Indians, too, recognize "particular proclivities of a person" with respect to "spiritual strivings." While the individual is usually subordinated to a person's hierarchical role within a family, most Indians have an "inner spiritual self" (Roland 1988: 289) that valorizes the individual. This Hindu second language of individualism in the spiritual realm is apparent in *bhakti* sects which allow the individual to achieve salvation through devotion irrespective of caste, gender, or other social groupings, in pilgrimages in which familial responsibilities become subordinate to an inner spiritual quest, and in Hindu religious philosophies that urge detachment from family ties that are mere illusion (Roland 1988: 307-310; Ramanujan 1989: 54; Wadley 1983).

When thinking about family life, most men focus most of the time on social pressures as driving actions. But aren't there second languages that emphasize the individual even in family life? How do men balance the first language of social pressures with a recognition of individual autonomy? In what way do men valorize the individual in their interactions within their families even if they also emphasize family duty?

EQUALITY BETWEEN BROTHERS IN JOINT FAMILIES[4]

Despite the emphasis men place on younger brothers being guided by elder brothers (Derné 1993), relationships between brothers are sometimes characterized by equality. While equality between brothers is inconsistent with the emphasis on elders guiding juniors within a family, brothers who are similar in age often live as near equals under their father in a joint family, enjoying the pleasure of a one-to-one relationship with one another. Like Raj Kumar Singh, many brothers live together "laughing and talking," sharing "each other's pains and sorrows" (chapter 3). Ramesh Mishra, 35, is an eldest son who lives with his parents, wife and children, and his brothers and their families. Ramesh describes his relationship with his brothers as "a relationship of friendship more than a relationship of brothers." By emphasizing friendship, Ramesh recognizes the equality he feels with his brothers. By contrasting such a relationship with the expected relationship between brothers, Ramesh emphasizes that it is an elder brother's duty to guide and control his younger brothers.

For Ramesh, like a few other men, sports is an arena for acting out the equal relationship between brothers. Ramesh talks with relish of the pleasure he gets from playing soccer with his brothers. "We are sportsmen," he says, "and we enjoy playing football together." Newly married Kumar Yadav, who is also an eldest son living with his parents in a joint family, enjoys wrestling with his brothers:[5]

> We do exercises together in the morning. When we do it for two hours, we get such bliss [*ānand*] as if we are in heaven. My main rival in wrestling is my [younger] brother. My brother has become a very good wrestler and we pull and push with each other.

These shared leisure activities are an indication of the pleasure and closeness that sometimes exist between brothers, pleasure that may provide relief from a cultural world that focuses on adherence to social pressures.

While Ramesh and Kumar emphasize equal relationships with their brothers, this emphasis remains secondary to their focus on being guided by their parents within joint households. Kumar says, for instance, that he wouldn't do even "the smallest" thing without asking his father.

Ramesh similarly focuses on the importance of following his father, emphasizing that families break when individuals try to have their own way:

> In the household in which there is only one *mālik* [head of household], the family will not break, while in the house where there are two or three *mālik*s, everyone wants to impose his own point. It is very natural that in those places separations will occur.

While Kumar Yadav and Ramesh Mishra have an elaborate second language to understand their easy, equal relationships with their brothers, this second language doesn't challenge the priority of the first language holding that one should be guided by family elders. Indeed, the equal relationships between these men and their brothers may be possible precisely because these men can rely on their fathers to provide the social guidance that they value (Derné 1993: 182).

RECOGNIZING INDIVIDUAL DESIRES WITHIN JOINT FAMILIES

While Kumar Yadav, Ramesh Mishra, and others focus on the importance of being guided by their parents, other men emphasize how such guidance must be tempered by a recognition that individual family members also want some autonomy. For these men, joint families break not because of individuals trying to have their own way, but because of excessive pressure from the *mālik*. Rajendra Gupta, a 28-year-old living with his wife, parents, and younger brother's family, runs a prosperous general store and pharmacy. Rajendra prefers living in a joint family, but he also feels that the joint family

> is not right if everything is dependent on the parents. It's wrong if you have to ask [your parents] for five rupees. The joint family is right if you can spend your money and roam around [*ghūmnā*] as you like. The joint family is wrong if there is force from the parents for everything— that one should not go to the movies, or should not go moving around. In those circumstances, the joint family will break.

Deepak Mishra similarly focuses on the importance of freedom within the family. While emphasizing that his father, Sureshwar, is the *mālik*, Deepak says that "since the family is full of adults, the *mālik* does not obstruct us in any way. We are free to do whatever we want—roam around [*ghūmnā*], see films, whatever."

Deepak and Rajendra want to make choices, but they also continue to focus on the guidance and nurture that joint-family living provides.

An emphasis on compromise is a common way that men balance their desire to make their own choices with their desire to be safely guided by their families. Anand Singh, a 47-year-old living with his wife, six older brothers, and their families, says that, while "our elder brother is our boss," "tensions" necessitate compromise:

> We try to create tolerance of one another. [We tell each other to] listen to our elders. But sometimes the elders accept the points of those who are junior. Only then can the family move on.

Sunil Gupta, a 35-year-old who also lives in a joint family headed by an elder brother, similarly focuses on the importance of compromise, while accepting that his eldest brother should always be consulted first: "We tell our thoughts to the *mālik* and we listen to his talk. Somewhere he is flexible and somewhere we are flexible."[6]

Some heads-of-household say that they accommodate the desires of their juniors, often arguing that compromise is necessary to protect the family. Devi Prasad Gupta, a rich 76-year-old, operates a successful jewelry shop on the alley that leads to Banāras's most famous temple. He has a large quiet, cool house in the suburbs of Banāras. The day I interviewed Devi, his son played in front of his house with his daughter. Another arrived on a scooter bearing milk. Although he is the unchallenged head of the family, Devi recognizes the importance of considering his children's wants:

> If I don't do things according to my son's wish or if his wife's wants aren't fulfilled, then they will go separately because they will feel my pressure [*dabav*] on them. We should live according to the principle that they should feel this [pressure] as shade. [They should understand] that from living under me they are getting shelter and comfort.

For Devi, Sunil, and Anand, a recognition of individual desires tempers the importance placed on obedience to elders. While this second language recognizes individual desires, it doesn't challenge the first language that gives priority to joint-family living. For Devi, Sunil, Deepak, and Rajendra, a willingness to compromise is important because it stabilizes the joint family.[7]

Individual Sensual Desires

While most men emphasize that tempting love for one's wife might threaten the joint family, many men also recognize their libidinal and sensual desires (Roland 1988: 228-9). Indeed, one-third of the men I interviewed reject the notion that a husband and wife should limit their mutual interactions (see also Seymour 1980: 128), and more than a third value close mutual relationships with their wives.[8] While many village ethnographies report that men must limit their conversations with their wives,[9] nearly all of the men I interviewed talk with their wives on many topics, often enjoying the interaction. Twenty-three-year-old Raj Kumar Singh is delighted with his marriage, and enjoys bantering with his wife:

> We talk about her blood relatives. We talk about how each of us passed our childhood. Or we talk about any subject which comes up. Sometimes we quarrel with each other. Then, the man consoles her. . . . For example, [the man will say,] "You are very beautiful, you are this, you are that. Let's go to the movies for entertainment." In this way, the man consoles the woman.

Some older men with more responsibilities in their families discuss family decisions with their wives. Shyam Gupta, a very well-off fifty-year-old living with his wife, two sons, and daughters-in-law, comments, for instance, that he and his wife "talk about any family problems that come up, and share our thoughts about anything exciting that happens." While many village ethnographies report that men do not feel it is right to be seen with their wives in public, nearly all of the urban men I interviewed believe it is acceptable to go to the cinema with their wives, and many men say that they occasionally roam around [ghūmnā-phīrnā] with their wives.[10]

Some men focus on sexual relationships with their wives as an important part of living the good life. Like many youngest sons, Anand Singh cultivates the mischievousness that would be unbecoming to an eldest son. He enjoys bragging to me about how much he enjoys sex with his wife, calling any limitation between husband and wife "unfathomable:"

> I take enjoyment with my wife. In the morning, we kiss and love [pyār karnā; mohabbat karnā] [each other] until I go to the shop. Her best quality is making love [English phrase.] She never refuses. Whenever I want, I just say it and she makes herself ready to please me. If I don't receive love [pyār] after working the whole day, then life is useless, isn't it?

Anand values his loving relationship with his wife: "If you give much love [pyār], you will receive much love [pyār]."

Other men focus on the pleasure of trusting relationships of understanding with their wives. College-educated Ramesh Mishra feels that "having a relationship is very important" because only then can there be "mutual understanding" between husband and wife. Vinod Gupta similarly values a close relationship with his wife as the means to the good life:

> No limitation need be placed on the mutual contact of husband and
> wife. As much as the husband and wife know each other, then their
> love [English] will become intimate [*ghanishṭh*]. . . . As much as they
> know each other very closely, then they will obtain that much of a
> happy life. . . . To respect each other's feelings is the way of passing
> the good life.

Several older men with married sons also value their relationships with
their wives. Shyam Gupta says, for instance:

> My wife and I get along [*paṭnā*] with each other very well; it means a
> lot of love [*prem*] is there.

Shom Mishra, 45, says that there is "no danger" from the "intense passions" between husband and wife. Although Shom notes that "the physical relationship [between husband and wife] cannot last forever," he is
certain that the "idealistic relationship" with his wife can be maintained.
Shom says that by talking with his wife he creates "an environment" in
which "there is a natural and automatic cooperation."

Other men describe with pleasure how their wives provided com-
panionship. Anil Gupta, 76, continues to live with one of his sons,
whose wife he likes most. Although Anil did not become close to his
wife until after his parents died, he nonetheless lovingly describes going
on pilgrimages and to the movies with her. When she died, Anil felt "a
very big internal pain that was so much I could not tell anyone."

My own observations of men enjoying close, playful discussions
with their wives indicate that men's statements that they have close
relationships with their wives reflect a reality one would not expect
from village ethnographies that emphasize mutual avoidance of husband and wife. One afternoon in the hot season, I sat with R.P. Mishra in
his cool house. R.P. is a college-educated 35-year-old with a white-collar service job. He spends much of his leisure time playing sitar and
attending musical concerts. A younger son, whose brothers have separated from his household because of their white-collar jobs in distant
cities, R.P. lives with his parents, wife, and several young children. On
this day, I sat in his house as he played with his three young daughters.
His wife Lakshmi came in and bantered with him in a good-natured
way. We all discussed which Hindi films we liked. Lakshmi teased R.P.
that she would like to see more films but that the problem was money.
R.P. and Lakshmi spoke about love marriages, Lakshmi asserting that
"although there is much love before the marriage, the love can't last
long."

Bhipul Gupta is a 62-year-old heading a nuclear family consisting of
his wife and unmarried son. An image of Krishna adorns his simple

store that stocks screws, tires, tubes, and other bicycle parts. Bhipul has short cropped grey hair that is thinning, and a nice smile. Bhipul enjoys a close relationship with his wife Ratna. Bhipul says he is with Ratna "the whole day and night." He talks with her about many topics, but especially about finding a bride for their 18-year-old son:

> If the party of a girl comes to our house and I have talked with them, I tell my wife about it. I tell her who came asking about marrying our son and I ask for my wife's advice. . . . There are always all sorts of talks about the household.

Ratna joined us after the interview. Ratna's demeanor evoked confidence. She wore a *sārī* with a warm blouse underneath, and sported red glass bangles. She continues to place bright red *sindūr* (which indicates her married status) in the part of her gray hair. Ratna, moreover, has not developed deference lines under her neck that come from continually looking down. Ratna and Bhipul interacted comfortably, throwing ideas to each other for a long time. They discussed topics of local interest such as the case of a man who had abandoned his wife and children to go to America. While the majority of men feel that they must limit their relationships with their wives to protect the joint family, a substantial minority act on a second language that emphasizes benevolent love for a particularly special individual.

Yet, even men who become close with their wives tend to give priority to the first language that focuses on familial guidance. While Vinod Gupta enjoys an open relationship with his wife, he insists that it will never get in the way of his obligations to his parents:

> No, this [talk] is wrong. I do not observe limits. I remain open with my wife. Even though I keep it open, it is not necessary that I will forget my mother and father.

Anand Singh similarly insists that his love for his wife will not threaten the joint family in which he lives as a junior member:

> The man should not be the slave of the wife. If he does as the wife says, his family will be hurt. The family will be harmed because the wife came from outside. Therefore, I should live accepting my family's things, not her things. Only then can the family work. Man should have such control over himself that he does not give much importance to his wife.

Thus, men who have a second language that recognizes their love for their wives also place a lot of emphasis on their duties to their families.[11] Their love for their wives, moreover, usually does not lead them to criticize the ideology of male dominance that I describe in chapter 2.

BREAKING FROM JOINT FAMILIES

The second language which emphasizes individual desires is apparent in men's recognition that such desires often contribute to the breakup of joint families. Men who value joint-family living nevertheless expect that brothers will eventually separate (see also Shah 1973: 31; Sharma 1980a: 4-5). Sureshwar Mishra, the *mālik* of a sizable joint family, thinks that living separately is not right in society's eyes. He categorically says that "as long as the parents are alive, everyone should live together." But even Sureshwar recognizes the individual desires of brothers, saying that after parents die, children will "do whatever they wish." Raj Kumar Singh enjoys laughing and talking with his brothers. He is so committed to joint-family living that he insists that his wife "look after each brother equally." Yet, even Raj Kumar recognizes that his relationship with his wife will eventually doom his attachment to the joint family: "Now everyone is one. But when my wife has a child, the relationship will spoil a little. It is natural that the blood will pull the blood."

The emphasis so many men place on loving their wives and attaining autonomy within a joint family makes it likely that individual desires contribute to joint-family splits (see also Mines 1988: 571). Yet, even Nandu Gupta, who talks of how his desire to be treated as a special person precipitated his separation, emphasizes the imperatives of family duty. Dileep Singh separated from his parents so that he could better provide for his own children, but he, too, continues to emphasize how he fulfills his duties to his parents. He says, for instance, that he contributes to his family's wedding expenses. Like Dileep, most men downplay individual desires so much that they are reluctant to talk about how their individual wants played a part in their decision to separate (see chapter 7). Nevertheless, the fact remains that almost all men eventually separate from their brothers. Among the men I interviewed it is rare for brothers to continue to live together sharing one hearth when their own children have grown. Only three of the ten men who head households that include their married sons have any of their brothers still living with them. Few fathers who are living with their parents are also living with their uncles. Second languages valorizing individual choice and autonomy are one reason that most men are able to separate from their parents and brothers without feeling anxious and uneasy for very long.

CULTURAL ARENAS THAT CELEBRATE THE INDIVIDUAL

Men often develop close relationships with their wives and eventually separate from their brothers, but this movement away from the family group often produces anxiety. As Kakar ([1982] 1990: 80) argues, the cultural emphasis on being guided by one's family leads many Indian men to experience anxiety when facing "the demands of autonomous functioning."[12] This anxiety is often acute in the first days, weeks, and years of marriage, since, as Kakar ([1982] 1990: 81) argues, "the demand of establishing a close emotional bond" with their wives is often men's "first truly individual act . . . in which the family could not participate." Establishing that bond, Kakar argues, "threaten[s] to isolate [young men] from the web of their familial and group emotional ties."[13]

One reason men overcome this anxiety may be that many young men participate in a variety of cultural arenas that prepare them to emphasize the individual. Joseph Alter (1992: 196) demonstrates, for instance, that the wrestling world in Banāras contests the dominant focus on group membership. In wrestling bouts the individual "writes his own destiny in terms other than those prescribed by social precedent and cultural mandate," thus challenging the cultural world in which the "individual is subordinated to the social whole." Wrestling is a popular activity of many young men in Banāras, and a few of the young men I interviewed, like Kumar Yadav, are wrestlers. But many more enjoy watching Hindi films, another cultural arena that celebrates the individual.

India is the world's largest producer of feature films. On an average day, fifteen million Indians enjoy watching Indian films in the nation's 11,000 cinema halls (Kakar 1989: 26). Young unmarried men make up the Hindi film's largest audience, and some young men attend films several times a week (Khare 1985: 143). Twenty-four-year-old Prem Singh says, for instance, that he sees films "10, 15, or 20 times a month. When I have time, I see them." In this section, I draw on fieldwork and interviews I conducted with male filmgoers in Dehra Dun (North India) in 1991 (see Derné 1994c, forthcoming a), but the filmgoing experiences of many young men whom I interviewed in Banāras in 1986 and 1987 is similar. In 1986 and 1987, I attended films with the men I interviewed, and asked men about their "entertainment," a line of questioning which often led to a discussion of filmgoing. I asked men whether they saw films, whom they saw films with, and what appealed to them in Hindi films. The biggest hit of 1986 was *Ram Teri Ganga Maili* [*Ram, Your Ganga is Polluted*], a love story that focuses on the struggles of a couple whose marriage is opposed by the man's father—despite the fact that the couple already has a son.[14] I asked most of the men I interviewed whether such a love marriage could succeed and whether it was proper for the father of the hero to try to destroy the marriage of the hero and heroine.

How does the cultural world of Hindi films celebrate the individual? Does it challenge the priority given to social fear over unbounded love?

How does filmgoing cultivate a recognition of the individual? How do men respond to Hindi film themes that emphasize love?

Filmgoing provides space for the individual by allowing the male filmgoer to escape from the authority of home and work. For young men living with their parents, filmgoing is a time outside of the usual constraints of joint-family living. As junior members of their parents' households, young men must be constantly attuned to the demands, expectations, and judgments of family elders. Most live in tight quarters that provide little opportunity for privacy. Filmgoing is one of the few ways that men escape the constant attention of their limited social circle. Unmarried male filmgoers rarely attend films with other family members, and the dark of the theatre provides anonymity. Away from social pressure, filmgoers delight in horseplay with friends. They shout, whistle, and talk bawdily.

The culture that surrounds Hindi films focuses, moreover, on individual stars. About two dozen English and Hindi magazines are devoted exclusively to the Hindi film world. These magazines continually comment on what hero or heroine is number one, who is dating whom, and what the stars' favorite foods, drinks, and politics are. Male filmgoers I interviewed in 1991 speak of their favorite stars as possessing very special qualities. One unmarried 24-year-old describes the action hero Amitabh Bachchan as having "his own talent and his own way of acting. He doesn't copy anyone." A married 32-year-old similarly says that the romantic hero Jeetender is his favorite hero because "he moves deep into the story."

Film themes also focus on individuals (Dissanayake and Sahai 1992: 23). Action films present individuals who struggle alone against injustice. Many films assert that individuals are not determined by their family background, by presenting one family member as good and another as evil. The focus on the individual is particularly strong in recent Hindi film love stories. Since *Ram Teri* was released in December of 1985, love stories have been the biggest hits of the Hindi film world (Jain 1990; Derné forthcoming a). These love stories focus on individuals making their own choices and reverse the exemplary-dangerous distinction between social fear and love, as they tell stories of heroes and heroines whose love is above parental feuds, parental greed, and family differences.

While the collectivist framework for understanding action focuses on how parents guide children in their choice of education, career, and marriage, recent Hindi film love stories celebrate the individualism of heroes and heroines who make their own way. One of the biggest hits of recent years, 1989's *Maine Pyar Kiya* [*I Fell in Love*], tells the story of a hero, Prem, whose love for the heroine, Suman, leads him to abandon his parents (see Jain 1990; Derné 1994c, forthcoming a). Prem decides to leave his parents to pursue Suman and refuses to give his father "any explanation." When Prem approaches Suman's father asking for her hand in marriage, he asks to be seen as an individual. "Separate me from my father," Prem pleads. "Today, I am a common boy who has come to ask for your daughter's hand." When Suman's father refuses to allow his daughter to live on Prem's father's "hollow wealth," Prem declares that he will make his "own world." As Prem struggles to earn a living at hard labor, he refuses his father's help, telling him, "this is my struggle, father." After Prem has proven his ability to earn, the heroine's father accepts him as a son-in-law. When Prem's father comes looking for his son, Suman's father tells him "I don't know where [your son] is. I only know that boy who today built his own person and existence [*hastī*] separate from his father, and I am proud [*nāz*] of him." Suman's father evaluates Prem as an individual separate from his family and in doing so he invests making one's own person with importance.

The theme of making one's own choices independent of family is pursued repeatedly in recent Hindi film love stories. The refrain of a song of another big hit, 1988's *Qayamat Se Qayamat Tak* [*From Destruction to Destruction*] portrays a boy making his own way:

> Papa says, "you will make a big name. Son," [he says,] "do this kind of work." But no one knows what my destination is.

Indeed, the hero and heroine of *Qayamat Se Qayamat Tak* make their own decisions. When the heroine's father forbids her from seeing the hero, the hero asserts children's right to make their own choices. "Rashmi," the hero tells the heroine, "the right to make decisions about your life and my life is not your father's or my father's. We're their progeny, not their property." While the first language for most men emphasizes reliance on family guidance, films paint a picture of a world in which young men and women make their own decisions.

By focusing on the tyranny of family authorities, recent films give love priority over social fear (Derné forthcoming a). In the 1990 hit *Dil* [*Heart*], the hero's father objects to his son's love so much that he withdraws his financial support. But the hero places more importance on his love for the heroine than on fear of his elders. After the heroine's father has the hero arrested on trumped up charges, the hero declares in a popular song: "we are lovers. We are not fearful of the world [*ham pyār karne vālle; duniyā se naḍarne vālle*]." The heroine, too, is motivated by love rather than social fear. When her father bars her from seeing the hero, she tells him:

if you don't let me meet him, you can't stop me from killing myself. Those who love [pyār] are not afraid [ḍarnā] of anyone and even until now no one has stopped them.

The heroine's father is outraged when the hero comes to his house:

Rascal, progeny of a pig, how dare you have the boldness to thrust yourself into my daughter's room. . . . I will kill you, you bloody bastard.

But the heroine is resolute: "Fire the bullets, father; now we are not afraid [ḍarnā] of anyone."

In *Qayamat Se Qayamat Tak*, the hero and heroine also reject social fear in favor of love. Like *Dil*, *Q Se Q Tak* tells the tale of two young lovers whose families oppose their marriage because they are feuding. The hero's father is humiliated that his son has gone to his enemy's door "begging for love [mohabbat]," and he threatens to kill his son. On hearing this, the hero asks his beloved if she will abandon her "love [pyār] in the fear [ḍar] of this threat." As in the other love stories, the heroine refuses to be guided by the fear of her parents, giving priority to love: "I can't live without you," she tells her beloved.

In *Maine Pyar Kiya*, too, the hero, Prem, forfeits his family's support to be with his beloved. Like the hero's father in *Dil*, Prem's father warns his son about the "heartless [bedard], cruel [zālim] world outside." Realizing that the fear of jeopardizing the family honor doesn't sway Prem, Prem's father asks his wife to use her love [mamtā] to stop him. Having rejected social fear, Prem still places importance on his mother's love, and turns to her for support: "Ma, I am right, aren't I? You are with me, aren't you. Now, I do not fear [ḍarnā] anything."

Besides giving priority to love instead of social fear, Hindi films also advance alternative notions of love. First, they present love as focusing on a particular beloved. The statement from the heroine of *Q Se Q Tak*—"I can't live without you"—is repeated in the songs and dialogue of many movies. When threatened by her father, *Dil*'s heroine refuses to obey him, saying that if she and the hero can't live together, they will "die together." While most of the men I interviewed describe love as directed toward anyone for whom they have a duty to love, recent Hindi film love stories describe love as a feeling for a uniquely special person.

Second, while the men I interviewed are wary of equality between husband and wife, recent Hindi films celebrate equality as an important basis for marriage. In *Maine Pyar Kiya*, the heroine works side by side with the hero, asking "Isn't your struggle my struggle, too?" In *Dil*, the hero and heroine (who at the time are estranged from their parents) fight about whether the heroine should wear a bracelet his mother had sent. The hero opposes her wearing it because his family is boycotting them. The old cautionary tale of the instability of equal relationships appears to be reasserting itself as the hero is angry and storms out of the house, abandoning the heroine. But in the end, each tries to let the other have his or her way. The heroine tells the hero she is happy and urges him to take the bracelet, but the hero refuses.

The importance of equality between a man and a woman is a central theme of 1990's *Aashiqui* [*To Fall Madly in Love*]. When the hero, Rahul, saves the heroine, Anu, from her imprisonment in a hostel for orphans, she refuses his offer of support because she wants to support herself:

> I don't want to be a burden on you. If you want to help me, then let me stand on my own feet. Give me [help] finding a hostel and a job. That's enough.

The hero's mother, who is having difficulty paying the bills after being left by her husband, confirms the heroine's desire for independence. She tells her:

> It is important that we women stand up on our own feet. I don't have a job, so what can I do? Don't give up your job.

Rahul's mother urges the sort of equality between husband and wife that most of the men I interviewed regard as dangerous. "I tell you one thing from experience," she counsels the couple, "relationships are successful if there is equality [*barābarī*] between people."

Is the precedence given to love between husband and wife in Hindi films new? Do Hindi film themes indicate a movement away from family duty? Or do they merely help men use a time-tested second language, which allows them to recognize their own desires along with family duties? While the Hindi film world is a topsy-turvy world which reverses the normal order, these reversals are not new. Kathryn Hansen's (1992: 169) study of 19th and 20th century Nautanki theater of North India shows, for instance, that popular culture has long celebrated the "love, which most fully stretches and exercises the human heart." Hansen (1992: 144-145) rightly recognizes that the "prevalence of romantic tales" in Nautanki is "paradoxical" since North Indians usually disapprove of "the union of hearts and bodies by individual choice." While Nautanki tales, like Hindi film stories, demonstrate the existence of tension in Hindu society "between individual interests and group loyalties," they do not imply that viewers will give preference to the former. Hindi films help viewers recognize individual desires in some contexts, but this doesn't mean that viewers will give priority to the individual.

Both Nautanki theatre and modern Hindi films temper their celebration of love by recognizing the "hard wall of opposition erected to hold back" love's "mighty emotional flood" (Hansen 1992: 169; see also Derné forthcoming a). Hindi film stories continually remind viewers of the costs of marrying for love. In *Ram Teri*, the heroine is sold as a dancing girl and shot. In *Q Se Q Tak*, the opposition of the families is so strong that the hero and heroine end up dead at the end of the movie. In *Aashiqui*, the heroine is repeatedly reminded that her mother's love for a man dishonored her mother so much that she was run over by a train, leaving the heroine an orphan. In films like *Maine Pyar Kiya* and *Dil*, the hero and heroine must give up the financial support of their families to follow their love. As the hero's father tells his son in *Dil*:

> Because you have married the daughter of my enemy, you can no longer live in this house. Before you go, think about how very hard it is to earn enough to eat. You have become so totally blinded by love [*pyār*] for this mere girl that you are going to give up everything.

Like Nautanki theatre (Hansen 1992: 149-150), Hindi films portray "romantic love" as only possible "beyond society's boundaries" "in the barren wilderness or in heaven." In *Q Se Q Tak*, the hero and heroine learn of their feelings for each other in the far-away vacation resort of Mt. Abu. Before the tragic end of the film, the hero and heroine can only survive by living in an old, abandoned temple outside town. In *Ram Teri* the hero falls in love with the heroine while he is on a college fieldtrip in the hills, away from the watchful eyes of parents. The hero and heroine of *Ram Teri* survive the many ordeals that the hero's family places in their path, but the film's final scenes show them abandoning society by leaving the hero's family in Calcutta as they row out into the Bay of Bengal.

These films may emphasize love's joys, but they also express the dominant view of love as a madness that should not be allowed to jeopardize family honor (see also Hansen 1992: 149-150). In *Q Se Q Tak*, for instance, the hero's uncle begs the hero's father to forgive the hero because the hero's actions were caused by the "stupidities [*nādānī*] of youth," whether they be called "love [*pyār*] or craziness [*pāgalpan*]." Films often remind viewers of the possibility that love can be used to manipulate young people. In *Maine Pyar Kiya*, the heroine's father accuses the hero of making fun and frolic [*khilwāḍ*], rather than feeling real love [*pyār*] for his daughter. The hero's father accuses the heroine's father of deliberately leaving his daughter to bewitch the hero:

> You left your daughter here so that she could trap [*phansānā*] my son in the net [*jāl*] of her love [*prem*], so that she could make herself the daughter-in-law of this family.

Hindi films also support the belief that love can ruin a family's social position. In 1989's *Chandni*, for example, the hero's mother lectures the hero about the dishonor he will bring the family by marrying Chandni:

> Remember one thing, son, we cannot make a girl of such a low family our daughter-in-law. She is not fit to be the daughter-in-law of any good family [*ghar*]. If you marry Chandni, a mark [*kalank*] will come on our family [*vansh*] that will never be undone [*dhulnā*].

While films challenge the priority given to family honor, they nonetheless remain restricted by conventional paradigms, perhaps unwittingly reinforcing the popular belief that love is incompatible with family honor and joint-family living (see also Hansen 1992: 199-205).

In fact, most filmgoers continue to focus on the importance of following social pressures, rejecting Hindi films' celebration of young men who reject their parents' wishes (see Derné forthcoming a, c). While films provide a lens through which men see equality and love as exemplary, most men focus on the importance of maintaining family support by bowing to social pressures. Because Hindi film culture is continually attacked by critics, conservatives, educated people, and elders, filmgoers often see films as meaningless entertainment.[15] Twenty-nine-year-old Gopal Mishra sees films a couple of times a month, but he still says that he gets "nothing out of films. When I have no work, I go and sit in the cinema. I spend five rupees and nothing seems good." For most men, films are mere fantasy with nothing relevant to teach about their everyday lives. An unmarried 22-year-old male filmgoer told me in 1991 that "films are a fantasy world that is very different from reality." Other filmgoers repeatedly insist that films are "not real," "just stories," or "only provide a little entertainment for three hours."

Men often use the collectivist framework for understanding action to distance themselves from the fantasies they see on the screen. When I did the fieldwork that is reported in this book, *Ram Teri Ganga Maili* was at the height of its popularity. While *Ram Teri* celebrates the love of the hero and heroine, the men I interviewed in 1986 and 1987 insist that such a marriage could never succeed (see also Derné forthcoming a). Twenty-six-year-old Jyothi Gupta says, for instance, that the marriage in *Ram Teri*

> could never succeed. Because the boy and the girl are not of the same caste, they will have no honor [*izzat*] and will not be able to live in society. The couple will not even be able to find a place to live.

In discussing the same film, Gopal Mishra comments that it was "proper" for the hero's father to attempt to destroy his son's marriage by having the hero imprisoned on false pretenses. Although the hero and heroine already have a son, Gopal insists that the

> marriage will not succeed in the Indian environment. In this atmosphere, everyone will see it as a love marriage. Such a marriage has no future.

Nineteen of the men I interviewed in 1986 and 1987 had seen *Ram Teri*, but only six offer an unqualified condemnation of the father's efforts to ruin the marriage. Five men approve of the father's attempts to destroy the marriage, five men mention that the marriage could never succeed, and three men reject the film as a fantasy that has no connection with how Indians actually live.[16] While films celebrate love marriages, most men continue to use the dominant first language which holds that the consequences of dishonor are so horrible that a love marriage could never be successful.

The men I interviewed in 1991 are deeply involved in the Hindi film culture, but these men, too, continue to emphasize the importance of maintaining their respected place in their families (Derné forthcoming a).[17] One unmarried 21-year-old filmgoer whom I interviewed in 1991 enjoys love stories, but insists on the incompatibility of love and joint-family living:

> Mostly love marriages are not successful because as long as you have mutual love [*pyār*] you will want to marry, and you will want to remain in that true way of mutual love. But after the marriage it cannot be obtained in the familial situation. Most girls think that the boy will love them the way he loved her [*pyār karnā*] before marrying her. But that can never be.

The advice offered by advice columnists in Hindi film magazines also indicates the continued importance of the first language of family guidance (see also Derné forthcoming a). One 24-year-old Delhi man writes that he is in love with a woman other than the one his parents had chosen for him. Despite the film world's emphasis on love, the columnist advises him to

> marry the girl your parents have chosen. If you marry the other one you will not be prepared to endure her improper pressures. . . . Although you like the girl it wouldn't be right to marry her. In the coming time, your beloved will marry in another place.[18]

The second language giving love priority complements the dominant first language, exposing a tension in Hindu culture. While it helps some men come to terms with their desires, it does not overthrow the dominant first language, which continues to emphasize family duties.[19]

CONCLUSIONS

North Indian Hindu men have access not only to a language that recognizes how actions are driven by social pressures, but also to second languages recognizing individual desires. This suggests that cultures are not consistent, unified wholes, but include tensions between conflicting tendencies.

Most Hindu men have less facility using the second languages of exemplary love and individual desires. For most men, these second languages are less rich, familiar, and legitimate than the dominant first language of group pressure. Kakar ([1982] 1990: 275) argues, for instance, that, while Indians are "more individual . . . than they realize," the "cultural highlighting" of the group makes it difficult for many Indians to recognize their individual autonomy.[20] Some men experience individual desires but do not act on them because they give preference to the dominant language of group guidance.[21] But many others are able to use the elaborated second languages of volition and autonomy that I describe in this chapter to talk about and act on their own wants.[22] The importance that Anand Singh, Ramesh Mishra, Surjit Singh, and others attach to love (even as they sometimes also focus on the importance of bowing to social pressure) suggests that second languages valorizing exclusive love sometimes allow Hindu men to play that note on their emotional keyboard.

Culture, then, provides not just core values, but contrasting values, as well (Hewitt 1989: 72). In Hindu culture, conformity to family pressure is a core value, but there is a fascination with both the dangers and the seductiveness of freedom. Men live with their culture's central contradictions and struggle to resolve them. By manipulating Hindu culture's core and contrasting values creatively, men are able to make diverse choices as they construct family relationships. In the next three chapters, I explore how men balance group pressure and their own wants. While men usually conform, they sometimes marry for love, violate the norm of husband-wife avoidance, and break with their parents. My consideration of the range of stances that Indians take to the reality of social pressures begins by considering the various ways Hindu women resolve the tension between group demands and individual interests.

6

True Believers, Cowed Conformers,
Innovative Mimetists,
and Unapologetic Rebels:
Women and Men Respond
to the Threat of Dishonor

While bringing him tea, Lakshmi Mishra jokes with her husband R.P. that the service she is giving him illustrates the benefits of arranged marriages and joint-family living. Lakshmi presents herself as a devoted homemaker who meets her husband's needs, and honors him by serving tea when he has a guest. Does Lakshmi embrace the dominant gender ideology so completely that she finds her true self in serving her husband? Or does Lakshmi's joking acceptance of her position merely reflect her coming to terms with an unhappy situation that she feels she can not change? Is it possible that Lakshmi is trying to boost R.P.'s ego and faith in her so that she can persuade him to negotiate with his mother to decrease her housework burden or separate from the joint family he values should "tensions" later arise? Might a woman like Lakshmi ever contest the gender culture that circumscribes women?

The range of stances that Lakshmi Mishra might take to norms of Hindu gender culture suggests that the collectivist framework for understanding action is not always internalized. Rather, skepticism is one common response to cultural messages (Swidler forthcoming; Derné forthcoming a). Individuals often use their culture by keeping their distance from it. What stances do individuals take toward the reality of social pressure? What are the constraints faced by those who choose to buck social norms?

In this chapter, I describe four stances that women and men take toward the collectivist framework for understanding action and the gender culture that subordinates women. "True believers" (Jadwin 1992; Bailey 1991: 216; see also Scott 1990: 24) wholeheartedly believe that they should be guided by social pressure. They think about their honor, seek the guidance of others, and enforce social rules by dishonoring those who act unconventionally. They believe that joint-family life, arranged marriages, and restrictions on women are an unambiguous good. But others manage to keep some distance from gender culture and Hindu ethnopsychology. "Cowed conformers" recognize that their individual desires conflict with the demands of honor or gender culture, but, seeing the real consequences of dishonor, they still bow to social pressure (see Scott 1990: 24). "Innovative mimetists" (Jadwin 1992; see also Irigaray 1985: 76; Scott 1990: 32-33) reject social rules, but try to avoid the consequences of dishonor by mimicking adherence to social standards. Finally, "unapologetic rebels" openly buck social pressures.

In this chapter, I consider these four stances, as well as the real constraints that prevent more people from bucking cultural rules. The collectivist framework for understanding action generates a form of social control—dishonor—that even those who reject the framework as their personal orientation must contend with. Even individuals who are skeptical about the benefits of social guidance are often swayed by considering the real threat of dishonor. That so many women and men rebel and so many others only unhappily comply with social dictates that they resent suggests the strength of second languages that celebrate the individual.

WOMEN'S STANCES

How do Hindu women respond to the cultural system emphasizing the impropriety of women going outside the home? How do they respond to the imperative that they obey their husbands and live in joint families? Do women take various stances toward social pressure? The fact that women and men take a similar range of stances toward social pressures suggests that the four responses I outline are general stances to cultural constraint.

TRUE BELIEVERS

Some ethnographic evidence suggests that some women are sometimes "true believers" who focus on the protection and honor they gain by being restricted to the home. Some women pride themselves on their strict observance of *parda* [seclusion], and regard modesty as an important component of their self-definition.[1] Indian feminist Madhu Kishwar ([1984] 1991: 11) argues that, since "restrictions [on women's movements] are made a mark of higher social status and respectability, women themselves are made to feel that they have a stake in secluding themselves from the outside world as far as possible" (see also Minturn 1993: 325). Ursula Sharma (1980b: 217) describes some of the North Indian women she studied as proudly asserting that they "hardly sti[r] outside [the] four walls" of their courtyards. Lindsey Harlan (1992: 19) similarly reports that the Rajasthani Rajput women she studied greatly value the "reserve" which they see as the "sine qua non of dignity."

Harlan (1992: 202) reports that the women she studied are always "mindful" of their responsibilities as *pativratas*—women who have taken a vow to protect and obey their husbands. Rajput women, Harlan (1992: 202) reports, regard stories of satīs [women who immolate themselves on their husbands' funeral pyres] as models that "empowe[r] women to perform their domestic roles." Harlan (1992: 203) reports that the stories women told her "illustrate the widely shared belief that through giving up the self, women gain character and power." Some women believe that sacrificing themselves for their husbands' families makes women "great, superhuman beings" (Harlan 1992: 202). Jacobson (1982: 98) similarly reports that young women often veil within the home to remind themselves and others that they are "expected to be subservient and humble as [they carry] out the duties [their] elder affines prescribe for [them]." While recognizing young wives' ambivalence to joint-family living, Jacobson (1982: 103) reports that women sometimes feel that they "have a stake in holding together a family unit that is providing adequately and fairly for all its members."

Harlan describes some women who might be called pragmatic true believers. These women reluctantly sacrifice the imperative of obeying their husbands in order to advance the larger goal of serving their husbands' interests (Harlan 1992: 156-172). Women often told Harlan (1992: 92-3) that a young wife sometimes neglects the worship of the kuldevīs [family goddesses] of their husbands' families because the worship of familiar natal kuldevīs provides the most effective way to protect their husbands' welfare. Women often neglect the prohibitions satīmātās [venerated women who died on their husbands' funeral pyres] sometimes demand against children wearing clothes or parents using a cradle in order to follow the larger duty of caring for the husband's family. Other women controvert their husbands' wishes by prohibiting their husbands from drinking alcohol or having sex with other women (Harlan 1992: 157-158). Harlan (1992: 158) argues that these pragmatic true believers renounce their "selfish" "desire to please their husbands" in order to better serve their husbands. Harlan (1992: 155, 204) rejects the notion that women's explanations are cynical rationalizations. Even as women reject social norms by worshipping their parents' kuldevīs, failing to practice satīmātās' prohibitions, and failing to join their husbands on their funeral pyres, they nonetheless continue to focus, she argues, on the pativratā goal of protecting their husbands.[2]

COWED CONFORMERS

Other ethnographic accounts suggest that some women feel isolated and unhappy in their homes, but believe they are unable to do anything about their situation (Luschinsky 1962; Bennett 1983; Sharma 1980a;

Liddle and Joshi 1986). These women complain about *pardā* [seclusion] and their husbands' efforts to control them. They wish to be free from their husbands' authority. Such women are cowed conformers who focus on the consequences of leaving their husbands or violating restrictions on their movements outside the home. It is their consideration of consequences that leads them to sacrifice their own desires, grudgingly adhering to the restrictions they face.

Ursula Sharma's work in North Indian villages indicates that many women conform to limitations on their movement because of a concern with honor. One woman who wished to earn extra money by doing tailoring work for people in her village sacrificed her earning potential when her mother told her that "people might talk if they saw you wandering about there where you don't know anyone" (Sharma 1980a: 46-47). Other women say that they are careful to be chaperoned because of their concern with "what other people will say" about them (Sharma 1980b: 228). Many upper-class women who had spent part of their lives in cities only observe restrictions on their movements when threatened with being observed by their relatives (Sharma 1980b: 230). At other times, they move about freely. These women conform not because they want to, but because they have to.

Purnima Mankekar's (1993a, 1993b) reception study of New Delhi women and men watching the serialized television version of the religious epic *Mahābhārata* indicates that debates about women's position sometimes take place within families. A mother who works as a stenographer in a government office praises Sita, the heroine of the religious epic *Rāmāyaṇa*, for the suffering she endures for her *pativratā dharma*—the duty toward her husband.[3] But her daughter, Uma, a secretary in a private corporation, asks why Sita had to "submit at every step" (Mankekar 1993b: 552; see also Omvedt 1993: 231).[4] While torn between the belief that Indian women should be committed to their husbands and a focus on women's independence, Uma nonetheless believes that "as a young woman she [is] better off emulating the 'independence' of 'American women.'" Uma praises the "fiery strength" of Draupadi, a heroine of the *Mahabhārata*, as "appropriate to contemporary times" (Mankekar 1993b: 553). Mankekar (1993a: 483) found that many women contrast Sita's humility and respect for elders with Draupadi's fire and willingness to challenge her in-laws. She argues that the television depiction of Draupadi's disrobing after she is gambled away by her husband enabled many women to "confront and critique their own positions in their families" (Mankekar 1993a: 479).[5] Many women see themselves as choosing between tolerating injustices and feeling angry at them. "We can't tell what path we should take," one woman reflected.

"Should we tolerate or not?" (Mankekar 1993a: 483). Uma is moving toward the unapologetic rebel stance, while women like her mother remain true believers. Those women who tolerate treatment that they know to be unjust take the stance of the cowed conformer.

INNOVATIVE MIMETISTS

Despite the ethnographic evidence for conformity, there is also evidence that some Hindu women seek to avoid the restrictions that constrain them. Ethnographers describe some women as innovative mimetists who mimic adherence to the standards of patriarchal culture to manipulate their husbands.[6] These women hope that by appearing to be dutiful, obedient, stay-at-home wives, they can cajole their husbands into persuading elders to lessen a wife's chores and even into leaving parents altogether. If a husband comes to love his wife he may bring her gifts that should (by the standards of the patriarchal culture) first be offered to a mother or sisters (Bennett 1983: 178; Luschinsky 1962: 476). He may ask his mother to give his wife easier chores (Luschinsky 1962: 398). He may even come to share his wife's desire to break from the joint family that oppresses her (Bennett 1983: 179; Sharma 1978: 221; Luschinsky 1962: 477). Without knowing Lakshmi Mishra very well, it is impossible to know if her focus on serving her husband is an end in itself or part of a larger strategy.

While men often blame women for family tensions in order to maintain the fiction of male solidarity where none exists,[7] wives also sometimes try to persuade their husbands to reject the elders' authority in the family so that they can escape their heavy housework burden, and their mothers-in-law's authority. Some husbands tell me that their own wives pressure them to separate. Twenty-five-year-old Krishna Das Singh, who continues to live with his parents, says, for instance, that

> my wife thinks, "my husband earns fifty rupees a day. We will eat comfortably. We will enjoy and move around and see pictures. I shouldn't have to serve my father-in-law and mother-in-law. I will not have to work as hard and will only have to cook two *chapātīs*."

Other men describe how closeness between husband and wife precipitated splits in their own families. Phoolchand Mishra believes, for instance, that his brother separated from the parental household because his brother's wife "want[ed] to cook food for fewer people." Men are not reliable narrators in these accounts. They may be blaming women for separations that were actually caused by conflicts among men. Yet, the reports of female anthropologists, and an analysis of women's oral traditions suggest that women sometimes mimic deference to manipulate their husbands.

Hindu women have told female anthropologists that "sex, as a means to have children and as means to influence their husbands in their favor, was their most effective weapon in the battle for security and respect in their husband's house" (Bennett 1983: 176-7; see also Das 1976a; Luschinsky 1962: 398; Jacobson 1982: 101-102; Minturn 1993: 304; Sharma 1978). These female anthropologists describe cases in which women work to get close to their husbands with the aim of influencing them. Raheja and Gold's (1994: 20) recent study of women's oral traditions in villages in Rajasthan and Uttar Pradesh (North India) suggests, moreover, that women's oral culture stresses "the desirability of disrupting patrilineal unity in favor of a stress on conjugality" (see also Tyagi 1993). Raheja and Gold (1994: 73) argue that women's songs celebrating the "powers and pleasures of sexuality" are an implicit challenge to "the power of senior over junior men, the power of men over women, and the power of older women over younger brides."

Lisa Jadwin (1992) argues that because women who resist patriarchal authority often find themselves vilified and defeated, they choose instead to mimic standards of female virtue. Lynn Bennett (1983: 176) found that Nepali women often succeed in establishing close relations with their husbands by acting appropriately docile. "The public ideal of . . . devotion and service to the husband" coincides, she says,

> with a woman's private strategies to secure her own position in the household and perhaps even, eventually, get her husband to split off from the joint family altogether. All depends on winning the husband's affection, and women know that their wifely services and the deference that increases his self-esteem and prestige within the family are a good path into their husband's heart.

It is a woman's "own private political motivation," she argues, for a wife to "please her husband through service and humility." As Jadwin (1992) recognizes, women often are mimetists who deliberately assume the feminine role, concealing their unacceptable agendas, in order to manipulate patriarchal authority.

Raheja and Gold (1994: 127) report that, while men's songs urge a man "to thwart any attempts by his wife to fracture the solidarity of his own natal kin," women's songs celebrate the possibility of a partition in the husband's family. In one song, the young wife sings, "I don't like to fight, Mother-in-law. Even if you divide our family in the morning, even if you take all the rooms in the house, just give me my husband's room." Some women's songs suggest that a husband's "faith in his own natal kin lead[s] to disaster." "Don't listen to your mother and your sisters," one song urges the husband, "or your house will be destroyed" (Raheja and Gold 1994: 129-130).

Despite this subversive intent, some women's songs show how women can use the symbols that subordinate them to challenge the roles that restrict them. One song that questions the moral validity of restrictions on the development of intimacy between husband and wife suggests that these limitations can be circumvented if a woman is so heavily veiled that she cannot be seen by her husband's family. This song, Raheja and Gold (1994: 127) argue, shows that veiling, the emblem of the wife's subordination to her husband's male kin, can be used to circumvent that subordination by facilitating sexual contact with her husband.[8] By repeatedly referring to husbands as "beloved" and "lords," these songs suggest that women can break joint families through the devotion to their husbands which is socially sanctioned.

Liddle and Joshi (1986: 191) indicate that even professional women sometimes "underplay their abilities in order not to upset their male colleagues." Professional women sometimes maintain the "illusion" of "submissive[ness]" when in the presence of their husbands' elders. One woman says, for instance, that she is "two-faced" when she goes to her in-laws. "I cover my face when I go," she says, "but I don't go that often" (Liddle and Joshi 1986: 181). Another woman's use of the same phrase similarly reveals her mimetic strategy:

> You mustn't "show off" or try to show up your husband. So you have to be two-faced. At work, I make decisions. At home, I stay in the background. (Liddle and Joshi 1986: 181).

Liddle and Joshi (1986: 194) see these women as "consciously keeping to themselves the evidence which contradicts men's deficient knowledge of them."

UNAPOLOGETIC REBELS

Finally, unapologetic rebels in the women's movement sometimes actively and publicly protest restrictions on their movements outside the home, denying the image of women as docile and necessarily restricted to the home. While many of the professional women Liddle and Joshi (1986: 183) interviewed had to sacrifice some of their independence because of family commitments, many others work to change society. One woman says, for instance, that she's "very intolerant of the differences in how men and women are treated" and "wish[es] to change" women's position. Another woman told them that merely being a daughter or wife doesn't consume my energy and potential. I don't conform to the stereotype of women in society. I want to change it (Liddle and Joshi 1986: 182).

Indeed, sometimes women's actions contest the dominant gender ideology. Liddle and Joshi (1986: 217) describe women who resist pressure to marry, and others who leave their husbands. As one woman told them: "In the end I simply couldn't tolerate [my husband] anymore. I left my husband because of all the problems" (Liddle and Joshi 1986: 222).

Women's groups have also been active in the public sphere, challenging the restricted role men try to impose on them (Kishwar and Vanita 1991; Calman 1992; Omvedt 1993; Basu 1992). Women have participated in the independence struggle and reform movements. They have been leaders in the labor movement and in struggles over the high price of goods.[9] Women have protested alcoholism by demolishing liquor shops.[10] Women's groups have organized protests targeting depictions of violence against women in Indian film, harassment of women on trains, dowry, bride burnings and wife-beating to name a few examples.[11] These public, bold actions of women contest the dominant image of women as shy, ashamed, and docile. Unapologetic rebels face the consequences of bucking social pressure directly and unashamedly.[12]

Since even women who face strict limitations sometimes rebel, it should be no surprise that, as I show below, men, too, take a range of stances toward social pressures. But what is it that constrains men and women from rebelling more often?

REAL CONSEQUENCES OF DISHONOR

Does Lakshmi Mishra's husband R.P. embrace the collectivist framework for understanding action so completely that he automatically seeks the advice of his father when he has to make a decision? Does R.P. ever distance himself from Hindu gender culture or ethnopsychological beliefs? If Lakshmi and R.P. were to buck social norms by separating from R.P.'s parents (as R.P.'s brothers have done), what constraints would they face?

Like many women and most men, R.P. is very concerned with honor. R.P. says, for instance, that if a young man refuses to marry a woman after seeing her photograph, it would destroy her family's honor [izzat, maryāda]. R.P. says that in the past a concern for social prestige [samājik pratishthā] kept women from working outside the home, and he still assesses whether women should work outside by considering "what the time is saying." How does the threat of dishonor constrain?

Boycotting people who break with social norms expresses and generates the framework that sees action as rightly driven by social pressures (chapter 3). But being boycotted also has real consequences. The most intractable cost of being boycotted is difficulty arranging marriages of one's sons and daughters or brothers and sisters (see also Kolenda 1978: 92, 1993: 116; Billig 1991: 346). Deepak Mishra says, for instance, that the harms of dishonor

> are many. If I have a son and I do any wrong things, no one will allow him to marry with them. Therefore, one must watch what one does in society. The biggest reason is that there will be difficulties for the children's marriages. If I don't protect my honor in society, then there will be difficulties for my sons and daughters.

Men constantly report that those who marry for love jeopardize their relatives' chances of marrying. Nandu Gupta puts it this way:

> If my brother marries for love, it is so big a dishonor [*badnāmī*] in society that it is difficult for other girls in my family to marry. [People will say,] "look, he has done a love marriage. Their *khāndān* is not good if these types of boys are in the house." Arranging their marriages becomes difficult.

Many point out that those who marry for love will face problems arranging the marriages of their own children. Jyothi Gupta repeats a question voiced by many:

> When one who has done a love marriage has a child, where will that child marry? There will be great difficulty.

Jyothi tells of a neighbor whose love marriage delayed his brother's marriage. Given the extensive nature of the examination of the families of potential brides and grooms and the idea that family is the best indication of what kind of spouse a person will make, love marriages probably damage the marital prospects of other family members.

A family's prosperity partly depends, moreover, on the network of social ties that are formed and strengthened through marriages. Alliances with other families remain important in everything from getting a job to receiving credit.[13] The person who loses his honor may have difficulty finding work, renting a house, or getting a loan.[14] K.K. Mishra describes the consequences of dishonor as gravely affecting one's ability to succeed:

> If they marry for love, then the society never looks on them approvingly. Even though they may look very modern—they may speak English and wear suit-boot [i.e. modern clothes]—90% of the people

have the very old faith. Mostly in front of the people [who have married for love], they will say that they have done good. But behind their backs they will complain: "Look, he has done a love marriage and gone against his parents." Wherever he goes, he will have to bend down [*jhuknā*].

Krishna Das Singh describes similar problems for those who marry for love:

Those who object to love marriages do so much to the boy and girl that it becomes difficult for them to live in the society. Going on the road becomes difficult for them. No one will give them a room to rent, saying that they have a bad character and are wrong.

These consequences of dishonor are often seen as lasting for generations. Ashok Mishra says, for instance, that a man must observe social restrictions so that his children can prosper:

One should move with one's society because one's children will also have to live in that society. If a man does any wrong works, his family's honor [*izzat*] will be finished. Coming generations will have to bear the burden [*jhelnā, sahanā*] of his evils. The society will forever look on that family with a bad look. If the honor [*izzat*] has gone, it will never come again. Even if a man dies, his children, parents, brothers, wife and whole family [*khāndān*] will have to bear his evils.

Ashok Mishra, a true believer, focuses on how dishonoring acts are "evil." But he also describes the consequences of dishonor that anyone acting dishonorably has to face.

MEN'S RESPONSES TO THE THREAT OF DISHONOR

The Hindu men I interviewed all have access to a first language of group guidance and at least some familiarity with a second language of individual autonomy. They all face the real threats of being dishonored. But, like women, individual men construct diverse stances to the threat of dishonor.

TRUE BELIEVERS

True believers, like Ashok Mishra, embrace the dominant framework for understanding action as their personal orientation. They have internalized the framework for understanding action and see it as the best plan for living. When faced with a choice, they seek guidance from their elders, and ask them what would be honorable in a particular situation.

For true believers, the economic and social consequences of dishonor are not as important as their felt belief that maintaining one's honorable place in a group is the best way to live. Kumar Yadav says, for instance, that he wouldn't even do the smallest bit of work without asking his father. As I show in chapter 3, most men unselfconsciously seek parental guidance about whom to marry and what sorts of educational and employment opportunities to pursue.

Often men are "pragmatic true believers" who temper the focus on being guided by social pressures with some recognition of individual desires. In the last chapter I describe how Deepak Mishra, Rajendra Gupta, Anand Singh, Sunil Gupta, and Devi Prasad Gupta focus on compromise as a way of protecting the joint family. These men truly believe that being guided by the joint family is the best way to live, but they also think that to protect the vitality of the joint family, they must allow for some individual choice. While this recognition of individual choice is at odds with the dominant collectivist framework for understanding action, their aim is to protect the joint families that they value.

Other true believers recognize their individual desires, but willingly sacrifice them for the sake of maintaining a respected place in their social group. Through this process, which Stanley Kurtz (1992: 61) calls "renunciation on the way to the group," most Hindu men come to emphasize group participation so much that they voluntarily sacrifice their self-interests.[15]

Often men who recognize internal wants at odds with their parents' directions willingly give priority to their parents' wishes to protect their honorable place in their families. Rajesh Yadav recognizes that if he separated from his parents, he could "spend as much money as [he] earns on [himself] alone." Despite these "advantages of living alone," he refuses to even consider separating from his family, emphasizing that the advantages of living separately "are not granted social status [*samājik star*]." The problem, he says, is that "when one lives separately, others feel that one has left one's parents." Similarly, Vinod Gupta sees advantages to love marriages: "In today's age," he says, love marriages are "right in one way" because it is "good if the boy likes the girl." But Vinod concludes that it is more important to marry "in agreement with one's parents" because

> if we live outside of our society, culture and civilization, we will die. I could only marry where the family members of the boy and the girl agree. Only then would the society give us the respect [*pratishṭhā*], honor [*sammān*], and status [*darjā*] of husband and wife. If it was not an arranged marriage, society would not have given us the status of husband and wife and this type of marriage could only be unsuccessful.

Although Surjit Singh believes an arranged marriage will not bring him happiness in "a true sense," he too willingly accepts such a marriage to protect his honored place in society. Surjit imagines himself as enjoying interacting with women, but he is similarly willing to sacrifice these desires as well:

> [Whether or not a man can talk with a woman] depends on the influence of each city. Because the area in which Banāras is located is a little backward, here the families regard it as bad if you sit with girls. So, we are unable to talk with them.

Like Rajesh and Vinod, Surjit Singh willingly sacrifices his individual desires to protect his honored social position.

COWED CONFORMERS

Other men, however, long to act on their individual desires. These men keep cultural dictates at a distance. They conform not because they give priority to group membership, but because they find the consequences of dishonor too fearful to risk. Often lacking the cultural and social resources that I describe in chapter 8, cowed conformers bow to social pressure to avoid the real consequences of dishonor.

Rajesh Yadav, Vinod Gupta, and Surjit Singh could be either cowed conformers or true believers in the cases I have just described. If Rajesh Yadav does not consider separating from his parents because he gives priority to group membership, he is a true believer. But if it is his calculation of the costs of dishonor that causes him to conform, he is better understood as a cowed conformer. Similarly, Vinod Gupta could be considered a cowed conformer if recognition of the economic and social consequences of dishonor are what cause him to marry according to his parents' wishes. I suspect that in these instances both Rajesh and Vinod are true believers, given their statements with which I open chapter 3. For Rajesh and Vinod, it is the importance they place on maintaining their group membership that drives them.

In this section I consider several men who attempted to follow socially illegitimate desires, but who retreated into conformity when forcefully reminded of the consequence of dishonor. The strength of second languages that focus on individual desires is apparent in the stories of all of these men, since all recognize their own desires. But the fearfulness of the threat of dishonor is also strongly evident since each feels that he must subordinate his personal desires.

Krishna Das Singh, 25, is the youngest of three brothers who live together with their parents. Krishna would have liked to reject the marriage his parents arranged for him, but was ultimately persuaded that his family's honor would not allow it. Given that Krishna continues to be dissatisfied with his marriage, it is not surprising that he does not like arranged marriages:

> It is I who has to marry and only I can know what I have to do and how I have to do it. I have to pass my life and I know better than my parents how to pass my life.

Krishna says that arranged marriages run because of the "fear [*bhay*] of society." But for Krishna social fear is not exemplary. Arranged marriages, he says, only cause a "big mental heat in man's heart."

When Krishna's marriage was set, he objected to his parents:

> I married the woman my parents wanted me to marry but I didn't like it. I objected to them that my marriage should not be happening there and that there should not even be any talk of marriage in that place. . . . I broke all the house's pots and pans and rejected the marriage hundreds of thousands of times. I was upset and I ran away from my house. But they didn't accept this and they arranged the marriage.

Despite these strong objections, Krishna was ultimately persuaded to marry because of his concern with his family's honor:

> I was compelled [*mazbūr*] to marry although I had no liking for the girl then and I do not like her to this very day. My parents started to say, "Our honor [*izzat*] will go. We have fixed the marriage." In our society when four people come together and fulfill their customs, it is understood that the marriage has happened—whether I am there or not. If they fixed it, even if I am not there and they gave their word, then the marriage must be done. If they back out, there is much dishonor [*beiz-zatī*] in the society.

In the face of such pressure, Krishna began to sympathize with his wife's plight:

> I [began to] think that if I left her, there would never be any honor [*izzat*] for her in the society. It would become extremely difficult for her to find someone else to marry. I thought that I should not cause problems for an unknown woman. I thought, "let's go anyway. I will manage."

Krishna's parents' culture work aims at defining the marriage they had arranged as the only one that could be legitimate. They draw on the first language of social guidance by appealing to Krishna to consider his family's honor, as well as the reputation of the woman and her family. The fact that Krishna tried to reject social pressures and speaks of compulsion [*mazbūr*] when describing why he ultimately agreed to the marriage indicates that Krishna is a cowed conformer, at least in this instance. He bowed to social pressure not so much because he gave priority to group membership, but because he regarded the consequences of dishonor as too fearful to contemplate.

Krishna's friend, Nandu Gupta, was also initially unhappy with the marriage his parents arranged for him. Having remarried after the death of his first wife, Nandu now lives in a nuclear family with his second wife and young children. When he married his first wife, Nandu disliked her:

> The wife I got was dwarfish. I hated her very much. I said, "Where has my father arranged the marriage? I will not keep her." You cannot believe it, but even after living in a house with her for a year and a half, I had never had any relation with her. . . . She used to say to me, "come, I have arranged the bed." But I had so much hate for her that even then I didn't want to see her.

Social pressures were exerted:

> My wife's father was approaching everyone saying, "you have to make him understand that . . . now that he has married her he should not leave her."

Unlike Krishna, who continues to dislike his wife, one day Nandu had a "conversion" (see Stromberg 1985, 1991) experience that led him to love and accept his wife:

> One day she was trying to feed me and in anger I threw the *thālī* [metal plate] in her face. Blood started coming from her mouth. When my mother saw this, she asked my wife, "What happened? Has he beaten you?" She said, "No, he has not beaten me." After that I went to the roof of my house and thought. There, I got an inspiration [*prerṇā*]. "What fault has she done?" Later, I went to the temple and I saw another who was very educated but whose wife was handicapped. After seeing this, the feeling [*bhāvnā*] came into me that my wife is better than this. She is beautiful and healthy also, it is only that she is very short. After that my love [*prem*] for her became very deep.

Nandu Gupta, who originally disliked his wife, faced social pressures to accept the marriage. Although Nandu sees himself as having made a choice to accept his wife—a choice made clear by a feeling he experienced as an individual, appeals to honor appear to be decisive. Both Krishna and Nandu are cowed conformers who feel constrained by a concern with honor to accept marriages that they originally opposed.[16]

Conclusions

The demands of honor press on both men and women. Both must contend with the real consequences of dishonor. Both know that if they appear to act dishonorably they can jeopardize the marital prospects of their brothers and sisters, sons and daughters.

Although all Indians must contend with the threat of dishonor, responses vary. True believers, who emphasize group identity, see themselves as appropriately guided by a concern with their honor. Rajesh Yadav realizes the advantages he would gain by separating from his household, but focuses instead on the competing advantages of maintaining status in his family. Vinod Gupta recognizes the benefits of marrying for love, but, like Rajesh, concentrates on the advantages of maintaining his place in his caste and family. Cowed conformers bow to social pressure because of the consequences of dishonor. Krishna Das Singh fought to reject the marriage his parents arranged for him, but ultimately felt that the consequences of separating from his family and his society were too great.

A few people, unapologetic rebels, brave the consequences of dishonor. But others, the innovative mimetists I focus on in the next chapter, seek to have their cake and eat it. They act on their illegitimate desires, but try to maintain their honor, by hiding the illegitimate nature of their actions.

7

Culture Work and Strategies of Action: How Hindu Men Buck Social Pressures

While the threat of dishonor is an important constraint, some individuals nevertheless manage to get around social norms and act unconventionally. Most of the men I interviewed assent to arranged marriages as a routine. While some men like Krishna Das Singh and Nandu Gupta were originally unhappy with the marriages their parents arranged for them, most accept the system of arranged marriages without question. Yet, my interviews also reveal two love marriages—one done by Ramesh Mishra and one done by Kishan Gupta's brother, Raja. Ramesh and Raja are not unapologetic rebels. While they marry for love, they do not unashamedly declare that this is what they are doing. Rather, they hide the unacceptable nature of their actions by feigning adherence to social norms. What strategies do men like Ramesh and Raja use to get around social norms and dominant cultural understandings? How do these innovative mimetists avoid the consequences of dishonor by concealing their unacceptable agendas? While they manage to rebel, how are men like Ramesh and Raja still constrained by the dominant framework for understanding action?

Ramesh Mishra, 35, is the eldest of five brothers. Ramesh's hair is turning silver, and his round face is engaging. Ramesh, who married 10 years ago, lives with his wife, four young children, his four brothers, their wives and children, an unmarried sister, and his parents. Each brother gives his father Rs. 1000 a month, from which he runs the family's expenses. All five wives share the household chores. Ramesh's brothers are all in white-collar service jobs, and Ramesh, who was once a lecturer at a central school, operates a successful general store. Ramesh says proudly that the store he started with Rs. 300 is now worth Rs. 50,000 after only four years of labor.

Ramesh earned a master's degree in physics from Banāras Hindu University (B.H.U.). Men and women study together at the graduate level (but not at the undergraduate level) at B.H.U. While most young unmarried men have little opportunity to meet unmarried women, Ramesh came in contact with unrelated women who were doing graduate work at B.H.U. Ramesh's day-to-day interactions with women in school may have nurtured an ease interacting with women that many young men lack. During his studies, Ramesh fell in love with a woman who was studying for her master's degree in Sanskrit.[1]

Like Ramesh Mishra, Raja Gupta is the eldest of several brothers. Raja, 38, is the eldest male in a small joint family consisting of his mother, his wife and children, his brother and his brother's family. Raja's family, like Ramesh's, is solidly upper-middle-class. Raja and his family operate a successful studio photography business in a central business area of Banāras. The success of the business is apparent in the phone connection, electronic equipment, and television in Raja's house. Like Ramesh, Raja is college-educated, having received his B.A. from B.H.U. Raja met the woman he later married in the neighborhood in which his family's business is located. Indians commonly say that neighbors sometimes have the opportunity to talk to each other from rooftops, and Raja's love marriage appears to have been facilitated by this type of proximity. According to Raja's brother, Kishan, Raja met with his wife for 11 years before they finally married. Both Raja and Ramesh, then, had relatively uncommon opportunities to get to know unrelated unmarried women—opportunities that were essential to making a love marriage possible.

Both Raja and Ramesh say that they loved their wives before marrying them, but both also insist that they didn't have sexual relationships before marriage. For instance, while Ramesh says that "friendship is good," he insists that "to go forward from friendship is bad." It is only after a pause that Ramesh hastens to add that going forward is wrong only if it is "before marriage."

After they fell in love, both Raja and Ramesh insisted that they would only marry their beloveds. As Raja's brother puts it, "after meeting my *bhābhī* [elder brother's wife], my brother decided that he would marry only her and no other. *Bhābhī* decided as well that she would only marry my brother."

Ramesh Mishra's bride was of the same Brāhman subcaste as Ramesh. Raja Gupta's bride, however, was a Brāhman—a higher caste than Raja's Vaishya caste. The caste difference between Raja and his beloved may have made it more difficult to present the marriage as an arranged one, leading to a long delay in accomplishing the marriage.

OBTAINING PARENTAL CONSENT

Both Ramesh and Raja were careful to get their parents' consent to marry the bride of their own choosing. Neither was willing to marry in court—a legal marriage in modern India. In both cases, the young men initially faced opposition from their parents. Ramesh says that his parents were of the "old way of thinking. In the beginning," he says, "the marriage was not good in their eyes." Ramesh insists, however, that he married only after gaining "the consent of both my parents and my wife's parents."

Kishan Gupta similarly says that Raja's marriage could not "take place until my parents were ready for it." Raja's marriage, in fact, took place only after his father's death, and although Kishan insists that his father had consented to Raja's marriage before his death, it is possible that this presentation of the marriage as having had the father's consent is merely a convenient, if untrue, version of events.

The men I interviewed commonly regard love marriages as inoffensive as long as the couple obtains their parents' consent. Conservative Ashok Mishra comments, for instance, that a "love marriage that is done with the consent of the parents is right." Similarly, Devi Prasad Gupta, 76, reasons that should one of his sons have chosen his own bride, this would have been acceptable as long as Devi himself had given his permission:

> What is the difficulty? If I give my permission, then it is okay. I don't see that as a special problem.

Obtaining parental consent, then, is an approach which is widely recognized as making a love marriage acceptable. By obtaining one's parents' permission, one acts in accordance with a framework that sees action as rightly supervised by superiors in the family hierarchy.

MANIPULATING EXISTING CULTURAL STORIES AND VOCABULARIES

While I cannot reconstruct with certainty the arguments Raja and Ramesh used to convince their parents to accept their love marriages, Kishan's and Ramesh's statements justifying their love marriages reveal the sorts of arguments they may have made. Raja and Ramesh refer to shared, commonly understood cultural components to justify their actions. They address their parents' real concerns about love marriages and make arguments that operate within the dominant framework for understanding action to do so.

Raja and Ramesh both had to convince their parents that the proposed marriages would not damage the family's honor, jeopardizing other family members' marital prospects. Ramesh comments, for instance, that his parents agreed to the marriage only after he convinced them that the marriage would not "harm our honor [*izzat*; *mān maryādā*]. Until they were convinced of this, they objected that the marriage would trouble the family."

For whatever reason, perhaps because Raja proposed to marry a woman of a different caste, Raja found it difficult to convince his parents that a love marriage would not be dishonoring. Ultimately, it was decided—perhaps by Raja himself, or perhaps by Raja's parents—that Raja would have to delay his marriage until after his sisters had married. Raja's brother, Kishan, puts it this way:

> There was the question of society. We had to see the society. We had to recognize that in the future we might have problems in the brothers' and sisters' marriages. Therefore, there was some objection. Finally, though, all of our sisters were married before brother married. Seeing the society, brother arranged the marriages of our three sisters and got himself married only afterwards. Had he married first, there would have been difficulties arranging our sisters' marriages.[2]

Both Ramesh and Raja had to be concerned with maintaining their families' honor, and for Raja's family the biggest concern was arranging good matches for Raja's sisters.

To argue that his marriage would not be dishonoring, Ramesh manipulates existing cultural stories, using reasoning that makes sense within the dominant framework for understanding action. Ramesh focuses on the fact that his beloved is of the same caste as himself in order to manipulate existing cultural stories that hold that love marriages fail. Accepting the dominant understanding that love marriages usually fail, Ramesh argues that this is because the man and the woman are typically of different backgrounds. He argues that because he and his wife are of the same caste and background, they would not face any difficulty obtaining "mutual understanding" which he sees as vital for a successful marriage. "Whatever way the marriage is arranged," he says, "it is useless if there is no mutual understanding between husband and wife." Ramesh conjectures that arranged marriages, like love marriages, might face difficulties if the man and the woman are of different backgrounds:

> If one is from a higher family and another is from a lower family, there will be difficulties whether the marriage is a love marriage or an arranged marriage. When marriages occur between families of the same status, no complications arise—whether it be an arranged marriage or a love marriage. This is because [the boy and the girl] understand each other's family's circumstances. But if the situation and circumstances of the boy's family and the girl's family are different, then understanding is impossible and fighting and separation are born.

Ramesh's culture work aims at presenting his love marriage as an exception from common stories which discredit love marriages. In making this argument, Ramesh uses a vocabulary that makes sense within the collectivist framework for understanding action: Ramesh focuses not on the personal characteristics of the woman he had chosen to be his bride, nor on his own personal, individual happiness that he hoped to gain by marrying her, but instead on the family of the woman he had chosen to marry. Appeals to his own happiness or appeals which focus on his beloved's personal characteristics, while making sense within the American framework which sees action as chosen by the individual in accord with his or her own interests and desires, would make little sense according to the Hindu framework which sees action instead as determined by the individual's social ties.

Influenced by the gender culture I describe above, Ramesh's parents might have been concerned that a love marriage would disrupt the family. They might have been afraid that if Ramesh loved his wife too much he might neglect his responsibilities to his parents. Ramesh addresses these concerns directly by forcefully assenting to the norm that men must avoid entangling themselves in their wives' complaints:

> When outside women come for marriage, difficulties arise. Therefore, we [men], try to say our own points and to not give any attention to the women's talk.

Ramesh, further, reasons that he is more likely to neglect his wife than his parents: "I have lived 35 years with my parents, so how could I forget them? If I could forget them, I could forget my wife just as easily."

The effect of Ramesh's culture work is that his father respects him and his mother respects his wife:

> Although in the beginning [my parents] felt bad [about the marriage], when they saw that it was not bad for our honor [izzat, mān maryādā], they had no problems. Now, my father respects me the most of all my brothers. He doesn't do anything without taking my advice. My wife's situation is the same. For any work, my mother and my sisters-in-law take advice from her.

Ramesh, then, succeeded in maintaining his respected place in his family.

Ramesh Mishra uses complicated, sometimes innovative, arguments to establish the propriety of his marriage. He draws, however, from shared cultural components to convince his audience that his marriage is proper. He frames his arguments around the importance of the family's honor and the importance of living harmoniously within one joint family. He manipulates existing cultural stories about why love marriages fail, using reasoning that makes sense within the understanding that individuals are primarily members of social groups.

Using the Traditional Wedding Ritual

The consent Raja and Ramesh obtained from their parents and their wives' parents allowed them to perform the wedding ritual in the traditional way, including the *barāt* or wedding procession that goes from the groom's house to the bride's house. The conspicuous *barāt* often includes the groom atop a horse, a musical band equipped with portable electric generators, bright lights, and groups of male friends and relatives who dance enthusiastically. The *barāt* is important in socially declaring that a marriage has taken place, hence assuring that public pressure will guide and control a marriage.

Both Raja and Ramesh emphasize the importance of using traditional public wedding rituals. After nervously admitting that his "marriage was a love marriage," Ramesh hastens to add that his marriage

> happened in the arranged way even though we knew each other from before. The marriage happened in the ritually correct, *vedic* way and with the consent of my parents. . . . The wedding happened as an arranged marriage—the *barāt* went and the *pandits* [Hindu priests] performed the ceremony.

Kishan, too, only reluctantly admits that his brother's marriage was a love marriage, emphasizing that it, too, followed the traditional form:

> It was a love marriage, but first the parents accepted it and then it took place. . . . The *barāt* went in the usual way and the marriage happened in that way only.

Both Raja and Ramesh, then, present their marriages as being done with the consent of their parents by following the traditional public form.

To fail to follow the established public wedding ritual would imply that one were marrying as an individual without the consent and guidance of society. According to the collectivist framework for understanding action, such individual actions might appear threatening. Many of the men I interviewed comment that the showy wedding procession is essential precisely because, as Ramlal Mishra puts it, "the whole society must witness the fact that this boy's marriage is happening with this girl." Deepak Mishra similarly reasons that without a wedding procession,

> the boy might be able to claim "I did not marry her. I am not her husband." The girl, too, might say, "he is not my husband." If no one witnesses the marriage and something happens afterwards, then no one will know that the two are husband and wife. Therefore, the *barāt* goes. Then, all people realize that a marriage has taken place.

Because the Hindu framework sees action that lacks social consent as dangerous, Ramesh and Raja are careful to publicly demonstrate their respect for society by adopting the traditional public forms. Because of the understanding that marriages must be controlled by social pressure, Ramesh and Raja are careful to include the *barāt*, a public demonstration which allows "society" as Vinod Gupta puts it, "to witness the fact that" two people have married.

Both Ramesh Mishra and Raja Gupta direct culture work at convincing elders of the propriety of action, use a vocabulary that makes sense according to the framework for understanding action that most men embrace, and use traditional public forms to mask the unconventional nature of their actions. The rest of the chapter suggests that these three elements are general characteristics of the strategies of action Hindu men use to accomplish diverse goals. What is the nature of men's culture work and strategies for acting unconventionally? How are men's culture work and strategies of action constrained by the collectivist framework for understanding action?

CULTURE WORK: WHAT PEOPLE USE CULTURAL COMPONENTS FOR

Max Weber (1949: 81) rightly directs our attention to the human drive for meaning.[3] People are always evaluating the actions of self and others as good or bad, right or wrong, just or unjust, natural or unnatural. Meanings are not self-evident. Rather, individuals must work to attribute meaning to action. Individuals are not merely passive beings weighted down by culture, but actively draw on common cultural resource to justify diverse actions (Obeyesekere 1981: 110; Swidler 1986).

People use cultural components to attribute meaning to action. *Culture work* is the combination and manipulation of cultural components such as stories, beliefs, and values to attribute meaning to particular actions.

Culture work which aims at attributing positive meaning to conventional actions is relatively easy. Stories, values, and other justifications are simply taken out of the "tool kit," dusted off, and used. Krishna Das Singh's parents did culture work in their appeal to Krishna to accept the marriage they had arranged for him. Krishna's parents told him that he had to accept the marriage to avoid jeopardizing the family honor. Nandu Gupta's wife's relatives similarly focused on honor to convince Nandu that he could not leave his wife. Both Nandu's and Krishna's relatives used readily available cultural components to attribute positive meaning to arranged marriages.

Men can easily marshal evidence from the *Rāmcharitmānas*, Tulsi Das's medieval Hindi version of the religious epic *Rāmāyaṇa*, to justify arranged marriages, restrictions on women's movements outside the home, and the imperative that a wife obey her husband.[4] The men I interviewed respect the *Rāmcharitmānas* as a source of moral directives. Twenty-six-year-old Ashok Mishra says, for instance, that "from reading the *Rāmcharitmānas*, we get high teaching about how one should behave with one's parents, *bhābhī* [older brother's wife], and *bahū* [daughter-in-law], and how one should behave with one's *devar* [husband's younger brother] and others as well." Fifty-four-year-old Nathuram Mishra says that people who "believe in God do not like love marriages," by emphasizing that the proper "social system of marriage" was demonstrated by the *Rāmāyaṇa*'s description of the wedding of Ram and Sita. As Ashok Mishra says, "when it comes to marriage, it is important that we follow the example of him whom we call *bhagwān* [God] Ram." Some men also refer to the *Rāmāyaṇa* to justify restrictions on women's movements outside the home (see also Lutgendorf 1987: 652-663; Derné 1988: 364-366). Nathuram Mishra quotes a verse from the epic to suggest that chaos is the result of granting women freedom. Men similarly refer to the *Rāmāyaṇa* to justify a wife's obedience.[5] Gopal Mishra says, for instance, that Sita, the heroine of the *Rāmāyaṇa*, is the ideal woman because "she doesn't do any thing other than what her husband has ordered." For Gopal, "the customs and traditions" of India "are based on the relationship of *bhagwān* Ram and Sita. Because Sita always obeyed [her husband] Ram's orders, all wives of Hindustan must do what their husbands tell them to do."

While a person seeking to justify conventional acts has an array of existing stories, beliefs, and values to draw on, the man wishing to justify a love marriage will have to work harder to manipulate cultural values and stories to justify unconventional action. Like Ramesh Mishra and Raja Gupta, most men who act unconventionally are forced to manipulate cultural components in a way that uses vocabularies and strategies of action which are consistent with the dominant framework for understanding action.

STRATEGIES OF ACTION

Ann Swidler (1986: 273) argues that a focus on "strategies of action"—"persistent ways of ordering action through time"—is vital for understanding "culture's causal effects." Swidler (1986: 276) rightly criticizes sociologists' "excessive emphasis on the 'unit act,' the notion that people choose their actions one at a time according to their interests or values." Rather, she argues, "action is necessarily integrated into larger assemblages."

Routine patterns of action are one type of such larger assemblages of action. Most of the time, most individuals take for granted the propriety and meaningfulness of their actions. Hindu men take for granted the propriety of joint-family living, arranged marriages, restrictions on women's movements outside the home, and limitations on contact between husband and wife. These routine patterns of action are so general in Hindu society that individuals need no strategies for accomplishing them. If a man habitually restricts his wife to the home, he needs no strategy for acting that way. He simply acts. The individual needs a strategy of action only when embarking on a novel path.

Strategies of action are used when individuals have no routine pattern of action to follow. A strategy of action is a way of responding to a novel situation or of pursuing an action which has not yet become part of the individual's repertoire of routine actions. Strategies of action are general tactics that people use to pursue diverse, but particular, goals. While the particular aim of the strategy is novel, the strategy of action itself is not. My focus is on how strategies of action are used to present or frame unconventional actions so that they are comprehensible and unthreatening to others. As Goffman (1971: 85) argues, the individual "goes about constrained to sustain a viable image of himself [or herself] in the eyes of others." Because the social framework for understanding action is a shared, commonsense understanding, those whose actions do not appear to fit the dominant framework may be mistrusted as lacking normal human attributes (see Goffman 1974: 188).

The social framework for understanding action limits the strategies of action available to individuals by determining the picture individuals need to present of themselves to avoid being distrusted as someone whose actions make no sense. As seen through Hindu men's framework for understanding action, individuals who follow their social group are trustworthy and those who act independently of it are anomalous, confusing, and worthy of suspicion. Because of the understanding that individual volition is threatening, Ramesh Mishra, Raja Gupta, and other men are constrained to present their actions as in accord with some social group, even as they act unconventionally and separately from their social group.

THE DIRECTION OF HINDU MEN'S CULTURE WORK

An important feature of Hindu men's strategies of action is that the culture work they do is directed mostly at persuading others that one's actions are proper and acceptable. Where individuals are seen as choosing action on their own, culture work tends to be directed toward the self. But where individual actions are seen as the responsibility of the group rather than the individual, culture work must aim at an audience more than at the self.

An important element of Ramesh's and Raja's strategies of action is to aim their culture work at their parents. Rather than marrying in court, Ramesh and Raja aim culture work at convincing their parents that their particular love marriages would not be improper.

VOCABULARY OF CULTURE WORK

A second characteristic of Hindu men's strategies of action is the use of a legitimate vocabulary that makes sense within the dominant social framework for understanding action. The commonsense understanding that actions should be driven by one's social group generates a vocabulary of legitimate action, focusing on such concepts as honor and tradition. True believers who embrace the dominant framework for understanding action as their personal orientation spontaneously use this vocabulary because they believe that action should be driven by considerations of honor. Because this vocabulary is rich and familiar, moreover, many use it to justify their actions even as they act based on an individual volition they sense only vaguely.[6]

But even those who do not embrace the dominant framework as their personal orientation must still use the legitimate vocabulary to justify their actions. They must, after all, address their culture work toward an audience for whom this vocabulary is salient. Because social practices assert that people acting on their individual volition are not to be trusted, innovative mimetists are constrained to use a vocabulary of honor and tradition to prove that they should not be seen as dangerously individualistic.

Other men use Ramesh Mishra's and Raja Gupta's strategy of making arguments that work within the dominant framework for understanding action to justify unconventional acts. Sunil Gupta intends to give his son a chance to meet the woman he will choose to be his wife before marrying her. To justify this departure from tradition, however, Sunil emphasizes the demands of honor:

> Even if [my son] does not want to see the girl, I will show him. I have seen marriages in which the boy refused to marry the girl. In those cases, the social reputation [*pratishṭhā*] goes down. It is not the reputation of the boy which becomes less, but of the boy's parents.

Sunil's unconventional decision to show his son the woman he chooses for him is framed around consideration of the family's honor.

Men similarly use the vocabulary of tradition to justify unconventional actions. A number of men whose families are less than ideally joint comment that it is a tradition that when a family becomes large, brothers separate. Ramchandra Mishra, 32, operates a small cloth shop, in which his children often play while he works. Ramchandra, who wears a simple kurta-pajama, enjoys religious recitations. On two occasions, I accepted his invitation to attend performances of the *Rāmcharitmānas*. Ramchandra, who lives with his parents, wife, children, and younger brother and his wife and children, recognizes that

> when my children become big, then the tension [between us] will be increased. After this, there will be a division. It is tradition. We move according to the tradition that when a family becomes big [the brothers] separate.

While individual men's interests and conflicts between brothers are behind many joint-family splits, men tend to present separations as driven by tradition.

Another way that men de-emphasize the individual inclinations that often drive actions is to focus on the demands of changing times. Anil Gupta talks of his sons' separations from his family as a response to changing times:

> In our people's time, the joint family had importance. In the new age, the joint family has no importance . . . [because] the modern form of society has changed.

Anil encouraged his sons to separate from the joint family once they had obtained white-collar jobs. But by presenting the separation of the family as in accord with society, Anil claims the actions were not spurred by his own individual initiative but by social trends.

Those who have decided that a son should meet his bride before marrying may also focus on how this is not an idiosyncratic individual choice, but the result of changing times. Sunil Gupta says that he will allow his son to meet the woman he has chosen for him "because the time is changing. Whatever my parents did was right, but now circumstances have changed." Vinod Gupta used a similar argument to convince his father to show him the woman he had chosen for him. Vinod insisted on meeting the woman: "While my brothers married with money and dowry, I told my family that I would marry only after seeing the girl." Despite his insistence, Vinod de-emphasizes his demand in explaining his father's actions, focusing instead on social trends: "I married with the changing times—I married after meeting my wife. My father-*jī* knew to change with the times." While Vinod is enough of a true believer that he did not consider marrying for love, he can also be an innovative mimetist. He wanted to meet his bride before marrying her and recognized that a focus on changing times was the best way to convince his parents to show him the woman they had chosen for him.

Another way of framing unconventional actions as in accord with the dominant understanding of human motivation is to assert that the actions are in accord with some respected group in society. Thus, men say—not always disparagingly—that educated people can marry for love, or allow women to work outside the home. Shyam Gupta, a 50-year-old heading a small joint family that includes his sons and daughters-in-law, comments that educated people accept that women can work outside the home:

> Interviewer: "But, here if a woman works outside the house, then the society does not understand this as good."
>
> Shyam: No, in the society there are two types of people—those who are educated and those who are not. Those who are educated regard it as very good that the woman is earning as well as the man. It is people from the lower classes [*nimnā shreṇī*] that do not understand it as proper.

Individuals can justify unconventional actions by declaring that their actions are appropriate for a person who belongs to a respected social group, an explanation which operates within the logic of the collectivist framework for understanding action.

Finally, men sometimes emphasize that actions which break with social norms do not fundamentally challenge their attachments to their families. Many men emphasize that separations from their families do not reflect enmity with their brothers or parents by focusing on tensions between wives as the fundamental reason behind separations (Berreman 1972: 175; Luschinsky 1962: 423-476; Mandelbaum 1988; Sharma 1980: 4-5). For instance, Phoolchand Mishra describes his relationship with his brother as "sweet," even though his brother has separated from his family. Phoolchand explains the separation by pointing to the brother's wife's unwillingness to do the joint family's work:

> Because there is only one stove, a lot of food needs to be cooked in the joint family. Some of today's women don't like to do much work. They like to roam [*ghūmnā*] around too much. They want to cook food for fewer people so that they have to work less. Therefore, my brother has become separate.

Many more emphasize that increasing family size, rather than enmity
between family members precipitated a separation. Rajendra Gupta, 28,
says that his father separated from his uncle many years before because
the house became too small for all of them to live in. Rajendra insists
that the separation was "not caused by any fight." Others who live separately focus on how separations were caused by unique circumstances.
For instance, five men who have brothers working in separate cities all
insist that the families must still be seen as joint, despite what they call
"temporary" separations based on the demands of their brothers' work—
"temporary" separations which in some cases had endured for more
than 15 years!

Strategies of action, then, use a vocabulary that focuses on honor,
tradition, and moving in accordance with contemporary trends and
respected social groups. These vocabularies are rich, understood, and
legitimate because they de-emphasize the individual volition men find
threatening. While acting based on individual desires, innovative
mimetists avoid the consequences of dishonor by presenting their
actions in ways that can be understood through the collectivist framework for understanding action that most men embrace.[7]

USE OF TRADITIONAL PUBLIC FORMS

A third important element of Hindu men's strategies of action is the use
of traditional public forms to hide the fact that actions are unconventional. Ramesh Mishra and Raja Gupta emphasize the importance of
using the traditional public wedding ritual. The strategy of adopting
proper public forms to mask a private reality is used by other men in their
attempts to present unconventional actions as having the approval of
society. Dileep Singh admits that he has taken his family to live in the
city because he can provide for his young children better than if he lived
with his brothers in a nearby village. Yet, he still insists that he doesn't
"live separately from anyone" by pointing to public occasions in which
the family is symbolically unified. These occasions include weddings, the
times his village relatives stay with him for festivals, and his own stays in
the village to work the farm. He emphasizes, for instance, that

> if there is any work of the family such as a wedding, we complete that
> work together. We arrange marriages together and complete the cere-
> mony together.

Sureshwar Mishra similarly minimizes the fact that two of his sons live
in separate cities by emphasizing that they live jointly when visiting

Banāras. Sureshwar, too, insists that the family should be seen as joint. Anil Gupta established separate homes for all of his sons, and admits that "everyone eats separately." Anil nevertheless insists that "in one way the family must be seen as joint because we are together at the time of marriages." Dileep Singh, Sureshwar Mishra, and Anil Gupta focus on occasions of family togetherness to mask the fact that separations have occurred in their families.

The collectivist framework for understanding action holds that individuals should not take responsibility for directing their own actions, but should act in accordance with their family and their society. By obtaining parental consent and embracing public wedding rituals, Ramesh Mishra and Raja Gupta present themselves as acting under the guidance and supervision of their elders in the joint family. With time—as both Ramesh and Kishan imply in their hesitation to admit that the marriages were love matches—the convenient fiction may be adopted that the marriage had been an arranged one after all. Indeed, Ramesh admits that few now see his marriage as a love marriage, saying, "I have done my own work and little by little people forget. No one remembers. Many things happen in life but not everything is remembered."

RAMESH MISHRA'S PERSONAL ORIENTATION TO ACTION

I have presented Ramesh as a Goffmanian actor, who actively manipulates meanings to advance his own interests. How is this possible given the Hindu understanding that actions should be guided by forces outside the individual? As I argue above, a variety of second languages in Indian society recognize the individual. While Ramesh does not have rich cultural tools to speak strongly in the language of individual volition, he has the experience of having his own desires, a second language with which to understand them, and a repertoire of strategies of action that allow him to pursue these desires, while presenting himself in a way that can be understood through the dominant first language. Ramesh's "overt verbal communication is generally dictated by considerations of structural hierarchy" (Roland 1988: 222)—he seeks his parents' advice, he assures them that he will not be too influenced by his wife, and he presents his marriage as an arranged one by using the traditional public form. But, Ramesh still has "room for maneuvering" (Roland 1988: 222) within this structural hierarchy.

While Ramesh uses the legitimate first language that gives priority to the group, he nonetheless embraces the secondary focus on the individual as his primary orientation. Ramesh's relatively individualistic orientation is apparent in several ways. First, he sees himself as developing his own ideas himself. Ramesh says that he got the notion that "mutual understanding" between husband and wife is essential "from inside myself." Second, Ramesh does not think that social norms must always be followed, posing the rhetorical question, "What difference does it make what people think?" Third, Ramesh does not see individual actions uncontrolled by social restraints as dangerous. Instead of focusing on the necessity of social pressures, Ramesh emphasizes that "man's [own] self control" is "very necessary." Fourth, Ramesh sees himself as evaluating whether traditions should be followed. Ramesh says that

> the breaking of tradition does not mean much. The important question is how to follow tradition in the present environment. Those traditions that cannot be followed in the present environment are better off broken.

Finally, in contrast with other men I interviewed, Ramesh believes that individuals can bring about changes in society by taking responsibility for their own actions. For instance, Ramesh believes that the dowry problem[8] could be solved if individuals decided to follow their own principles:

> One cannot stop anything by making laws. To change things, one has to change man's views.
>
> Interviewer: How will people's thoughts change?
>
> Ramesh: Man can make himself understand. One has to show oneself that he does not take dowry. Then it will change.

This illustrates Ramesh's orientation that actions are directed by individuals not by society—an understanding which differs in important ways from the understandings of most of the men I interviewed. While nearly every man I interviewed says that demanding dowry is a dirty thing, most feel that the individual is powerless to do anything about the problem as long as dowry is generally given and taken. Rajesh Yadav says, for instance, that

> both the giving and taking of dowry is a crime. One should not take dowry because although you are taking another's girl, someday you will have to give your daughter. Then, the same trouble [of raising dowry] will come to you. . . . The practice of dowry should be finished little by little. *But this is possible only when all individuals in society think in this way—only if everyone thinks in this way.* [Emphasis added.]

While Ramesh Mishra feels that individuals following their own moral convictions can change the dowry system, Rajesh embraces the dominant framework for understanding action by seeing individuals as powerless to change society. Rajesh sees the impetus for change as coming only from society as a whole.

Although Ramesh Mishra does not hold the dominant Hindu framework for understanding action as his personal orientation, he is nonetheless constrained to use strategies of action that present his unconventional acts as in accord with that framework. The social practices that tell Ramesh he must avoid being seen as too individualistic constrain him to present his actions as in accord with his family's dictates.

A COMPARATIVE NOTE:
STRATEGIES OF ACTION IN THE UNITED STATES

Although this takes me beyond the scope of this book, it is worth considering briefly how American strategies of action might be constrained by the American focus on individual volition. To do so, I briefly consider Hervé Varenne's (1977: 166-187) description of an American couple, Sue and John, who marry in the face of parental opposition. Varenne's ethnography of a Midwestern American town describes Sue and John's "love story." Sue and John fall in love and intend on getting married. But Sue's parents are opposed to the marriage because they feel that Sue should finish college first, and are uncomfortable with John's previous divorce and lack of "intellectualism."

In an important way, marrying in the face of parental opposition in American society does not parallel a Hindu love marriage. While Ramesh broke with his cultural tradition by marrying for love, Sue and John play out a variation on what Varenne (1977: 166) calls "the fundamental drama of [American] culture: the assertion of the individuality of a grown-up child through a break with one community and the creation of a new one" (see also Bellah *et al.* 1985). Despite this difference, Sue's strategy for marrying John and her parents' genuine attempt to prevent the marriage are still a nice illustration of how American strategies of action are constrained by the American framework for understanding action.

Both Sue and her parents use a common vocabulary that works within the individualistic American framework for understanding action. First, both Sue and her parents take it for granted that Sue has the right as an autonomous individual to decide for herself whether she wants to marry John. To justify her marriage, Sue needed only remind her friends of the commonsense wisdom that "everybody is free to do whatever they like" (Varenne 1977: 172). While Sue's parents opposed Sue's marriage, "they could not argue that [Sue] belonged to them by right or duty." Instead, they tried to convince her that "she was more like them than she was like John, and thus, rationally speaking, ought to [herself choose to] continue participating in their community" (Varenne 1977: 174). Second, both Sue's and her parents' arguments reflect the commonsense understanding that the ultimate test of whether Sue should marry John is whether she, individually, would be happy with him (Varenne 1977: 180). Ramesh Mishra did not mention the happiness he hoped to gain by marrying his wife because such concerns do not make sense within the Hindu understanding of action as driven by group pressure. By contrast, both Sue and her parents center their discussion on whether Sue would be happy marrying John. Third, Sue and her parents focus not on public forms but on inner realities. Sue did not see a large, religious wedding as essential, but was ready for a wedding that was "completely private, except for [her] closest friends" (Varenne 1977: 172). Similarly, rather than focusing on the public reality that Sue was practically living with John, Sue's parents focused on what they believed was Sue's inner self—an inner Sue whom they felt did not really love John (Varenne 1977: 173).

While their aims are opposed, both Sue and her parents work within the American framework for understanding action, according to which Sue has the right to make her own decisions based on what she thinks will bring her inner self the most happiness. Even as Sue's parents believe that they know what is best for Sue and try to force her to bow to their pressure, they are nevertheless constrained to work within the dominant American framework for understanding action which holds that Sue has the right to make her own decisions based on what she thinks will make her most happy.

FRAMEWORKS FOR UNDERSTANDING ACTION AND CULTURAL CONSTRAINT

Because the dominant social framework for understanding action shapes the image individuals need to present of themselves, certain strategies of action become characteristic of particular social groups within any society. While an individual may have only a limited number of strategies of action in his or her particular cultural repertoire, the class of strategies that can be effectively used varies from society to society. Because social frameworks for understanding action vary cross-culturally, characteristic strategies of action vary cross-culturally as well.

An important constraining power of culture lies, then, not in prescriptive cultural norms, but in commonsense but nonetheless cultural descriptions of the world, not in demanding particular actions, but in constructing the framework through which action is perceived (see also D'Andrade 1984: 93-97; Schneider 1976). Moreover, because much of the constraint comes from social practices that discredit those whose actions appear inconsistent with this framework, much of the force of culture comes not from the internalization of cultural descriptions but from the power of society apparent in such social practices.

LIMITATIONS ON THE ABILITY TO SUCCESSFULLY USE STRATEGIES OF ACTION

Both Ramesh Mishra and Raja Gupta were successful. They achieved parental consent and social acceptance of the love marriages they insisted upon. Others, like Krishna Das Singh and Nandu Gupta, objected to the marriages their parents arranged for them, but were unsuccessful in stopping them. Perhaps Krishna's tactics of "breaking all the pots and pans in the house" and running away from the house were merely less successful arguments than the ones Ramesh Mishra made, but it seems likely that other reasons were involved as well. The next chapter describes general resources that allow some men to use Hindu strategies of action more effectively than others. But there are some self-evident reasons that Ramesh Mishra and Raja Gupta were success- ful in marrying for love that can be noted here. First, some people have opportunities to act according to their wishes. Ramesh Mishra and Raja Gupta had opportunities to meet unmarried women—opportunities which Krishna Das Singh and Nandu Gupta did not have.

Second, the dishonor attached to particular choices varies. Ramesh Mishra's efforts at getting his parents' consent was relatively easy because the woman he chose was of Ramesh's caste. Raja Gupta may have had a more difficult time because his marriage was an intercaste one. Another man whom I got to know, Vijay Mishra, married a Vaishya widow. Because he had a stable teaching post, Vijay became an unapologetic rebel who simply married in court. His conservative rural family that made its living through religious activities found the mar- riage very dishonoring. "Because I have married a widow," Vijay says, "my brothers think that they will not be able to marry and so they have boycotted me." Had Vijay tried to be an innovative mimetist, he would have had little success. His family was too firmly opposed to the wed- ding.

While strategies of action which present actions as in accord with the framework for understanding action are effective in some circumstances, they are of limited use in others. Some love marriages are simply too discrediting. Thus, although Devi Prasad Gupta says that he would allow his son to marry a woman of his own choosing as long as the son first sought Devi's permission, he still insists that he would not allow his son to choose a woman outside of his caste:

> Why would [my son] marry out of caste? If he were of no account, then he might do a marriage out of caste. This might be okay in some people's minds, but it is not in mine. In my opinion [a marriage] is right only if it is in your caste because then [a family's] way of life and habits of eating are maintained.

In short, sometimes one can try to minimize the consequences of dishonor by pretending to be guided by some social group. Other times, the only options are to bow to social pressures or unapologetically rebel.

The approach I have outlined here is also limited by its focus on the dominant groups in society. One might ask how the framework for understanding action of the dominant group influences subordinate groups like women, lower-class or lower-caste people, or religious or ethnic minorities—even if these groups do not embrace that orientation as their own. How might subordinate groups' frameworks for understanding action affect them differently than the ways that the dominant group's framework constrains the dominant group? Might subordinate groups, who must be familiar with the dominant group's framework for understanding action as well as their own framework, have more cultural tools in their cultural repertoire?

8

Who Rejects Social Roles?
Innovators and Cultural Dopes

In this chapter, I explore the uneven hold of cultural norms: Why is the norm of arranged marriages characterized by more consensus than the norm of husband-wife avoidance? Who are the men who reject cultural norms? What explains why some men can perform culture work better than others?

My small sample revealed a range of individual variations: Older men and younger brothers are more likely to reject restrictions on husband-wife interactions than younger men and eldest brothers are; *Banārasī*s who were born in a village are more likely to question arranged marriages than *Banārasī*s who have lived in Banāras their whole lives; college-educated men, like Ramesh Mishra and Raja Gupta, are more likely than other men to depart from arranged marriages. My consideration of these individual variations suggests that experience is a social and a cognitive resource that creates the desire and the ability to get around cultural norms, that men who are members of respected social groups can use that membership to depart from traditional norms, and that honor controls public life more powerfully than it controls private life.

The explanations of individual variations proposed here are tentative for several reasons. First, my sample is small, and for some of the social groups I discuss it is very small. Second, the sample of urban, upper-caste Hindu merchants of Banāras was not designed to be random—although I think that there are no obvious biases. Third, because the interviews were open-ended, I did not elicit each individual's opinion on every particular topic that I eventually decided to analyze. So, while I can say, for instance, what sorts of people are likely to volunteer the idea that some love marriages work, I cannot say that those who did not volunteer this idea would necessarily reject it. Fourth, there are some "missing values" for all of my findings. I did not discover, for instance, whether some older men who headed their own families were older or younger brothers. My hypothesis that birth-order is important developed only from an analysis of variation.

The reader should approach this chapter with caution, but there are several reasons why the analysis of this small sample is plausible. First, the differences I observe are substantial. Because of my small sample, I cannot describe small differences between groups, but the differences I

142

do observe are sometimes large indeed. Second, my conclusions about who is more likely to be successful at culture work make sense given the strategies of action I identified in the last chapter. Indeed, I looked for and identified the differences described in this section because of my inference that I would find them. Third, my findings that people with more experiences—men who are older, men who have relations with older brothers' wives, men who have moved from village to city, and men who have college education—are more likely to break social norms are consistent with each other. Fourth, my findings are consistent with the work of other investigators (Mines 1988).

EXPERIENCE AS A RESOURCE

People often rely on cultural understandings to guide them when embarking on unfamiliar actions. They are especially dependent on cultural guides when they have no personal experience. Experience works in two ways. First, experience is a cognitive resource which helps people judge social norms critically. A married man who finds that his love for his wife does not lead him to neglect his elders may conclude that closeness between husband and wife is not always destructive. Second, experience is a social resource an individual can use in discourse. Experience provides a tool men can use in culture work justifying unconventional actions.

UNSETTLED TIMES: EMBRACING CULTURAL NORMS WHEN FIRST FACING MARRIAGE

The fact that older men are more likely to reject limitations on husband-wife interactions suggests how experience empowers. Nearly 40% of men over 29 say that there need be no limits on the husband-wife relationship, while less than 10% of the men under twenty-nine reject limitations on husband-wife interaction (see table 1). While less than a quarter of men under 45 say that there need be no limitations on interactions between husband and wife, nearly half of the men over 45 reject restrictions on interactions (see table 2). While nearly half of the men over 28 say that a husband may talk with his wife in front of his parents without restriction, none of the married men younger than 28 regard this as acceptable (see table 3). Why are older men more likely to reject the norm limiting interactions between husband and wife?

First, the cultural norm limiting husband-wife interactions aims largely at *young* husbands. Elders fear that a young wife, with little

TABLE 1

	Men ages 20-28	Men ages 29-75
Says he must limit his relationship with his wife.	12 (92%)	17 (61%)
Says he need not limit his relationship with his wife.	1 (8%)	11 (39%)

TABLE 2

	Men ages 20-45	Men ages 46-75
Says he must limit his relationship with his wife.	22 (79%)	7 (54%)
Says he need not limit his relationship with his wife.	6 (21%)	6 (46%)

TABLE 3

	Men ages 20-28	Men ages 29-75
Believes a husband must not talk with his wife in front of his parents.	10 (100%)	11 (48%)
Believes a husband can talk with his wife in front of his parents.	0	12 (52%)

invested in her husband's family, will manipulate her husband for her own ends. By contrast, men hope that an older wife will have developed a commitment to her husband's family.

Second, older men have more financial independence and, so, may be more able to stand on their own without parental support, allowing them to repudiate parental constraints. Mattison Mines (1988: 573) found that, while even young men "had strongly felt dreams for autonomy," most only feel "capable of leading a life separate from their parents' control" after they have "a sense of self sufficiency." Men need an alternative to family support, Mines argues, since "rebellion may precipitate total estrangement lasting for years, if not for a lifetime." College student R.L. Yadav has dreams of love, but admits that if you marry for love "in your boyhood," "the love [prem] will not run for long." For R.L., this is because young men lack the money to support themselves. "If you have money," he says, "then you can do everything and your love [*prem*] will be running for a long time—even for your whole life." Some young men, then, see self-sufficiency as providing the power to break with social norms.

Third, men may rely on cultural norms to guide them when they have no personal experience that suggests an alternative. During the "unsettled" time (Swidler 1986: 278), or "liminal" period (Turner 1969) of social transformation, cultural models play a powerful role in organizing social life (Derné 1985; Swidler 1986). Similarly, during the "unsettled" times in the life cycle when individuals are unfamiliar with new roles, received cultural norms are direct guides to action.[1] Without experience of marriage, young married men usually use cultural guidelines which strongly emphasize the dangers of closeness between husband and wife. When accumulated experience of a decade or more of marriage tells men that talk between husband and wife is not dangerous, but is enjoyable, men may reject the dominant cultural norm that limits interaction between husband and wife.

Many younger men feel that their inexperience renders them unable to make independent evaluations of cultural guidelines. Twenty-six-year-old Jyothi Gupta operates a bicycle shop in the bustling center of Banāras. Jyothi, whose marriage has just been arranged, lives with his brothers and parents in a joint family. Jyothi refuses to venture any opinion on proper husband-wife relationships saying, "How can I know about these things now? I will come to know about these things only after I have married." Jyothi, like others, does not feel entitled to evaluate cultural norms because of what he regards as his inexperience. As Shobnath Gupta, an unmarried 20-year-old, puts it, "I have not married, so what can I say [about married life]?"

Hindu men, young and old, see experience as a source of wisdom. Nearly half (22/49) of the men I interviewed mention that arranged marriages are better than marriages chosen by the bride and groom because of parents' experience. Tej Gupta says, for instance, that the advantage of arranged marriages is that the parents "who have passed their time [and] lived through these things" are able to decide on an appropriate bride. Narayan Singh similarly believes that, because "parents know about the world [and] have experience," they will arrange a good marriage. Experience, then, is culturally emphasized as providing wisdom.

Hindu men see experience as the basis of authority. Junior men often see themselves as subject to the directions of their elders. Gopal Mishra loves to laugh and talk, but he wanted me to interview his father, saying that he knew more about Hindu culture. Gopal describes the pressures elders can bring on juniors, and elders' relative immunity from social criticism:

> If someone else is younger than me, I can tell him, 'Brother, this work is wrong. Stop doing it.' But if someone is elder [*buzurg*] than me like my father or uncle, then I cannot tell him even if he is doing something wrong.

Rajesh Yadav, who remains a bit dissatisfied with the ten-year-old marriage his parents arranged for him, comments on how he felt he could not object to the marriage because of his respect for his parents:

> Whatever marriage the parents arrange is right. A boy has so much respect [*adab*] and deference [*lihāz*] for his parents that he will never object to his parents' decision. A boy respects [*sammān karnā*] his parents so much that he will do whatever they say.

Rajesh can't help but imagine the way "it should be"—"the boy and girl should meet each other, and understand each other well"—but because he respected his parents' experience, Rajesh married "in shyness." Younger men say that, because they lack experience and authority in their families, they do not feel entitled to comment upon, let alone challenge, established norms.

While older men do not talk about what leads them to reject the norm of husband-wife avoidance, the fact that they are more likely than younger men to take such a stand suggests that experience transforms their understanding and empowers them to act independently. Older men's experience of relations with their wives as benevolent transforms their understanding, while their increasingly respected positions in their families offer greater flexibility to embrace unconventional beliefs. Responsible to fewer elders, older men—themselves the guardians of meaning—have more leeway to get around cultural norms. These conclusions are consistent with Mattison Mines's (1988: 572) recent work which shows that as Indians grow older they increasingly feel "some dictates of social conformity to be less compelling." Mines (1988: 574) found that, because older informants feel "less constrained by society and family obligations," they "become their own decision makers." Empowered by experience and authority in the family, older men's culture work can point to the wisdom of their experience to justify their rejection of the norm that they limit contact with their wives.

YOUNGER SONS AND THE NORM
OF HUSBAND-WIFE AVOIDANCE

Younger sons are more likely than eldest sons to be close to their wives. While only two of the eldest brothers I interviewed say that they talk freely with their wives in front of their parents, seven younger brothers report that they talk in this manner. While five younger sons think it is always wrong to talk with their wives in front of their parents, ten eldest sons embrace this strict prohibition.[2] Why do younger sons appear to be more likely to be close to their wives than eldest sons? First, the norm barring close husband-wife interaction is more imperative for eldest sons (see Trawick 1990: 64). Eldest sons are responsible for the joint family as a whole, while younger sons are supposed to be controlled by their elder brothers. Men see more danger for the family if the eldest son, who will eventually head the family, is too influenced by his wife (see Lutgendorf 1987: 573-4). They hope that if a younger son is manipulated by his wife, his older brother will make certain that the family's interests are not threatened. Younger brothers' experiences with their elder brothers' wives may, however, constitute a second important reason why younger brothers tend to become close to their wives.

Anthropologists uniformly report that Hindus regard the relationship between a man and his *bhābhī* [elder brother's wife] as close, affectionate, and sometimes sexually charged.[3] Films, plays (Hansen 1992: 28-29), and popular magazines celebrate the closeness of *bhābhī* and *devar* [husband's younger brother]. The English language magazine *Woman's Era* heralds the benefits of large families by reminding readers that every wife wants "her husband to have a brother." In describing the *bhābhī-devar* relationship, *Woman's Era* focuses on teasing sexuality, asserting that the *bhābhī* "inflames the thirst which a wife quenches. She is a mother and a sex idol in the same body. Flirtation with a . . . *bhābhī* adds color to a man's life" (Sharma 1991: 37).

While the men I interviewed respect their *bhābhī*s, many men have sexy, joking relationships with their *bhābhī*s. Surjit Singh, a 33-year-old who hopes to marry soon, likens his close relationship with his *bhābhī* to the relationship Indian men value most—the relationship with their mother:

> My relationship with my *bhābhī* is very good. She cooperates with me in everything like a mother. The love [*sneh-pyār*] of *bhābhī* for me is as a mother for her children. As long as I remain unmarried she . . . meets all of my difficulties.

Raj Kumar Singh, a recently married 23-year-old, insists—rather pointedly, and without prompting—that he has no sexual relationship with his *bhābhī*. His emphasis on how he enjoys joking with her suggests, however, the teasing sexuality that is often an important component of the relationship. "My relationship with her," he says laughingly, is

> good, good, and good. Our relationship is really rolling. We joke— mostly about my wife and how she should be. We joke about sex [literally English: "the love system"]. But there's nothing beyond [joking].

Like Surjit, Raj Kumar likens his eldest *bhābhī* to his mother saying that "she is given first preference and respected [*izzat karnā*] as a mother would be."[4]

The often close relationship between younger sons and their *bhābhīs* is an important experience that older sons do not have. Indian men have little opportunity to interact with women outside their immediate families. In Banāras, men do not usually attend schools or universities with women, and even in places where coeducation is common, a man usually has little experience interacting with women since parents try to limit daughters' contacts with young men (Mukhopadhyay 1994). For younger sons, the often sexually charged relationship with their *bhābhīs*—women who are defined as sexual creatures—is an important experience that may lead them to desire similarly close relationships with their own wives, and to reject cultural norms that demand that a husband and wife remain distant from each other.

Anand Singh, the 47-year-old youngest of many sons who focuses on close sexual ties with his wife, enjoys what he calls a "very close" relationship with his eldest *bhābhī*. Anand describes his eldest *bhābhī* as the *mālkin* [female head of household] who "tells everyone in the family what to do." Not only does Anand proclaim that there is "no sort of prohibition, nor any sort of limit" on his relationship with his *bhābhī*, but he also obviously enjoys "joking [*mazāk karnā*]" with her. "I hurl abuses [*gālī*] at my eldest *bhābhī*, and also get beatings too. All sorts of jokes are rolling between us [*mazāk chalnā*]." Perhaps Anand's experiences with his *bhābhī* developed expectations that led him to focus on closeness with his own wife.

Because they have *bhābhīs*, younger sons are more likely than elder sons to have the experience of a close, sexually charged relationship before marrying. This experience may lead them to desire close relationships with their own wives—a desire that leads them to violate the norm of husband-wife avoidance.

EXPERIENCE AND THE REJECTION OF SOCIAL ROLES

In what other ways does experience lead men to reject dominant cultural norms? While roughly one-third of the men I interviewed reject the norm of husband-wife avoidance, all of the unmarried men I interviewed say that they will allow their parents to arrange their marriage. Unmarried men have little experience interacting with unrelated women and lack any knowledge of alternative ways of marrying. People may need their culture most when approaching a first-time action like marrying. Thus, there is more variation in cultural ideas about proper husband-wife relations then about whether marriages should be arranged by parents because understandings of husband-wife relations are mediated by real experience.

Moving from village to city is another important experience that allows people to assess cultural beliefs. Perhaps the experience of the difference between rural and urban life leads men who have moved to Banāras from rural areas to reject conventional wisdom about family life.[5] Most strikingly, more than 80% of urban men born in rural areas believe at least some love marriages are successful, while less than one-third of the men born in the urban environment believe some love marriages work (see table 4). Although the differences are not as great, urban men of rural origin are also more likely to reject the norm of husband-wife avoidance, and to reject the notion that women should never work outside the home (see tables 5 and 6). Seeing the differences between rural and urban life may allow urban men of rural origin to regard cultural norms as socially constructed, rather than inevitable, and to see that other ways of life are possible.

COLLEGE EDUCATION AS A REFERENTIAL RESOURCE

Experience not only shapes understanding, but provides a resource people can refer to in discourse. One way that men reject cultural norms is by using a strategy of action that presents actions as occurring with the guidance of some respected social group. Indians who are college-educated can do culture work that justifies their actions by emphasizing that these actions are appropriate for the group of educated Indians.

College-educated men are more likely than other men to depart from a strict arranged marriage. All three of the people I knew who married for love had obtained postgraduate education. College-educated men are also more likely than their less educated counterparts to successfully insist that they be allowed to meet their brides or see their brides' photographs before the wedding (see table 7). Yet, college education does not change attitudes toward arranged marriages. College-educated men are no more likely to believe that some love marriages might be successful than are those who lack a college education (see table 8). It appears, then, that education provides a resource that allows men to act on their ideas at least as much as it changes their ideas. Eighty percent of college-educated men who believed that love marriages are sometimes successful persuaded their parents to at least see their bride's picture before the wedding, while less than half of the men who believed love marriages sometimes worked, but who lacked college education, successfully insisted on seeing their bride's photo. Of the

TABLE 4

	Men born in cities	Urban men born in villages
Believes love marriages always fail.	21 (68%)	2 (18%)
Believes some love marriages work.	10 (32%)	9 (82%)

TABLE 5

	Men born in cities	Urban men born in villages
Believe women should never work outside the home.	10 (30%)	2 (25%)
Believe it is acceptable for women to work if they are poor or if they are highly educated.	14 (42%)	3 (38%)
Believe that it is completely acceptable for women to work.	9 (27%)	3 (38%)

TABLE 6

	Men born in cities	Urban men born in villages
Says he must limit his relationship with his wife.	24 (71%)	6 (60%)
Says he need not limit his relationship with his wife.	10 (29%)	4 (40%)

men without college-education, at least three who wished that they would be able to meet their wife before the wedding, lamented the fact that they would be unable to do so.

Some men recognize that college education empowers by allowing men to claim membership in an educated group. Krishna Das Singh, who objected strongly to the marriage his parents arranged for him, views education as a resource that might have allowed him to marry for love:

> The people who are uneducated understand love marriages as worthless. But among those who are educated, love marriages happen and many people come to the function. There are good parties and people

TABLE 7

	Some college and above	No college
Respondent didn't see his bride or her picture before marrying. He also didn't want to show his son his bride before the wedding.	9 (47%)	10 (63%)
Respondent met his wife, saw her photo, said he would meet his wife, or showed his son his bride before the marriage.	10 (53%)	6 (38%)

NOTE: Table includes only men under 45, since no men over 45 had any college education.

TABLE 8

	Some college and above	No college
Believes love marriages always fail.	9 (47%)	8 (50%)
Believes some love marriages work.	10 (53%)	8 (50%)

NOTE: Table includes only men under 45, since no men over 45 had any college education.

> come wearing suits and ties. They manage the marriage from all sides and don't understand it as wrong. But uneducated people have the opinion that love marriages are wrong.

Krishna's description is fanciful, but he still rightly suggests that group membership is a resource which an individual can use to justify unconventional actions.

College-educated men are also more likely to reject the norm of husband-wife avoidance. They are more likely to talk with their wives in front of their parents and to say that they need not limit their relationship with their wives than are men who lack college education (see table 9). Perhaps the ability to refer to oneself as an "educated person" for whom the norms of "educated" Indians are appropriate may facilitate the rejection of cultural norms limiting interaction between husband and wife. That education is largely a resource for culture work, rather than an experience that shifts understanding is indicated by the fact that col-

lege-educated men are actually less likely to reject the idea that closeness between husband and wife may lead the husband to neglect his
parents (see table 10).

The sample size I have examined here is small, and the differences
between those who attended college and those who did not are not that
great. Nevertheless, the evidence points in the same direction—college-
educated men are more likely to see a picture of their bride before marrying, are more likely to allow their wives to work outside the home,[6]

TABLE 9

	Some college and above	No college
Limiting relationships with his wife:		
Says he must limit his relationship with his wife.	11 (74%)	12 (86%)
Says he need not limit his relationship with his wife.	4 (27%)	2 (14%)
Talking with a wife in front of parents:		
Believes a husband must not talk with his wife in front of his parents.	8 (57%)	9 (82%)
Believes a husband can talk with his wife in front of his parents.	6 (43%)	2 (18%)

NOTE: Table includes only men under 45, since no men over 45 had any college
education.

TABLE 10

	Some college and above	No college
Believes too close a relationship between husband and wife causes tensions in the joint family.	10 (71%)	8 (67%)
Rejects the idea that a close relationship between husband and wife causes tensions in the joint family.	4 (29%)	4 (33%)

NOTE: Table includes only men under 45, since no men over 45 had any college
education.

and are more likely to reject the norm of husband-wife avoidance. The ability to claim membership in the respected group of educated Indians may assist the college educated in the culture work that they do to reject social norms.[7]

PUBLIC CONSTRAINT, PRIVATE FREEDOM: BEYOND WATCHFUL EYES

There is consensus about whether marriages should be arranged and whether women should work outside the home. There is more disagreement about whether a husband and wife should limit their contacts and about what arrangements make the joint family operate smoothly. Why? One reason is that the latter norms are mediated by real experience. Another, however, is that whether or not a husband and wife should have close relations in the family and whether a family should run hierarchically or democratically are private, not public, matters.

Hindu men see cultural norms as constraining because they believe that rejecting them threatens their honor. Only actions that are observed by others are subject to the threat of dishonor. Because only public actions can cause dishonor, norms that regulate public behavior are the most powerful (see also Shweder 1991: 249; Sharma 1980a: 45).

Indeed, many of the men I interviewed recognize that private behavior is often negotiable. For example, Amrit Mishra regards drinking alcohol as wrong, but only if it is done in public (Chapter 4). Men similarly reason that fighting among women is dishonorable—but only if it is observed by others.[8] Deepak Mishra says, for instance, that "if there is always fighting, the honor [izzat] will go away because of the things outsiders [bāhar log] will say if they hear of it." Yet, Deepak also feels that this is not the most important cause of dishonor because

> fighting can happen in the house between us, and outsiders [bāhar log] will never know. If I went out and beat someone or had a wrong relationship with any girl or murdered someone or picked a pocket, any of these things would be enough to ruin the family honor [izzat]. All these things take place outside the house, not inside it.

Shyam Gupta is one of many who mentioned in an initial interview that fighting within the family could cause dishonor. Even then, Shyam qualified this, by saying that only fighting which was heard by outsiders would harm the family. "If [a woman] speaks with a sharp voice, or if there is any fighting in the house, and if people nearby [agal bagal *log*] or outsiders [*bāhar log*] hear of it, then the honor [*izzat*] of the family is struck down [*āghāt*]." Because the constraint that presses to obey cultural norms comes from the threat to one's honor, cultural norms are less strictly followed when others can not learn of impudent behavior.

Men's emphasis on how dishonoring it is to have a disobedient wife is probably related more to their desire to control their wives than to a concern with family honor. The fact that men talk as if fighting between the house's women is dishonorable even though such fighting is often private suggests that the charge that a woman is dishonoring her family is more a weapon to control a wife than a reflection of a real concern with family honor.

CONCLUSIONS

When are cultural dictates most powerful? First, to reject cultural imperatives, an individual must want to do so. Individuals who lack experience must rely on the dominant cultural ideas they hear repeatedly. Without knowledge of alternative ways of marrying, men embrace arranged marriages. Without the experience of married life, which could temper the focus on the dangers of love, young married men embrace limitations on husband-wife interactions. Without the experience of a sexually teasing relationship with their older brother's wife, eldest sons often do not become close with their own wives.

Second, to reject cultural imperatives, one must be able to do culture work that presents unconventional actions in an acceptable way. Experience facilitates the arguments men make in discourse. Older men can refer to the wisdom of experience to justify their rejection of cultural imperatives. Membership in a diversity of respected social groups is a similar resource for culture work. If one can argue persuasively that unconventional behavior is accepted by a respected social group, one can present an action as guided by that group rather than by dangerous individual inclination. Thus, college-educated men are more likely than others to successfully demand to see a photo of their brides before their marriages are set.

Third, people are more able to reject cultural imperatives which concern the private realm, since these imperatives are rarely significant for a family's honor. Less culture work needs be done to justify close interactions between husband and wife since such close interactions are not observed by outsiders. But in public, when honor is on the line, individuals cannot as easily reject cultural imperatives.

9

Family Structure, Ethnopsychology,
and Emotion Culture:
How Do They Make Each Other Up?

So far, I have emphasized how practices associated with joint-family living are generated by Hindu men's focus on group primacy, group control, and group solidarity. In chapter 3, I show that men's emphasis on group control leads many to use family pressure to control wayward family members. Forty-four-year-old Arjun Gupta says, for instance, that

> when any tensions arise [in the family], we [men] sit together, think, and solve the problem. . . . If my younger brother did something wrong, then all four brothers say to him, "You are doing wrong." This has a mental effect [*mānsik asar*] on him [and] . . . he comes again to his place.

In chapter 4, I describe how men's emphasis on group solidarity leads them to emphasize that members of a joint family should care for each other's children as if they were their own. Forty-seven-year-old Anand Singh says, for instance, that his wife must care not only for their own children, but for his brothers' and *bhābhīs'* children as well: "If they cry, she should take them in her lap and love [*pyār*] them." In chapter 4, I describe how men's commitment to joint-family harmony leads many to be wary of unbounded love with their wives. Yet, these practices associated with joint-family living—group pressure, multiple caretaking, and limitations on husband-wife interactions—do not merely reflect Hindu men's collectivist ethnopsychology; they also help generate men's emotions and commonsense understandings.

An important project of contemporary social theory is to link larger social structures with micro interactions that reproduce those structures.[1] Connell (1987: 17) argues that social scientists must try to understand how "personal life and collective social arrangements" mutually constitute each other. Shweder (1991: 73) similarly describes one of cultural psychology's projects as developing an understanding of how "psyche and culture, person and context, . . . practice and practitioner live together, require each other, and dynamically, dialectically, and jointly make each other up." In this chapter, I suggest that joint-family living, Hindu men's cultural construction of human motivation, and Hindu men's emotion culture reproduce, require, and bolster each other.

My main focus will be on how joint-family living is a collective arrangement that puts men in situations that make their emotion culture

156

and collectivist framework for understanding action compelling. I emphasize that when men use this emotion culture and ethnopsychology, they become active agents who bolster the joint family. But before focusing on the importance of joint-family structures I need to briefly reiterate how the collectivist framework for understanding action requires joint-family living and a focus on social fear as exemplary and love as dangerous, while this emotion culture, in turn, requires joint-family living, and a collectivist ethnopsychology.

I have argued throughout this book that most Hindu men value the guidance of social pressures. This collectivist framework for understanding action leads men to see social fear as an exemplary emotion that prompts people to be guided by the opinion of others, and to see love for one's spouse as a potentially dangerous emotion that could tempt one away from the benevolent guidance of elders. The collectivist framework for understanding action similarly bolsters joint families since the man who values the direction of family elders usually chooses to live in a joint family to facilitate parental guidance. The collectivist framework for understanding action requires, then, both joint-family living and the understanding that social fear is exemplary and love for one's spouse is potentially dangerous.

This emotion culture, in turn, requires joint-family living and a collectivist ethnopsychology. Men who see social fear as the only way to guarantee correct behavior want to live in a joint family where they can be continually subjected to the pressures that prompt *ḍar* [fear/respect/love]. They are wary of living separately where one is isolated from the group pressures that deter antisocial behavior. A man who sees exclusive love for his wife as a potentially dangerous emotional flood is wary of living outside of a joint family where he might be dangerously vulnerable to his wife's charms. Similarly, the person who sees social fear as the basis of morality sees action as rightly driven by social pressures. When it is heartfelt, then, Hindu emotion culture requires both joint-family living and the collectivist framework for understanding action.

In this chapter I suggest that the structure of joint families similarly requires the ethnopsychology and emotion culture that most Hindu men rely on to understand the world. How does living in a joint family lead men to see actions as rightly driven by social pressure? How does the structure of Hindu joint families create persistent dilemmas that lead men to be active agents who constitute and reconstitute the dominant emotion culture which holds that social fear is exemplary and one-on-one love is dangerous?

JOINT-FAMILY LIVING AND THE COLLECTIVIST
FRAMEWORK FOR UNDERSTANDING ACTION[2]

Since frameworks for understanding action constrain strategies of action
and influence the human psyche, it is important to consider the social
structures that generate ethnopsychological beliefs. Using psychoanalytic reasoning, and a modified Durkheimian approach, I suggest here
that family structure is important in shaping ethnopsychological understandings. Most young Hindu couples live in a household with at least
one other married couple (Kolenda 1967: 386), and most Hindu children
spend the early years of childhood in extended families (Kakar [1978]
1981: 115; Standing 1991: 27; Seymour 1993). Joint-family living
makes a range of family members available for the care of young infants
and facilitates prolonged infancy. The hierarchical structure of joint
families, moreover, places young men under the constant surveillance of
superiors. These joint-family patterns structure interactions which generate the collectivist framework for understanding action.

THE DURKHEIMIAN EXPLANATION

In *The Elementary Forms of the Religious Life*, Durkheim (1912 [1915])
argues that intense social gatherings bring about group conformity and
moral respect for sacred objects (Collins 1988: 111). For Durkheim
(1912 [1915]: 465) the social group can only make its influence felt
when "it is in action," and it is only in action when "the individuals
who compose it are assembled together and act in common." While
Durkheim focuses on the intensity and duration of gatherings that bring
together whole societies, Randall Collins (1988: 109) argues that
Durkheim's arguments may be applied to any social group, whatever its
boundaries. The joint families in which Hindu men live are precisely the
sort of groups that might lead to pressure to conform to group culture.
Collins (1988: 114, 1975: 75) argues that when individuals spend a
large amount of time in the presence of particular other people, there is
strong pressure for conformity. One reason Indian men emphasize
adherence to social pressures may be their participation in dense interactions with others in the joint family. By facilitating social gatherings
with important others, joint-family living may heighten men's consciousness of the group, leading them to emphasize being guided by
group dictates.

   In *The Division of Labor in Society*, Durkheim ([1893] 1933)
argues that pressure for group conformity is strongest when individuals
interact with a limited range of other individuals (see Collins 1988:

114, 1975: 64-65). If individuals are enclosed in a social environment, their social horizons are limited, group norms are well defined, and individual freedom is restricted (Durkheim [1893] 1933: 302). Durkheim ([1893] 1933: 130, 226-227) focuses on the extent of differentiation within a whole society, arguing that in societies with little internal differentiation, uniform beliefs and practices are imposed upon all through the dictates of public opinion. By contrast, Durkheim argues, when the division of labor and urbanization give rise to diverse and cosmopolitan networks of social encounters ([1893] 1933: 256-260), social solidarity can not be based on sameness, and morality becomes abstract, generalized, and focused on individual rights and freedom (Durkheim [1893] 1933: 400). Hindu men regard members of a family as sharing important traits. For most men, interactions within the family are of primary importance. While Hindu men often move in cosmopolitan circles, the joint family remains the emotional center of their lives. Moreover, since fathers usually make important decisions about marriage and career for their sons, even interactions outside the home may be perceived as occurring within a limited network. Following Durkheim's reasoning, Hindu men's perception that they engage in a limited range of social encounters may contribute to the cultural focus on being guided by social pressures.

Authority in the joint family may also generate an emphasis on conformity. Collins (1975: 74) extends Durkheim's analysis, arguing that those who usually take orders in their interactions become externally conforming. Even when order-takers do not carry out the demands of their superiors, repeated interactions in which subordinates receive orders generate a sense that one is not entitled or even able to act independently (Collins 1990: 35-37; Scheff 1990: 121-122). Upper-caste Hindu men spend most of their young adult lives as subordinates in joint families that emphasize the authority of elder over younger. They take part in interactions in which elders give orders, generating a sense that conforming to group pressure is the normal state of things.

Since young adult Hindu men spend most of their time as subordinates in tight, crowded, watched joint-family environments, they come to view adherence to social pressures as important. The Durkheimian principle of social density (Collins 1975: 74-6, 154) suggests, then, that dense, emotionally charged interactions with many other family members might give rise to the focus on being guided by social pressures that I describe. Indeed, older Hindu men may be more likely to emphasize individual choices than younger men (see chapter 8, Mines 1988) because they often have the privacy that comes with seniority in a family or separation from the parental household.

PHYSICAL CLOSENESS BETWEEN INFANTS AND
CARETAKERS IN INDIAN JOINT FAMILIES

Psychoanalytic reasoning suggests a number of other ways that joint-family living might lead Hindu men to focus on being guided by social pressures (Kurtz 1992; Roland 1988; Kakar [1978] 1981). Although the specifics of these psychoanalytic approaches vary, all draw the same conclusion—that joint-family living leads men to be acutely sensitive to social pressures. Since I have not done ethnographic research about Indian child rearing practices, and am not an expert in psychoanalytic theory, my discussion here is indebted to the insights of Sudhir Kakar ([1978] 1981), Alan Roland (1988), Susan Seymour (1983, 1993), and Stanley Kurtz (1992).

First, joint-family structure leads infant Indian boys to receive prolonged physical nurturance from mothers and other caretakers. Sudhir Kakar ([1978] 1981), and Alan Roland (1988) suggest that this is because North Indian joint families isolate young women in their husbands' households. In North India, a young woman is married into a house (and often into a neighborhood or village) in which she knows no one, cutting her off from all previous emotional attachments with family and friends (Kakar [1978] 1981: 60, 72; Obeyesekere 1984: 432-34). In her husband's household, the bride usually comes under the strict control and authority of her husband's mother, who expects the young woman to bear the most burdensome chores in the joint household (chapter 2; Kakar [1978] 1981: 73-4; Obeyesekere 1984: 435; Roland 1988: 231). The wife's ties to her own husband are limited, moreover, by customs demanding that a husband limit interactions with his wife to prevent the blossoming of close ties that might threaten the harmony of the joint family (chapters 2 and 4; Kakar [1978] 1981: 74; Obeyesekere 1984: 435; Mandelbaum 1988: 16; Roland 1988: 231). In this isolated situation, the young wife may shower her infants with affection because each infant's birth improves her status in the family, and because this affection is positively sanctioned (Kakar [1978] 1981; Roland 1988: 231). Even a young wife knows, moreover, that when her son marries, he will bring a daughter-in-law into the household who will relieve her of her most burdensome housework. It is vital for a mother to cultivate her sons' devotion so that they will remain with her after marrying (Bennett 1983).

Basing their arguments on clinical work with adult Indian patients and Carstairs's ([1957] 1967) ethnographic work, Kakar ([1978] 1981: 79-82), and Roland (1988: 232, 263) argue that infant Indian boys consequently experience a long period of maternal indulgence. Susan Seymour's (1976, 1980, 1983) and Leigh Minturn's (1993: 284; Minturn and Hitchcock [1963] 1966: 107-112) careful naturalistic ethnographic accounts of Indian child rearing suggest, however, that physical indulgence often takes place without the mother's excessive emotional involvement. Seymour's (1976, 1980, 1983, 1993) ethnographic study of mother-child interactions in joint households in urban Bhubaneshwar (East India) shows that childcare is instrumental, that mothers are not highly responsive to their children's requests, that mothers are unlikely to praise infants, and that care-givers do not consider the infant's emotional needs as of paramount importance (see also Kurtz 1992: 48-49; Minturn and Hitchcock [1963] 1966: 107-112; Whiting and Whiting 1975).[3]

While Roland and Kakar overestimate maternal indulgence, the "sensuous physical closeness" (Roland 1988: 232) and prolonged infancy they (see Kakar [1978] 1981: 81) focus on is consistent with ethnographic descriptions of Indian child rearing. Although Seymour (1976, 1980, 1983, 1993) did not find maternal indulgence, she describes mothers, siblings, and other caregivers as providing infants with constant physical closeness, meeting infants' demands, and rarely employing physical punishment. When awake, infants are carried around on the hip of their mothers or other caretakers (Seymour 1980: 131; see also Kakar [1978] 1981: 80; Roland 1988: 232). Infants sleep with their mothers when they are nursing and either continue to sleep with her or with some other adult throughout childhood (Seymour 1980: 131-134; 1993: 56-7; see also Kakar [1978] 1981: 80; Roland 1988: 232). The mother's breast is offered on demand and no baby is allowed to cry for long.[4] In the early years, children's needs are met quickly, children are seldom physically punished, and there is little effort at toilet training.[5] Mothers or other caretakers often bathe, dress, and hand-feed children until they reach the age of ten (Seymour 1980: 135, 1993: 59).

Furthermore, as Seymour (1983: 270-273) rightly suggests, the structure of Indian joint families facilitates this physical closeness by providing a range of caretakers to look after children (see also Minturn 1993: 283). Her research shows that physical closeness between infant and caretaker is more common in Indian extended families than in nuclear ones, and that the expressions of positive affect that Roland and Kakar emphasize are greatest in larger households.

The prolonged mode of mothering in which an infant's every demand is met (even if by a range of caretakers and in an instrumental way) leads Indian men to be particularly sensitive to the demands of others. Roland (1988: 232-3, 263) argues that constant physical closeness

fosters a sense of self which is much more inclusive of we-ness, with a
closer interconnection of inner images of self and other; [and] outer
ego boundaries that remain much more permeable to constant affective
exchanges and emotional connectedness with others. . . . [The] acute
sensitivity to the moods and emotional states of the mothering person
derives from the more prolonged symbiotic mode of mothering, and
becomes the bedrock for the later sensitivity to nonverbal communication, *and to the approbation and criticism from others—all crucial to
the Indian conscience.* [Emphasis added.]

Seymour (1993: 59) similarly suggests that "prolonging a child's physical dependence on others" creates "a sense of interdependence in a
society that does not value independence and where one is never
expected to go off and live on one's own."[6] In short, the extensive physical closeness, positive affect, and prolonged dependence that joint-
family living facilitates between infants and caretakers lead to the focus
on being guided by social pressures that I describe in this book.[7]

CHILDREN'S EXPERIENCE WITH
MANY ADULTS IN INDIAN FAMILIES

Kakar ([1978] 1981: 127) and Roland (1988: 263) argue that for male
children, the period of maternal indulgence abruptly ends at about the
age of five. Increasingly separated from his mother, a son is confronted
not with a father with whom he can identify, but with the "whole assem-
bly of elder males in the family" (Kakar [1978] 1981: 133; see also
Bassa 1978: 338). Custom limits a father's expression of love toward his
son to prevent a father from giving precedence to his wife and child
over his parents, brothers, and sisters (Kakar [1978] 1981: 131). Consequently, an infant boy's main experience is with a group of elders. A
child has to relate to many adults, all of whom represent a source of
authority and gratification (Gore 1978: 368).

A young boy's early experience, then, is of being guided by the
social pressures of a large extended family. The young boy's upbringing
emphasizes not his individuality but that he is a part of a group (Gore
1978: 369; Asthana 1988: 159; Seymour 1983, 1993). Like Arjun
Gupta, most men believe that whenever an individual makes a mistake,
the group of brothers instructs him against doing wrong. For Arjun, it is
the "mental effect" of being criticized by a group that makes the
offender return "to his place." Roland (1988: 264) argues that this focus
on enforcing conformity through shaming teaches the child to be
"extremely circumspect around his or her elders." Thus, how a person
"will be regarded by others becomes a central inner dynamic, rather

than a feeling of inner guilt . . . , which is more characteristic of the Western superego" (Roland 1988: 264). Seymour (1993: 59) similarly argues that Indians' "sense of interdependence" is partly the result of the fact that parents make so many "critical decisions in a person's life." A child's experiences in a family that usually consists of not only parents but also aunts, uncles, and grandparents shapes a self-conception that focuses on being guided by social pressures.

Seymour (1976, 1980, 1983, 1993) and Kurtz (1992) argue that from the beginning children in Indian families have multiple caretakers (see also Luschinsky 1962: 121-125; Minturn and Hitchcock [1963] 1966: 107-108).[8] In the joint families Seymour (1993: 57) studied, children are held, carried, fed, and bathed by persons other than their mothers or fathers 42% of the time. Moreover, in joint households, mothers provide only 27% of the interactions that offer positive affect (Seymour 1983: 272).

The presence of multiple caretakers, which joint-family living facilitates, leads to Indian men's focus on being cared for by the family group. Kurtz (1992: 107) argues that multiple caretakers ultimately teach children that "consistent care resides not in a relationship to any single individual" but in a relationship to all the caretakers "taken as a group." Multiple caregivers teach the child to abandon selfish desires for a mother's breast in order to join a group that will unfailingly grant requests (Kurtz 1992: 77), while providing spontaneous positive affect (Seymour 1983: 273). Kurtz (1992: 144) argues that once children understand that care is provided by a group of caretakers, they detach from their natural mothers and the "self becomes a group self." Multiple caretakers lead many Indians, then, to develop a sense that they are cared for as a group, by a group.

The Durkheimian and psychoanalytic accounts both focus on how prolonged, intense family interactions with many caretakers might lead people to develop a sense of self that focuses more on considering the demands of others than on individual autonomy. The two accounts are complementary explanations of how joint-family living might generate the ethnopsychological understandings of upper-caste, upper-middle-class, North Indian Hindu men.

JOINT-FAMILY LIVING AND HINDU MEN'S EMOTIONS

Joint-family living also shapes men's emotion culture. One reason that Hindu men emphasize a love that extends toward many in the family may be their childhood experiences with many caretakers. Kurtz (1992:

170) argues that the American notion of love as directed toward an exclusive other is the "logical outcome of the pattern of one-to-one intimacy between parent and child." Hindu infants, by contrast, are cared for by many caretakers in a family. Consequently, as Kurtz (1992: 255) argues, the adult love of most men is not for one alone, but for many in a family.

Another reason for the strength of the emotion culture which cautions of love, while embracing social fear is that these emotional paradigms correspond with structurally persistent dilemmas generated by the basic institution of joint-family living.[9] Because Hindu men must constantly work to keep the joint family from splitting, they have an elaborated paradigm describing how unbounded love between husband and wife threatens the joint family.

Men are attached to joint-family living, but the joint-family structure which subordinates young wives by making them do the most burdensome household tasks creates a persistent dilemma. Men want to live in a joint family with their parents, but they also become close to wives who often want them to separate from their parents. In developing strategies for facing this structurally persistent dilemma, men repeatedly focus on the imperative that love be tempered by social fear and be directed toward many in the family, constituting and reconstituting the dominant emotion culture. As men use these emotional paradigms to cope with the structurally persistent dilemmas they face, they bolster the joint families in which they live.

Because men are concerned with the threat that women pose to joint-family living, they often warn each other of the dangers of closeness between husband and wife, elaborating a paradigmatic scenario of a wife cultivating her husband's love in order to manipulate him. Men repeatedly remind each other that a wife may tear a family apart by seducing her husband. In answering an open-ended question about why joint families break, one-third (17/49) of the men I interviewed mention that women cause tensions that split families. Thirty-five-year-old Sunil Gupta's warning about how wives threaten a family is typical:

> When four brothers marry, four women come from four houses. They are of separate natures. They will be from separate environments. They will want to separate. They will put pressure on their husbands, saying "you should separate from the family. I do not like living in a crowd."

Rajesh Yadav similarly reiterates a cautionary tale about how fighting among women might cause a family to break:

> One woman will tell the other to cook. The other will say, "No, you cook." The first one says, "I have to go outside to do some work" and

the others say it also. They complain to their husbands. Before marriage, brothers are completely one. But after marriage, a man's wife attacks his mind. If he lives with his wife 24 hours a day, a man will never be able to understand whether it is his brother's fault or not.

Ashok Mishra says that women "see that other people have such and such clothes and eat such and such food. They create fights between brothers and talk in such a way that mutual tension is born. Without this [talk of wives] there is no tension between brothers." Men continually talk, then, about the threat that attachment to one's wife poses to the joint-family lifestyle that they value.

To insure that the love for a wife does not get the upper hand, men continually caution each other against becoming too close to their wives. They tell each other that a husband must always ignore his wife's complaints in order to protect the joint family (see chapters 2 and 5). Amrit Mishra cautions, for instance, that

> since wives have come from separate places, they cannot adjust among themselves. If we five brothers do not pay attention to their talk, then the joint family can work for a long time. But if we constantly listen to our wives' talk, then the family will not manage to run very long.

Sunil Gupta warns that "if one obeys one's wife's talk, it will create tension and fighting, and one will become separate." Arjun Gupta similarly cautions that the "family will be harmed" if the husband "listens to his wife's talk." The emotion culture which holds that love must reflect in many directions and that love between husband and wife must always be tempered by social fear arises through men's telling of cautionary tales that they hope will protect the joint family.

Men emphasize the goodness of love that reflects in many directions because this focus helps bind members of a joint family together instead of tearing them apart as might happen if there were an emphasis on exclusive love between husband and wife. Men emphasize the importance of being guided by social fear because this orientation tempers the intense passions between husband and wife that might fracture the joint family.[10]

The effects of social structures on emotions are mediated, then, through the interactions in which individuals participate (Gordon 1990: 147; Derné forthcoming b). Hindu men confront the persistent dilemma that women do not share men's attachment to joint-family living. The social structure of joint families which oppresses young wives leads many men to define the situation as one in which love is dangerous, as they imagine the scene of a wife manipulating her husband. Men's conception of love between husband and wife as dangerous if exclusive, egalitarian, or based on a special characteristic is constituted by the discourses and strategies men build around the paradigmatic scenario of a wife who has too much influence over her husband. When men like Anand Singh (chapter 5) protect the joint family by warning each other about the dangers of becoming the "slave" of their wives, they actively construct the idea that too much attachment between husband and wife is threatening. When men warn each other that the family is harmed if they listen to their wives' talk, they construct the notion that intimacy between husband and wife can prove dangerous. By using this emotion culture as a guide to action, men, in turn, bolster the joint families in which they live.

CONCLUSIONS

Culture, emotions, and family structure make each other up. Hindu men's collectivist ethnopsychology, emotion culture, and attachment to joint-family living each requires the others. The collectivist framework for understanding action requires joint-family living and a focus on social fear as exemplary and love as dangerous. Joint-family structure fosters dilemmas that lead men to see love between husband and wife as potentially dangerous. Joint-family childrearing that includes prolonged dependence, positive affect, and extensive physical closeness provided by multiple caretakers leads adult men to de-emphasize the individual and emphasize social fear. This de-emphasis on the individual and emphasis on social fear, in turn, lead men to want to live in joint families.

A focus on how men confront persistent tensions inherent in a social structure may, moreover, be a fruitful way of exploring how macro structures are reproduced on the micro level. Joint-family living continually forces men to face the persistent problem of wives who are dissatisfied with their lives in joint families. Men are active agents who develop strategies for facing this problem by emphasizing that love is dangerous if it is not tempered by social fear, or is directed too exclusively toward one's wife. This culturally constituted emotional paradigm, in turn, bolsters joint-family structure. When men see love as dangerous, they refuse to listen to their wives' complaints, reconstituting the joint-family structure that subordinates women. When men are wary of love that is not subordinate to social fear, they are careful to resist the temptation to separate from their parents, reconstituting the joint family as the arena in which men spend most of their lives. Emotions, then, may be an important link between macro structures and micro interactions, as they guide agents to take actions that bolster existing structures.

10

Conclusion

Catherine Lutz (1988) urges a focus on ethnopsychology—common-sense knowledge about mental processes and motivations. One aim of this book has been to show that a focus on social frameworks for understanding action helps us answer important questions in anthropology and sociology. In particular, a focus on these frameworks is a useful way of understanding cultural constraint.

In this conclusion, I review what this study of Hindu men's discussions of women, marriage, and family suggests about how culture works. First, consideration of men's investment in male dominance suggests that culture often reflects the efforts of privileged groups to protect their privilege. Second, consideration of culture's contrasting tendencies suggests that culture provides individuals with a diversity of languages that allow them to construct diverse actions. Third, while culture provides core contradictions, which individuals can manipulate, commonsense understandings of human motivation nevertheless constrain people and shape social life. I conclude with the tentative suggestion that ethnopsychology not only influences individuals' psyche and individual strategies of action; it may also have important effects on the macro level as well.

Cultural Ideas as a Tool of the Powerful

One of my aims has been to suggest how a focus on the interests of the powerful contributes to our understanding of the construction of gender culture. Dominant men use cultural ideas to bolster their power. They construct the meanings that are attributed to gender in their interactions with their wives, sons, daughters, daughters-in-law and male acquaintances. Men tell their wives that they may venture out only if accompanied by another family member, criticize daughters-in-law for acting too openly outside the home, and warn daughters against jeopardizing their marriage prospects and the family honor by talking with boys and laughing too much.

Men do so partly because they think that they benefit by restricting their wives to the home. Men, like Phoolchand Mishra, are pleased that when they come home from work, their wives are there to make them tea. Phoolchand Mishra, Vinod Gupta, Vikas Mishra, Anand Singh, and others fear that if women go outside the home, they might lose interest in serving their husbands within the home. Men's emphasis on how women must be restricted to protect their family's reputation are often not the result of cultural tradition, or the threat of dishonor, but are driven by men's understanding of their interests as men. Dominants' day-to-day interactions are sometimes aimed, then, at maintaining cultural ideas that bolster their power over subordinates.

THE COMPLEXITY OF INDIAN MEN'S ETHNOPSYCHOLOGY

It has long been recognized that Hindu men's commonsense understandings de-emphasize individual volition, but my research suggests that Indians often value adherence to social pressures from respected elders in a family, rather than seeing themselves as moved by hierarchy, physical substance, or the objective laws of *dharma*. Although men usually focus on how social pressures guide their decisions about family life, they also have access to the focus on *dharma* that Shweder (1991) describes, the attention to physical substances that Marriott (1989) describes, and the focus on hierarchy that Dumont ([1966] 1980) describes.

Because culture emphasizes not just core tendencies, but opposed tendencies, Indian men are often also aware of their own individual desires. While men, like Surjit Singh, often emphasize that these desires must be subordinate to the imperative of following social pressure, many men come to focus on their own desires as a guide to action. Ramesh Mishra found so much joy in being with his beloved that he married her against the initial objections of his parents. Nandu Gupta realized that he would be happier in the privacy of a small home, and separated from his family. A full one-third of the men I interviewed become close to their wives, rejecting the norm that husband-wife relations should be limited.

Ethnopsychological understandings do not constitute a unified, consistent whole. While some commonsense understandings are more familiar, elaborated, and legitimate, most people also have access to contradictory second languages with which they can understand the world.

As Hindu men resolve tensions between individual desires and family duties, they construct the commonsense understandings and emotional paradigms that this book describes. Aware that many men are pulled to their wives by individual desires, men often reiterate that love for one's wife must be subordinate to larger family interests. By repeating this concern, men construct an emotion culture in which one-to-one love is dangerous and social fear is exemplary. Similarly, men like Surjit Singh are aware that arranged marriages sometimes bring a man and woman together who are not well-suited to each other. Because men must continually confront this dilemma of arranged marriages, they justify arranged marriages by claiming that love can never be the basis of a successful marriage, that a boy's emotion is an unreliable guide to choosing a spouse, and that love marriages are never successful. As men continually repeat such talk, they constitute and reconstitute the idea that love blinds people to reason and that people should be guided by family elders. As men continually confront the tension between individual autonomy and group orientation, they engage in discourse that constitutes and reconstitutes the dominant focus on the value of group guidance and the danger of individual autonomy. This suggests that ethnopsychology and emotions may be important links between macro structures and micro interactions that reproduce those structures.

Since Hindu men's culture contains both core and conflicting values, men can use it to construct diverse actions. In constructing relations with their brothers, for instance, some men emphasize hierarchy, others emphasize equality, and others temper the focus on hierarchy with recognition that juniors should be given some autonomy. When men feel pulled toward their wives, some emphasize the imperative that the relationship between husband and wife must be limited, others deny that closeness between husband and wife threatens the joint family, and others embrace closeness with their wives, which sometimes precipitates splits from their parents.

CULTURE IN ACTION

The recognition that cultures contain contrasting tendencies is difficult to reconcile with the idea that culture powerfully constrains the lives of individuals. This book's main argument is that a focus on social frameworks for understanding action helps us understand how culture constrains.

Although most men embrace joint-family living, arranged marriages, restrictions on women outside the home, and limitations on interactions between husbands and wives, some men contest these dominant understandings. Although the collectivist framework through which action is seen as driven by the social group is the primary orientation of most Hindu men, some, like Ramesh Mishra, reject this framework. Despite this variation, informal, commonsense understandings of what determines individual actions still constrain in important ways.

The social framework for understanding action limits the strategies of action available to individuals by determining the picture individuals need to present of themselves to avoid being distrusted as someone whose actions make no sense. Because of the understanding that individual volition is threatening, Hindu men are constrained to present their actions as in accord with some social group, even as they, like Ramesh Mishra, reject important social imperatives by marrying for love.

An important constraining power of culture lies, then, not in prescriptive cultural norms, but in commonsense but nonetheless cultural descriptions of the world. Social frameworks for understanding action generate a vocabulary of legitimate action. Because of social practices that discredit those whose actions appear inconsistent with the dominant framework, even those who contest dominant understandings are constrained to use this vocabulary of legitimate action. An important constraint of culture comes, then, not from the internalization of cultural descriptions, but from the power of society apparent in practices that discredit those whose actions appear at odds with important cultural understandings.

Shaping Social Institutions and Collective Strategies for Change

I have argued that frameworks for understanding action shape self-conceptions, emotional paradigms, and the strategies individuals use to act unconventionally. How might these frameworks shape social institutions and collective strategies for change? While my work focuses on understanding cultural constraint at the individual level, it is worth speculating about how frameworks for understanding action might also influence and constrain collective strategies for change, the programs used to combat social problems, and the way social institutions work.

For instance, frameworks for understanding action may constrain not only the strategies individuals can use to buck social pressures, but also the strategies groups use to affect social change. When people are faced with conditions they want to change, the best way of doing so is not self-evident (Snow *et al.* 1986; Derné 1991). People need to choose between competing paths.

Because American men tend to focus on how people choose actions on their own based on their own calculation of what will make them

most happy, "when Americans try to get something done," as Swidler
(1986: 281) argues, "they are likely to create voluntaristic social movements" like religious revivals, reform campaigns, and voluntary local
initiatives that created much of American public schooling (see also
Bellah *et al.* 1985: 167; Varenne 1977 29-35). These strategies, Swidler
rightly notes, "rest on the cultural assumption that social groups . . .
are constituted by the voluntary choices of individuals." By contrast,
many Americans see social movements which focus on group justice as
illegitimate (Thurow 1980). Even in accomplishing collective acts, then,
Americans may be constrained by the individualistic framework for
understanding action that focuses on individual choices.

Indian social movements appear to be similarly influenced by the
Indian focus on collectivity. Lower-caste groups, for instance, often
focus on raising the status of the group (rather than the status of the
individual) by adopting upper-caste customs, asserting an elevated group
origin, embracing alternative religions like Buddhism or Islam, or cre-
ating new religious groups in which people can claim membership (Juergensmeyer 1982; Rudolph and Rudolph 1967; Berreman 1976; Srinivas
1969; Mujahid 1989). The focus on group pressure is apparent in
women's groups' tactics of boycotting offenders as a way of protesting
dowry extortions, wife-beating, and liquor sales (Manimala [1983] 1991:
126; *Manushi* 1979 [1991]: 179; *Manushi* [1981] 1991: 226). The social
movements and tactics people choose to improve their position, then,
may be shaped by whether the dominant lens through which people
understand human motivation focuses on the individual or group membership, individual choices or social pressures.

By alerting people to some aspects of human experience rather than
others, frameworks for understanding action may also influence the
political vocabularies that are effective in a particular society, and hence
the social programs used to combat social problems. Because American
policy makers needed to present old age insurance to a public that saw
the world in terms of autonomous individuals, they needed to describe
the social security system as an insurance program that everyone pays
into, rather than as a need-based safety net (Zollars and Skocpol 1990).
Because American policy makers understand individuals as choosing
actions on their own, the American system of criminal justice focuses on
altering the individual's cost-benefit calculations by punishing offenders
(rather than, for instance, developing shaming mechanisms) (Braithwaite 1989; Bayley 1976). Some American efforts at controlling pollution focus on manipulating the cost calculations of individuals and corporations by, for instance, providing credit for meeting pollution-cutting
standards to corporations that buy polluting cars from individuals (*USA*

Today 10 March 1992). To note one final example, the United States President George Bush spoke comfortably of solving the problems of American education by providing parents with "school choice." American policy makers, in other words, often confront social problems by manipulating the cost calculations individuals make. As Bellah *et al.* (1991: 61) have recently argued, this focus on the pursuit of individual advantages is often an impediment to Americans' ability to effectively understand and confront public problems.

In societies with a collectivist orientation, programs are more likely to emphasize duty to a social group. John Braithwaite (1989) has recently demonstrated, for instance, that the Japanese have effective crime control because they emphasize apology, compensation, and forgiveness, rather than punishment (see also Bayley 1976; Hartjen and Priyadarsini 1984). Braithwaite (1989: 137) similarly argues that Japanese regulatory agencies are able to change business behavior in a relatively short time because of the Japanese focus on reminding corporations of their moral responsibility to society. By contrast, Americans' "economic rationalism" of fines and tax incentives is ineffective because it lacks a moral component (Braithwaite 1989: 141-142). Similarly, the Indian focus on the social group makes state intervention a legitimate way of solving problems. Corporation malfeasance, for instance, sometimes results in calls to nationalize corporations (see for instance Rani [1983] 1991: 101). In contrast to the United States Republican Party's recent focus on "school choice," Indian courts have strictly limited competition for students by ruling that private colleges cannot charge more than what is charged in government-run colleges (*India Abroad* 21 August 1992, p. 29).

Frameworks for understanding action might also affect social institutions. For instance, business organizations might work differently where there is a focus on social pressure (Kakar [1978] 1981: 119; Roland 1988: 210; Haragopal and Prasad 1990). Roland (1988: 36) found that, because so many Indians like to be guided by superiors, Indian businesses often institutionalize the "active support, respect, and involvement of senior authority figures" in order to increase productivity. In short, frameworks for understanding action not only constrain and shape individuals, but may also affect social institutions, social movements, and social programs, as well.

APPENDIX:
FIELDWORK IN URBAN INDIA

This appendix has three aims—to provide a description of how I did my fieldwork and how I selected my respondents, to provide suggestions for future fieldworkers, and to emphasize that my ethical concerns with fieldwork were quite different from those of my respondents.

SETTLING IN

Because I had spent two months in Banāras in February and March 1986, I had a few contacts when I returned for fieldwork in the first week of November 1986. Two excellent Hindi teachers, several American scholars doing research in the city, and a number of Indian friends made my settling in relatively easy. I found a comfortable home in a Brāhmaṇ neighborhood near Assi Ghat. Assi is a closely knit, largely Brāhmaṇ residential neighborhood which is only a fifteen minute cycle rickshaw ride from the center of Banāras. I remained in Banāras until October 1987.

Some of my connections facilitated contact with respondents. The building I lived in was owned by Virabhadra Mishra, the respected *mahant* [head] of the Sankat Mochan Temple. Many of my respondents who lived in Assi chatted with me about *mahant-jī*. My association with him facilitated ease of contacts. A few other respondents associated me with Robert Thomas Wilson, an American South Asianist doing research in Banāras. Because of his facility with Hindi and his interest in the Rāmlīlā, he was a respected member of the Assi community. Respondents who knew of my associations with these respected people sometimes gave me some legitimacy as well.

RESEARCH ASSISTANTS

I was lucky to find a number of talented research assistants. In my initial enthusiasm, I hoped to get by with one research assistant. After a few months, however, I became frustrated with the assistant's occasional failure to show up for appointments, and the like. Like me, several other researchers whom I knew in Banāras also found it necessary to hire more than one research assistant if they hoped to work full time themselves.

My research assistants helped me translate interviews from Hindi to English, and assisted me in conducting interviews. While my assistants occasionally helped me with difficulties in understanding that occurred during the actual interview, the main reason for having a native speaker present was to alert me to any subtle reluctance a respondent might have about continuing the interview.

The presence of a research assistant might affect responses (Berreman 1962). Most of the interviews were conducted with the assistance of men who were relative outsiders to the Banāras upper-caste Hindu community, which probably encouraged men to discuss their unconventional views openly.

Seventy percent (34 out of 49) of the interviews were conducted with the assistance of a man who calls himself Nagendra Gandhi. Gandhi-jī has a B.A. in philosophy from a Calcutta university. He came to Banāras to study at B.H.U. in 1979. Gandhi is open-minded, and critical of some aspects of Hinduism. Gandhi's appearance indicates to others that he is an outsider. For about half of the interviews, he wore his hair long and with a beard. He joked that those who did not know him sometimes mistook him for a *sādhu* [itinerant holy man]. Those who knew him respected him as a free-thinker. Because of Gandhi's appearance and because he was an outsider without family in Banāras, his presence did not discourage the presentation of unconventional ideas. Gandhi was usually inconspicuous in interviews. He often had a number of insightful lines of inquiry at the end of the interview.

Nine interviews were conducted with the assistance of a Muslim, Parvez Khan. Parvez, also in his twenties and unmarried, was born in Banāras. He, too, usually took a minor role in interviews, but sometimes asked perceptive questions at the end of interviews. As a Muslim, Parvez was outside the Hindu community of my respondents. While my respondents might have been interested in presenting Hindu culture in a positive way, they didn't need to worry that Parvez's evaluations would harm their honor. Since both Gandhi and Parvez were relative outsiders, their presence did not represent an obstacle to the open expression of unconventional views.

Six interviews were conducted with the assistance of G. Ramchandra Pandit, an unmarried Brāhmaṇ in his thirties. Ramu has worked for undergraduate researchers in connection with the University of Wisconsin College Year in India program. Because Ramu—perhaps unknowingly—presents himself as a traditional Brāhmaṇ and an insider in Banāras, interviews conducted with Ramu's assistance might have encouraged the presentation of traditional views.

PRESENTATION OF SELF

I presented myself as a scholar. I usually wore Western slacks, a button down collar shirt, and glasses. I kept my hair short, and my face clean-shaven.

Robert Thomas Wilson (personal communication) suggests that Indians group Westerners into different castes. Indians see foreign scholars as the Brāhmaṇ caste of foreigners, government officials as the Kshatriyas, businessmen and well-off tourists as the Vaishyas, and hippie tourists as the Shūdras or untouchables. I tried to present myself as a member of the first (and perhaps most respected) group.

SELECTING RESPONDENTS

I approached men I interviewed at their place of business during business lulls and picked up a conversation that touched on my interests. Just as William Whyte (1943) found baseball a useful topic to gain entry into the world of men of an Italian slum in a city in the eastern United States, I found my facility talking about Hindi movies, the epic Rāmāyaṇa, and recent social issues useful. My talk about these topics demonstrated my inside knowledge of some parts of Hindu culture, as well as my facility with Hindi. This encouraged respondents to recognize that I was interested in them. These incipient friendships were the basis of asking about the possibility of conducting an interview.

I usually talked with a respondent a couple of times before interviewing him. I made pretty clear what sorts of topics I was interested in. This gave respondents time to think about what they might like to say. Thus, individuals did not talk about the first thing that came into their heads. In one instance, the man I interviewed thought about the topic in my presence. I had returned to interview Phoolchand Mishra at the printing press that he operated. He asked again about the questions I was interested in, and I told him. He proceeded to operate the printing press for a half-hour or so, thinking all the time. He then said that he was ready for the interview, and proceeded to speak almost without interruption for nearly an hour. I proceeded to ask questions only after this long, thoughtful presentation.

Forty-nine interviews were enough to reach saturation (Richardson 1988:211). After about fifteen interviews, I began to hear the same stories repeatedly. While the number of interviews is not big enough to fully explain differences in cultural ideas, it was large enough, I think, to exhaust most of the range of ideas.

CONDUCTING INTERVIEWS

Twenty-nine interviews were conducted in men's shops, eleven in their homes, six in tea-stalls or temple grounds, and three in my home. In most of the interviews, I had nearly complete privacy with the men I interviewed.

Interviews lasted forty minutes to more than two hours. I did follow-up interviews of a similar length with seven men.

Taping interviews was vital. First, it gave me a complete record of everything said. I did not need to make on-the-spot decisions about what was important. Second, I often missed subtleties during the interview that I picked up only when listening to the tape. Third, I noticed that men talked in more beautiful, expressive language when the tape started. They knew that I would listen to the tape later and so did not need to make as big an effort to insure that I understood every word.

No one was uncomfortable with the tape recorder once the interview had been going for a few minutes. The relative novelty of the tape recorder intrigued some. Perhaps half of my respondents asked to hear themselves on tape at the conclusion of the interview.

I did not pay respondents, but I did try to do something for them. I took photos of their family, bought something from their shop, or gave them something when I left. This sort of thing is expected in the Indian context since a relationship between people was established. I did not encounter any one who demanded things.

LANGUAGE

For this researcher, conducting interviews in a foreign language was helpful. I was very careful about every word in the interview schedule, which discouraged vagueness. More important, I often allowed momentary silences in interviews. These silences gave individuals a chance to fully present their ideas. In one test-interview conducted in English, I interrupted too often if the respondent got off track, or cut him short once I had what I thought was a clear answer. I learned from listening to interviews conducted in Hindi that one must give the respondent time to answer.

Respondents' Impressions of the Interviews

On a few occasions, men thought the questions were too personal. On a couple occasions, men commented that the interview lasted too long. Yet, most commonly, men said that they enjoyed the interviews and would like to get together to discuss the questions further. Friendships developed with a number of these men, with whom I saw movies and continued to visit regularly.

Focusing on Variation

I was very careful to tell the people I interviewed that I was interested in their ideas, not necessarily those of the society. I elicited respondents' ideas on every area of inquiry that concerned me and I did the generalization about respondents' ideas.

It was sometimes difficult to get people to talk about their own ideas. People would often tell me about "the way things are here," about "Indians generally" or about what I was or was not likely to "find very much of among Hindus." Despite this resistance, I think I was ultimately successful in getting my respondents to talk about their own ideas.

Ethical Concerns

I was careful to respect the privacy of my respondents. I have changed their names and some of their characteristics. I was also very careful not to insist that they answer questions that they did not want to answer. Here, let me note some of the issues which were problematic.

In a couple of early interviews, research assistants pressured respondents too strongly to answer questions that respondents did not want to answer. Although I had tried to impress on my assistants that our first obligation was to those we interviewed, sometimes getting the information was more important to the research assistant than respecting an individual's right to refuse to answer a question. I emphasize, then, that the researcher must go over this point repeatedly with his or her research assistants because a concern with respecting the individual's wishes not to answer a question is not necessarily an important indigenous concern.

The ethical concerns of the people being studied, moreover, may be quite different than the ethical concerns of American scholars. While American men are mostly concerned with individual rights, Indian men may be more concerned with the social acceptability of the study. Let me describe an interview to illustrate this point.

One day, Gandhi-*jī* and I were interviewing Vikas Mishra in his electrical repair shop. It was in the back of his tiny, dark workplace, and the front door was open. The space was not public—we could not be seen from the lane that the shop opened on to. But the space was not totally private either—we could be heard.

I had told Vikas that I would protect his privacy and that he could stop the interview any time he wanted. Near the end of the interview, Vikas began making political statements about government corruption and the downfall of Hindu culture. To me, these statements were innocuous. They were no more volatile than opinions voiced in the Indian press. Several people were within ear-shot, however, and were offended by Vikas's line of talk. Gandhi sensed this and insisted that we stop the interview and we did so.

From my cultural perspective, our primary obligation was to Vikas. Since he consented to the interview and was speaking freely, I thought we had met our obligations. From Gandhi's perspective, our primary obligation was to avoid offending society. Even though we had Vikas's full consent and he was speaking freely and in earnest, Gandhi felt we should stop because we were offending society. Of course, Gandhi was right. Not offending the general public is necessary for successful research.

My concern with gaining individual consent reflects my individualistic framework for understanding action. Because this individualistic framework was alien to him, Gandhi had to learn to be sensitive to these concerns. Gandhi, however, was much more sensitive than I was to the need to protect the research project's social acceptance. It was I who had to learn to be more sensitive to those sorts of concerns, which were self-evident for Gandhi given his collectivist framework for understanding action.

NOTES

CHAPTER ONE

1. See Stromberg 1986: 5, Swidler 1986, DiMaggio 1987, Clifford 1986, Keesing 1982, Geertz 1973d: 17, Obeyesekere 1981, Bailey 1983: 15.
2. Banāras, which is also spelled Benares, is also known as Vārāṇasi and Kāshī.
3. On the high population density of Banāras see Singh 1955: 38.
4. In late February 1986, a local paper reported that "the city . . . was a boiling cauldron of communal hatred through [February]. The city was battered by clashes for more than 10 days, disrupting normal life of the citizenry" (*The Pioneer* [Varanasi], 7 March 1986). In the spring of 1987, Hindu marches and strikes in support of the "liberation" of the Ram Janam Bhumi temple in Ayodhya by destroying a mosque, the Babri Masjid, were sources of communal tension (*The Pioneer*, 30 March 1987). The conflict over Ayodhya has been a continuing source of tension in Banāras as it has been throughout much of India. On the history of communal violence in the Banāras area, see Pandey 1990.
5. Whether or not a woman works outside the home is probably a family's decision rather than the independent decision of the woman herself (Kishwar [1984] 1991: 11). One man who encouraged his daughter to continue her education after she married was told by his daughter that her husband insisted that she didn't need to work outside the home:

> I told her, "In order to lessen the burden on your house and family you should [study to] become a lecturer." . . . But [my daughter] said, "My husband doesn't want that. He says that we earn enough." I insisted that if she got more education she would be able to help her family in a difficult time. But, since she kept insisting that her husband didn't want that, I stopped [trying to convince her] (see Derné 1994: 96-97).

Most men say that women should go outside the home only when their actions are aimed at benefiting the family as a whole (see chapter 2).
6. Caste Hindus consist of the Brāhmaṇ, Kshatriya, Vaishya and Shūdra *varṇa*s that are described in classical Sanskrit texts. Untouchables, the lowest group in the caste system, are not even mentioned in the sacred literature. The highest three *varṇa*s are referred to as "twice-born" castes since boys from these three *varṇa*s go through a "second birth" when they begin their religious studies and start wearing the sacred thread. Caste Hindus previously

barred Shūdra and untouchable boys from studying the sacred texts and wearing the sacred thread.

The four *varṇa* groupings corresponded to a hierarchical ranking of functions. *Varṇa* groupings defined Brāhmaṇs as priests, the intelligentsia, landlords, and bureaucrats; Kshatriyas as rulers and warriors; Vaishyas as merchants or businessmen; and Shūdras as peasant and artisan toilers whose job was to serve others. The lowest of all, untouchables, performed laborious, polluting tasks like carrying away dead animals, cleaning latrines, and toiling at the most menial agricultural labor. At a pan-Indian level the top three *varṇa*s constitute only about 15% of the population (Omvedt 1993: 9-10).

7. M.N. Srinivas (1969) first called attention to Sanskritization—the efforts of lower castes to improve their status by emulating the Brāhmaṇ style of life (Kolenda 1978: 99-100). *Ahīr*s, for instance, asserted their high status origin through a national organization, and have emulated Brāhmaṇ practices like the wearing of the sacred thread, abstinence from meat and liquor, and withdrawal of women from work in the market place (Pandey 1990: 91-93; Mandelbaum 1970: 442-445). Today, prominent *ahīr*s have achieved positions of political power in Uttar Pradesh, the state in which Banāras is located.

8. *Varṇa* describes India-wide categories, while a *jātī* is the actual caste community in a local situation. There are often several *jātī*s that represent a particular *varṇa* in any village or city.

9. One-third of the men I interviewed are in their twenties, one-third are in their thirties, and one-third are over 40. Of those over 40, there is a nearly equal distribution of men in their forties, fifties, and sixties.

10. Ten men head joint households that include their married sons. Two men whose sons remain unmarried head households that include married brothers and their wives.

11. I did not systematically select shops, banks, and post-offices from a particular area of town. I should mention that since I approached many people during the afternoon business lull when some shops are closed I may have interviewed fewer men who go home for lunch.

12. Only eight men declined to be interviewed and several of them said that they would like to be interviewed, but failed to show up for interview appointments. Another four men declined to have the interview taped. In these four instances, I conducted an abbreviated interview and took notes. There was nothing particularly unique about these four interviews, and since they were not taped, I did not include them in the analysis. (These four interviews bring the total to 53.)

13. I reflect on my fieldwork experience in the appendix.

14. The interview schedule I used appears as the second appendix to Derné 1988.

15. See, for instance, Swidler 1986, Stromberg 1986, DiMaggio 1987: 448, and Alter 1992.

16. See, for instance, Geertz [1966] 1973b, D'Andrade 1984, Douglas 1982b,

Lutz 1988, Shweder 1991, and Heelas and Lock 1981. See Derné 1994a for a review of these approaches.

17. See also Shweder and Much 1987, Berger and Luckmann 1966, Mills [1959] 1963, Dumont [1966] 1980: 6, and Derné 1994a.

18. See chapter 3, Douglas 1982b:5, Geertz 1975:5, Bellah *et al.* 1985:27, Bourdieu [1979] 1984: 424, and Fine and Sandstrom 1993: 26-27.

19. See White and Kirkpatrick 1985, Heelas and Lock 1981, Shweder 1991, Bellah *et al.* 1985, Berger and Luckmann 1966, Heritage 1984, Garfinkel 1967, and Zerubavel 1991.

20. While I could have hired a female research assistant to conduct interviews, I think that, because I am a man, women would have been unlikely to talk very frankly with me about life in their families.

21. As I show in the appendix, two of my three research assistants were also relative outsiders to the Banāras Hindu community.

22. Williams and Heikes (1993: 284) show, for instance, that American male nurses are more likely to describe gender differences as biologically inevitable when talking with a male interviewer.

CHAPTER TWO

1. *Mālik* literally translates as a head of a family or business.

2. See Liddle and Joshi 1986: Chapter 25, Kishwar [1983] 1991: 194, Omvedt 1980, Mukhopadhyay and Seymour 1994, and Sharma 1978, 1980a, 1980b.

3. This approach to culture follows Hewitt (1989: 69).

4. See chapter 6, Kishwar [1984] 1991: 11, Harlan 1992, and Jacobson 1982: 84-85.

5. See Kakar [1978] 1981: 118-110, Luschinsky 1962: 429-430, and Bennett 1983: 194.

6. See chapter 6, Jacobson 1982: 103, Luschinsky 1962, Bennett 1983, Sharma 1980a, Liddle and Joshi 1986, and Raheja and Gold 1994.

7. See chapter 6, Calman 1992, Manimala [1983] 1991, *Manushi* [1979] 1991, *Manushi* [1981] 1991, Omvedt 1980, 1993, and Raheja and Gold 1994.

8. I consider the range of women's stances to Hindu gender culture more fully in chapter 6.

9. My research confirms conflict theorists' argument that men often use ideas as weapons in their struggle to dominate women (Collins 1971: 3; 1975: 61; Hartmann 1976; Ortner and Whitehead 1981; Reskin 1988). My research suggests that a consideration of men's perceptions of their own interests as men is necessary for a full understanding of the constitution and reconstitution of a gender culture which subordinates women. This focus on the culture of male power (Nader 1974; Berreman 1981; Caplan 1985) reveals how men design their everyday talk about gender and family to be a part of the process that reproduces male privilege.

10. See, for instance, Seymour 1993: 63, Sharma 1989, Vatuk 1989, Kakar [1978] 1981, Rao and Rao 1982: 131-145, and Luschinsky 1962.

Throughout this chapter, my focus is on *men's* ideas. I do not mean to imply that women embrace joint-family living. While some studies suggest that women often find security in joint families (Jacobson 1982, for instance), others suggest that women often try to separate from joint families (Bennett 1983, for instance).

11. Twenty-nine of 41 men (71%) believe some limits must be placed on the relationship between husband and wife. Three of these 29 cite only the pressure of the husband's and wife's responsibilities and in all three cases, these men value a close relationship with their wife. Thus, 15 out of 41 (37%) men either have a close relationship with their wives or wish they could if they were free of the responsibilities of work. (I could not clearly place 8 men who refused to answer the question. Often unmarried men refuse to answer citing their lack of experience with married life, a fact I discuss in chapter 8.)

12. Of the 34 married men who discussed whether they talk with their wives, ten said that they could never talk with their wives in front of their parents. Eleven said that they could talk freely with their wives in front of their parents. Of the remaining 13, seven said that they could talk with their wives in front of their parents but only about some topics, while six said that they could not talk with their wives in front of their parents during the early years of their marriages. (I did not get a clear answer from five married men.)

13. See chapter 9, Carstairs [1957] 1967: 14, Kakar [1978] 1981: 74, Roland 1988: 231, Luschinsky 1962: 65, 342, Sharma 1980a, 1980b, and Mandelbaum 1988: 16.

14. Thirteen men explicitly reject the proposition that if a husband spends too much time with his wife he will neglect his parents. Seventeen men explicitly agree with it. Three men who don't explicitly state their agreement with this proposition mention that a husband must be careful to look after all of the relationships in the house, rather than focusing exclusively on his wife.

15. Raheja and Gold (1994: 77) describe the same metaphor in the North Indian villages they studied.

16. More than 90% of the men I interviewed mention that the ideal wife is one who remains controlled by her husband. Only two men, Bhipul Gupta and Anil Gupta, both in their sixties or seventies, see marriage as more like a partnership. I discuss the significance of these two men's age in chapter 8.

17. See Mandelbaum 1988, Kishwar [1983] 1991: 193-4, Sharma 1978, 1980a, 1980b, Carstairs 1957, Kakar [1978] 1981: 62, Luschinsky 1962: 65, and Harlan 1992: 20.

18. Eleven out of the 18 men I asked say that men do the marketing. Four say that women do the marketing, two say that children do the marketing, and one man says that vegetables are brought to the house by a vendor.

19. By adding -*jī* when talking about his mother, Sunil indicates that he honors and respects her.

20. See Sharma 1978, 1980a, 1980b, Carstairs [1957] 1967: 14, Kakar [1978]

1981: 62, Luschinsky 1962: 65, Mandelbaum 1988, and Harlan 1992: 42.

21. See Kishwar [1984] 1991: 11, Jacobson 1982: 82, 84, Sharma 1978, 1980a, 1980b, Luschinsky 1962: 338, Liddle and Joshi 1986, and Seghal 1985.

22. More than 80% of the men who cite specific examples of their behavior which could harm the family's honor cite one or more of these examples. I asked 34 men what they could do that might harm the family's honor. Thirty-one gave answers that cited specific actions. (The others said things like "any corrupt works" or "any bad works.") Eight cited theft or murder, 17 cited addiction to alcohol, marijuana or some other intoxication, and 8 cited being with prostitutes. At least one of these three things was mentioned by all but six men. Five men mentioned not obeying one's parents or elders.

23. I asked 34 men what their wives, sisters, or daughters-in-law could do that might harm the family's honor. Twenty-nine men cited specific examples. Eighteen men cited causing fighting or enmity in the house. Twelve cited talking with men. Six cited being outside of the house too much. Three men cited the failure to bring tea for the husband's guests.

24. As would be expected given the dominant framework for understanding action, many men think that the dishonorable behavior of a woman damages the honor of a husband's family (Sharma 1980a: 3; Kolenda 1993: 112). As Ashok Mishra puts it, "If my wife's behavior is bad, then my prestige [*pratishṭhā*] will be harmed."

Because they emphasize the family more than the individual, many men say that honor attaches primarily to families rather than to individuals. Gopal Mishra says, for instance, that

> individual honor [*izzat*] is not of any special importance. If I am an honest individual or do much in the society, that honor [*izzat*] is useless [*bekār*] if my parents don't get any benefit from it. But if I do things which improve the name of my mother, father, *khāndān*, and family [*parivār*], then that honor [*izzat*] is wonderful.

For Gopal, advancing individual honor without advancing family honor is pointless.

25. See, for instance, Collins 1981: 985, 1987, Bourdieu 1977, Derné 1994d, 1994b; Giddens 1984, Connell 1987: 17, 62-3, Scheff 1990.

26 Minturn (1993: 212-216) describes a similar incident in the village where she worked.

CHAPTER THREE

1. Despite the value placed on being guided by others in a joint family, joint families inevitably break. Although the separation of brothers into separate households is not a desired act, it is—especially after their parents' death—an expected one. Among the men I interviewed it is rare for brothers to continue to live together sharing one hearth when their own children

have grown. I explore breaks in joint families in chapters 5-7.

2. On urban India see Vatuk 1972: chapter 4, Rao and Rao 1982: 18-20, Gore 1968, and Standing 1991: 40. A representative sample of 1,365 undergraduate students in eight cities, including Delhi, Calcutta, Bombay, and Madras, found that 63% of the men (and 72% of the women) "want an arranged marriage" (Pathak 1994: 48, 59). Of course, as I suggest in the next three chapters, some men may want to marry for love, while knowing that they have little option but to embrace an arranged marriage.

3. While less common, men sometimes also refer to tradition to explain a young wife's subordinate position in the joint family. Shom Mishra says, for instance, that "it is a tradition that the daughter-in-law should make all arrangements for tea and breakfast before the mother-in-law rises." Although Shom says that his own daughters-in-law serve him and his wife well, he comments that these days many daughters-in-law neglect their husbands' parents:

> In today's system, the mother-in-law makes tea while the daughter-in-law is sleeping. If the wife considers it her right to sleep because she is the *mālkin*-to-be, then what will happen to the present *mālkin*? [The *mālkin*, or senior female in the family, is responsible for organizing women's work in the joint family.]

In stating his opposition to such a state of affairs, Shom refers to the importance of following Hindu tradition:

> Brother, [if the mother-in-law has to make tea for her daughter-in-law in this way], it is not superior. I wish that they would abide by the culture and the tradition as it is. There is benefit for everyone in this.

Shom's citation of tradition as a rationale for the daughter-in-law serving her mother-in-law expresses Hindu men's conception of action as guided by social dictates. A few men, moreover, even cite honor as a reason that a husband and wife must limit their mutual relations. Ramlal Mishra says, for instance, that by limiting contacts between husband and wife "the prestige [English] [of the family] will not be defamed."

4. Men similarly distrust equal relationships between brothers which are not firmly situated within a family hierarchy (Derné 1993: 182-183).

5. As Lindsey Harlan (1992: 32) notes, Hindus often see a family lineage as determining inherited character traits.

6. Richard Shweder similarly found that in explaining deviant behavior, Americans focus on the "dispositional properties of the agent," while Indians focus on the "contextual factors" that prompted the deviance. For instance in explaining why a motorcycle driver left an injured passenger at the hospital without staying to consult about the seriousness of his injury, Americans said that the driver was "irresponsible," "in a state of shock" or too "aggressive in pursuing career success," while Indians focused on the "driver's duty to be in court" (Shweder and Miller 1985: 55; Shweder 1991: 172-173).

7. See also Douglas 1982b: 5, Geertz 1975, Scheff 1990: 138-143, Bellah *et al.* 1985: 27, Bourdieu [1979] 1984: 424.

8. See Shweder and Much 1987, Berger and Luckmann 1966, Mills [1959] 1963, Geertz [1966] 1973a: 45, and Dumont [1966] 1980: 6.

9. The terminology of "languages" is Bellah *et al.*'s (1985). F.G. Bailey (1991: 214-215) similarly argues that the existence of a "predominant trend entails the existence of other contesting trends which are themselves surely included within the 'intellectual patrimony' of a 'society' or a 'given social group.'" See also Hewitt (1989).

10. While Richard Shweder found that Oriyas (East Indian Hindus) are much less likely than Americans to describe people in abstract, context-free terms, 20% of Oriyan descriptions of people are abstract and context-free. Thus, while there is a "tendency" for Indians to speak in context-dependent terms, they also have a language that recognizes individual traits (Shweder and Bourne 1982 [1991]: 146).

11. Even Shweder (Shweder and Much 1987: 227) notes, however, that his informants seek to discover what is required by *dharma* not only by examining "the historical experiences recorded in the Hindu scriptures" but also by consulting with "certain persons who have greater knowledge about the truths of moral law." It is possible that this focus on consulting elders is often the primary way Indian men evaluate what is appropriate and that the concern is more with maintenance of honor than with following the laws of *dharma*.

12. Even those who do not explicitly use religious texts often continue to focus on the religious sphere (e.g. Raheja 1988; Shweder 1991). Perhaps, as Margaret Trawick (1988: 193) argues, "scholars seeking indigenous Indian views of the world" still privilege written Sanskrit texts because they "were written by intellectual elites like us in a language akin to our own." As F.G. Bailey (1991: 213) and others (Berreman 1971) have argued, this "concentration on texts, on one or another version of a great tradition, blinds one to the culture in which people actually live: it blocks out the agency point of view."

CHAPTER FOUR

1. See Roland 1988, Kakar [1978] 1981, Hochschild 1983, Cancian 1987, Gordan 1990, Turner 1976, Shweder 1991, Trawick 1990, Lynch 1990b, Lutz 1988, Rosaldo 1980, and White and Kirkpatrick 1985.

2. In pursuing these questions I am following Ralph Turner's (1976: 991) emphasis on how "folk understandings of psychology" shape self-conceptions and Catherine Lutz's (1988) focus on how ethnopsychology influences emotional life.

3. For a fuller theoretical discussion of my argument in this section see Derné 1992a.

4. For a fuller theoretical discussion of the argument in this section, see Derné 1992a: 271-272.

5. See Derné forthcoming b, Hochschild 1983, and Lynch 1990a for reviews of these approaches.

6. I asked each man how love [*prem*] arose between a husband and wife who did not know each other.

7. Other recent ethnographic evidence also suggests the salience of social fear in North India. Sylvia Vatuk (1990: 72) describes, for instance, how the older North Indians she studied often "expect the young to display 'fear' [*ḍar*] and to 'respect them' [*izzat karnā*]. . . ." Owen Lynch's (1990c: 105) study of the Chaubes of Mathura (North India) describes an informant who spoke wistfully of previous days in which elders were "feared." I suspect that the focus on fear as an exemplary emotion is in fact common throughout North India.

8. Sylvia Vatuk (1990: 72) argues that elders' expectation that younger people will fear [*ḍar*] them is closely tied with their expectation that younger people will respect [*izzat*] them.

9. *Samāj ke ḍar* literally translates as "fear of society." When talking about their *samāj* [society], Hindi speakers often refer to any groups beyond the immediate family with which they identify themselves most closely. Often, this is their caste. I translate *samāj ke ḍar* as "social fear" to leave ambiguous which social group prompts fear. The fear/respect/love that men feel is for a society with which they feel an intimate connection.

10. On Rām līlā in Banāras see Lutgendorf 1990.

11. Nathuram uses *bhaybhīt* in addition to *ḍar* to speak of social fear. Hindi-speakers often use *bhaybhīt* to speak of a fright or terror. One Hindi-speaker told me that one felt *bhaybhīt* when one came upon a snake. But for Nathuram, *bhaybhīt* is an exemplary emotion that is combined with respectful obedience [*mānanā*], love [*prem*] and fear [*ḍar*].

12. Hindi-speakers have a range of words for love. *Pyār* and *mohabbat* are usually used to speak of the intense, passionate attachment between husband and wife or between unrelated men and women. *Sneh* and *mamtā*, which I translate as "affection," are used most often to speak of the more socially acceptable feelings of affection between parents and children. *Prem* is used equally often to speak of either sort of relationship, and *sneh*, *mohabbat*, and *pyār* can refer to either the love between husbands and wives or between parents and children. *Chāhat* [desire or longing] is another word men sometimes use to speak of love (see footnote 16 below). Hindi-speakers also often use the English word, "love." Until recently, the heroes of popular Hindi language films usually spoke of their feelings for their heroines by using the English words, "I love you." Although today filmmakers often use Hindi expressions (like "*Mai tum se pyār kartā hu*") to express love between hero and heroine, speaking of "love" by using English is still fairly common.

13. See also Averill 1985, Cancian 1987, Derné forthcoming b, Quinn 1992.

14. Some men, like Ashok Mishra, believe that recognizing a wife's special qualities indicates a discrediting "pride [*ghamaṇḍ*]."

15. Susan Seymour's description of parents' care for children similarly demonstrates a lack of emphasis on a child's special characteristics, and a focus on

spreading care within a family. Parents rarely treat a child "as an individual with special attention given to his [or her] particular feelings or needs." Instead, they treat the child "as simply one more member of the household, not the center of attention" (Seymour 1976: 788; see also Seymour 1980: 132, 1993: 55; Trawick 1990: 96; Kurtz 1992; Minturn and Hitchcock [1963] 1966: 107-112).

16. *Chāhat*, which is related to *chāhanā* [to desire or to want], usually refers to desire or longing. Love is a secondary meaning of *chāhat* and Phoolchand uses it in this sense. By referring to *chāhat* to mean love for society as well as for one's wife (see below), Phoolchand's use of *chāhat* is consistent with the emotional paradigm of exemplary love that I am describing.

17. See Carstairs [1957] 1967, Das 1976a, Hershman 1977, Mandelbaum 1988: 10, Rao and Rao 1982: 16, and Ganesh 1989.

18. Hindus throughout North India say that they need to keep their unmarried daughters from interacting with men in order to guard their virginity and protect their family's honor. After their daughters reach a particular age— which ranges from 5 to 13—the men I interviewed refuse to allow their daughters to play with boys.

19. For the men I interviewed, light skin is a sign of beauty.

20. See chapter 2, footnote 11.

21. See chapter 2, footnote 14.

22. *Lagāv* also translates as love.

23. The exemplary—dangerous dichotomy between social fear and love is ensconced in social practices. The custom of arranging marriages portrays love as dangerous by focusing on what might happen if a husband could choose his own wife. The practice of restricting women's movements outside, the home similarly helps reconstitute the idea that love is a powerful force that cannot be controlled if men and women come into contact with one another. The custom of limiting interactions between husband and wife to prevent the blossoming of dangerous love similarly helps constitute the idea of love as dangerous. The idea that love between husband and wife threatens the joint family and must be limited is similarly reconstituted whenever a father expels his son for neglecting his responsibilities or sends his daughter-in-law back to her parents' family for misbehaving.

24. See Derné forthcoming b for a discussion of emotional "scripts" (Gordan 1990: 155), "paradigms" (Averill 1985), "scenes" (Swidler forthcoming) and "scenarios" (Lutz 1988)

CHAPTER FIVE

1. There may have been some social pressure brought on Nandu to recognize that his father is the family's *mālik*. It was late in the interview when I asked Nandu if he was the *mālik* of his house. A bystander who had interrupted the interview cut in, saying that Nandu's "father is the *mālik*." It is only on this prompting that Nandu portrays his father as the *mālik*. In chap-

ter 7, I argue that Nandu is partly an innovative mimetist doing culture work that denies any separation has taken place.

2. White middle-class American men's focus on the individual's freedom and separateness similarly leads many Americans to desire limits and the security of social groups (Bellah *et al.* 1985; Hewitt 1989; Varenne 1977).

3. Other commentators have noted that Indians are often able to recognize both free will and the hand of fate (Daniel 1983; Babb 1983; Wadley and Derr 1989: 183.) Mattison Mines (1988, 1992) argues, moreover, that individualism is an important Indian value.

4. I explore the theme of this section more fully in Derné 1993.

5. On wrestling in Banāras, see Alter 1992.

6. See also chapter 3, where I describe 38-year-old Vinod Gupta's focus on compromise within the family.

7. Sometimes the focus on parental guidance in choice of a spouse is, similarly, tempered by giving the boy some sort of interview with the girl (see Vatuk 1972: 85). The four men who met their brides prior to marrying are strongly in favor of this practice. Rajendra Gupta says, for instance, that although the "traditional system is right, there is difficulty when there is force. Where the advice of the boy is taken, then there is no difficulty." Many unmarried men expect to be given a chance to see their brides. Surjit Singh says that

> I will see her. But the restriction is that you can only talk in front of other people—not alone. If I don't like the girl, then I can reject her.

Tej Gupta similarly says that his parents "will choose [my bride,] but I have the right to say 'yes' or 'no.'"

Some of the unmarried men's expectations may be unfounded. Tej Gupta's father, Arjun, says categorically that he will not allow Tej to meet the woman he will choose to be his wife:

> There is no way I will give him permission to try her. According to our *khāndān* [family lineage] and our family [*parivār*], that method cannot be used.

Given Tej's great respect for his father, it is likely Tej would settle for a chance to have a look at his bride-to-be's photograph.

8. See chapter 2, footnote 11.

9. Ethnographers report that in villages, a husband and wife should avoid and ignore each other during the daytime. They should not talk with each other in the day, and in some families a wife must veil herself in her husband's presence (Carstairs, [1957] 1967; Luschinsky 1962: 65, 342; Seymour 1983: 268; Sharma 1978, 1980a: 3-4, 1980b: 219; Mandelbaum 1988: 5).

10. All 19 of the men I asked say that they sometimes see movies with their wives. Nineteen out of the 23 men I asked say that they can move around with their wives.

11. In chapter 7, I discuss how Ramesh Mishra continues to give priority to his duties to his parents.

12. In chapter 3, I describe the helplessness Anil Gupta felt when his father and grandmother died.

13. Kurtz (1992: 214-215) argues that such anxiety is the result of the absence of the "normative, group-oriented process of Hindu development" in particular cases. A more healthy response, Kurtz (1992: 169-170) argues, is for Hindu husbands to "relate to a single wife . . . by seeing in her an embodiment of the group." He argues that husbands' "movement toward greater emotional intimacy with and exclusive interest in the wife represents not a developmental advance for which the man is unprepared but a regressive pull maturity obliges him to resist." But for many men, the pull toward a one-to-one relationship with their wives is important, if anxiety producing, and tempers men's focus on the group.

14. This section uses the anglicizations of film titles that Indian filmmakers use, rather than proper transliterations.

    Ram Teri is one of the two biggest hits of the last twenty years. On *Ram Teri*'s popularity, see Derné forthcoming c.

15. See Derné forthcoming a, c, Pfleiderer and Lutze 1985: 115-118, and Nandy 1981: 89.

16. Seven men disapproved of the father's efforts to stop the marriage, but two of these men nevertheless also insisted that the marriage could never succeed. The section concerning *Ram Teri* was open-ended, so men's responses were volunteered.

17. Of the 22 male filmgoers I interviewed in 1991, only 3 express an unqualified acceptance of love marriages. Several rely on their commonsense understanding that "a marriage could never succeed without parental consent." Others warn that boys who marry for love only take advantage of girls: "It is just one-sided," one young man says. "Boys do this behavior for amusement."

    Most of the male filmgoers I interviewed in 1991 also reject equality between husband and wife (Derné forthcoming a).

18. *Filmī Kaliyān*, August 1991, p. 74.

19. Hindi films' celebration of love may help some married men recognize an equal, loving relationship as fulfilling (Derné forthcoming a). Men who have already married according to their parents' wishes need not be concerned about the cautionary tales associated with love matches.

20. Bellah *et al.* (1985: 20-1) similarly argue that the "first language of individualism" makes it difficult for Americans to "articulat[e] the richness of their commitments" to others.

21. See also Roland 1988: 116-227, Ewing 1991: 141-142, Kakar [1982] 1990: 275, and Kurtz 1992.

22. Mattison Mines (1988: 568) similarly reports that Indians "frequently depict themselves as active agents, pursuing private goals and making personal decisions that affect the outcome of their lives."

CHAPTER SIX

1. See Jacobson 1982: 84-5, 97, Harlan 1992: 20, Minturn 1993: 96-97, Beech 1982: 117, and Sharma 1980a.
2. By focusing on women's tales of *satīmātās*, *kuldevī*s, and *bhakt*s [devotees of a deity], Harlan may have had access mostly to women's religious narratives. While her description of women's focus on protecting their husbands is one rich interpretation that women have access to, I suspect that in other settings women may try to reject the roles that constrain them. The women that Harlan (1992: 168) studied criticize other women for manipulating their husbands "for selfish ends," indicating that even true believers recognize that some women buck the roles that constrain them. While Harlan (1992: 161) describes women as "willing to perform" their duties "even if marriage is . . . torture by impalement," she also describes women as getting "what they want done 'by hook or by crook.'" Plenty of evidence from other ethnographers suggests that not all women are true believers who protect their husbands in whatever way they can.
3. In the *Rāmāyaṇa*, Sita's husband banishes her from his kingdom on the basis of a citizen's false accusations against her. Banāras is famous for its performances of Tulsi Das's 16th Century Hindi version of the *Rāmāyaṇa* (Lutgendorf 1990). Many of the men I interviewed make reading from the epic a part of their morning and evening worship. Throughout 1986 and 1987, the television version of the *Rāmāyaṇa* was popular in Banāras as it was throughout India. All seven of the men I asked could recount the outlines of the *Rāmāyaṇa* in detail. The *Rāmāyaṇa* tells of Ram's efforts to rescue his wife, Sita, from the clutches of a demon, Ravan. After Ram rescues Sita, he gives Sita a test of fire to show the world that Sita had remained faithful to him during the time she spent imprisoned in Ravan's kingdom. Gopal Mishra, who says that he always undertakes a ritual bath before watching the TV *Rāmāyaṇa*, says that Ram gave Sita the test of fire

> to show people that Sita had remained virtuous [*satītav*]. If Sita had been unpure [*apavitra*], she would have burned instantly in the fire. But Sita didn't burn. She was saved, proving the rightness of her character.

Yet, after Ram returned to his kingdom, a lowly washerman impugned Sita's character as he refused to allow his wife to return after staying out all night. According to Gopal Mishra, the washerman told his wife, "I am not a husband like Ram who will take you back when I don't know how you have spent the night." Gopal says that Ram, therefore, decided to banish Sita:

> Ram-ji thought, "although he is only a washerman, everyone is my citizen. If any citizen is making even a small allegation against me, I must remove that allegation." Therefore, he sent Sita to the jungle.

The men I interviewed see Sita as a desirable model for women precisely because she follows her husband's orders without question. Gopal Mishra says that Sita is "ideal" because her "first specialty" is being "faithful [*pativratā*]" to her husband:

> She doesn't do any thing other than what her husband has ordered. . . . Because Sita always obeyed Ram's orders, therefore all the wives of Hindustan always work only according to their husband's orders.

Amrit Mishra similarly says that Sita proves that the

> meaning of a pure [*shudh*] housewife [*grahaṇī*] is to obey her husband's orders, whether they are right or wrong. Sita-ji didn't know the crime for which her husband punished her [by sending her to the forest]. Since her father was a king, she could have gone to her father's place. But, when Ramchandra-*jī* exiled her to the forest, she went directly to that place.

4. Raheja and Gold (1994: 142) also describe North Indian women's lack of consensus about the desirability of Sita as a model for women (see also Omvedt 1993: 80).

5. The core narrative of the television *Māhabhārata* is the conflict between the Kaurava clan and the five Pandava brothers, their wife Draupadi, and their mother. The eldest Pandava brother gambles and loses each of his brothers and, finally, Draupadi herself. In the television version, Draupadi defies the order that she go the gaming house and has to be dragged in. One of the victorious Kauravas lunges toward her and pulls her *sārī*. But Draupadi's prayers prompt Lord Krishna to intervene, protecting Draupadi's honor (Mankekar 1993a: 473-475).

6. See Bennett 1983, Kakar 1981: 74, Luschinsky 1962: 332-3, Das 1976a: 9, 1988: 201.

7. See Berreman 1972: 175, Luschinsky 1962: 423-478, Mandelbaum 1988, Sharma 1978: 226, 1980a: 4-5.

8. These songs may also urge husbands to be mimetists. Raheja and Gold (1994: 133) report that while "men appear in some songs as publicly defying patrilineal dictums, they are portrayed in others as feigning, before an audience, adherence to norms concerning the priority to be placed on patrilineal solidarities rather than on intimacy and solidarity with the wife, while at the same time privately undermining them."

9. On economic struggles of women in Banāras, see *Pioneer* 1986.

10. See Calman 1992, Omvedt 1993, Shikhare 1986, and Manimala [1983] 1991: 132.

11. See Calman 1992, Omvedt 1993, Basu 1992, *Manushi* 1980, 1981, 1985, Kohli 1981, Sonal and Flavia 1982, and Manimala [1983] 1991: 126.

12. Even unapologetic rebels may, however, be influenced by the collectivist framework for understanding action (see chapter 10). Women's struggle against wife-beating, dowry, and liquor emphasize boycotting offenders

(Manimala [1983] 1991: 126; *Manushi* [1979] 1991: 179; *Manushi* [1981] 1991: 226), and many women's groups emphasize consensus in deciding what issues to pursue (Manimala [1983] 1991: 146).

13. See Roland 1988: 210-211, Béteille 1991: 19, Allen 1982: 5, Srinivas 1984: 27, and Papanek 1989.

14. I knew two people who were thrown out by their landlords for polluting a flat's kitchen by hiring a lower-caste cook.

15. Kurtz's (1992: 61) psychoanalytic study of childhood development argues that Hindu children move "away from infantile attachments to the mother . . . toward a more mature participation in the group." Kurtz (1992: 77) argues that the child sacrifices attachment to the mother in return for "the emotional sustenance of the group."

16. Nandu's focus on his own desires is at odds with the dominant framework for understanding action. He does not end up internalizing the framework that sees action as rightly driven by social pressures as his own personal orientation to understanding action.

CHAPTER SEVEN

1. On parents' concerns with daughters forming relationships with men while at college, see Derné 1994d; Mukhopadhyay 1994.

2. Raja married before Kishan, however, maintaining the usual superiority of older brother over younger.

3. See Parsons 1963: xlvii, Obeyesekere 1981: 110, Geertz [1972] 1973c: 434.

4. On the *Rāmāyaṇa* in Banāras, see Lutgendorf 1990; chapter 6, footnote 3.

5. See chapter 6, footnote 3.

6. Studies of the United States media similarly suggest that to be influential, writers and producers must tell stories and create images that make sense according to the interpretive schemes of larger cultural frames (Binder 1993: 755; Beisel 1993; Schudson 1989; Entman 1991).

7. Pragmatic true believers who want to be nurtured by larger social groups use similar explanations to minimize the psychic discomfort that accompanies a break with family duties (see Derné 1992a: 274-277).

8. Despite the Government of India's legislation outlawing dowry, a bride's parents still give dowry to the groom's family. The men I interviewed give dowry when their daughters and sisters marry, but they say that the groom's family often makes unreasonable demands (Derné 1994d). Dowry deaths— the murder of women in "accidental" cooking fires so that a family can arrange a second marriage for their son and collect a second dowry—and the mistreatment of women by their in-laws in order to extract more money from a woman's parents are widely recognized as pressing problems in India today. Dowry murder has emerged as a common rallying point for urban-based women's organizations (see Kishwar (1984) 1991: 32; Calman 1992; Omvedt 1993).

CHAPTER EIGHT

1. In the United States, young people who lack experience to guide them also rely on cultural materials, but their tool kit of cultural components contains diverse materials that they can experiment with (see Swidler forthcoming).

2. While the number of respondents is low, recall that many men were unmarried, that the parents of many men had already passed away, and that I didn't ascertain the birth order for many older men.

3. See Mandelbaum 1988: 5, Lutgendorf 1987: 573-4, Sharma 1978: 225, Shweder 1991: 163, and Kolenda 1990: 140.

4. What explains the close, sexually charged relationship between a woman and her husband's younger brother? While often describing how a woman's relationship with her *devar* is one of the few outlets for interaction in her husband's house, few anthropologists have noted why this close relationship might coincide with a woman's interests. In cultivating a relationship with her *devar*, a young woman may aim at cultivating sympathy for her plight in the household. Then, when a younger son marries, and the new bride frees the *bhābhī* from the most oppressive household chores, the eldest son's wife may hope that her *devar*'s understanding attachment to her will make him less likely to complain to his mother that his new bride's chores are unreasonably heavy. She aims to cultivate a sympathetic ally who will remember his *bhābhī* when his wife complains of her own burdens in the family. In-depth interviews with North Indian Hindu women would be necessary to establish that wives of eldest sons seek to cultivate a close relationship with their *devar*s for these reasons.

5. Two other possibilities come to mind. Those who move from village to city may be more likely to reject social roles because they are away from the watchful eyes of their families. Another reason might be that people who have moved from village to city are, by nature, innovators, having abandoned village ways to find success in the city.

6. All five men who say that they would allow their wives to work outside the home had attended college.

7. Other explanations are possible: It may be that because the college-educated need not rely as much on their parents for economic support, they are more able to afford the costs of bucking social pressures.

8. From my initial interviews, it appeared that women fighting in the home could cause a family dishonor. This seemed anomalous given the fact that such fighting is often private. To resolve this anomaly, I asked about fighting among the house's women in follow-up interviews. In the context of discussing honor—rather than discussing the proper behavior of a wife—most men did not see fighting in the home as dishonorable, noting that it would not be known to people outside of the home.

CHAPTER NINE

1. See Collins 1981, 1987, Bourdieu 1977, Giddens 1984, and Connell 1987.
2. This section modifies the argument I make in Derné 1992a. I am especially indebted to correspondence with Susan Seymour and Stanley Kurtz for improving the psychoanalytic argument. In the earlier paper (Derné 1992a), I accepted Roland's (1988) and Kakar's ([1978] 1981) psychoanalytic accounts uncritically. Seymour made me aware of ethnographic evidence that contradicts Roland's and Kakar's assumptions of maternal indulgence, and Kurtz suggested an alternative formulation.
3. Following Seymour's and Minturn's ethnographic descriptions, Kurtz (1992: 103) concludes that in India "physical indulgence in childhood" is "accompanied by a lack of maternal attention." Yet, there are several reasons to believe that boys nonetheless develop strong emotional attachments to their mothers. First, a young wife's isolated position in her husband's household gives her few other emotional outlets. Second, Indian family structure which grants a woman authority over her daughter-in-law gives women an interest in cultivating close bonds with her sons so that they will not leave the family after marrying. Third, many adult Indian men are extraordinarily devoted to their mothers (Kakar [1978] 1981; Luschinsky 1962). Men like Vikas Mishra, Raj Kumar Singh, and Ravi Mishra emphasize that ties to their mothers are what keep them living in joint-families. Gore's (1961) sample of one North Indian Hindu community found that 56% of men describe themselves as being closer to their mothers than to their wives, while only 20% described themselves as closer to their wives. Fourth, Minturn's (1993: 280-282) more recent work suggests that mothers are increasingly the primary caretakers of young children (although mothers still only report being the primary caregiver about half of the time). Her research also suggests that mothers are increasingly able to provide positive affect (Minturn 1993: 282). Seymour's and Minturn's work suggests that Carstairs, Kakar, and Roland overestimate maternal indulgence. Yet, many Indian men nonetheless develop the ties to their mothers that Kakar and Roland discovered through their clinical work.

    Even Kurtz (1992: 103) admits, moreover, that "the mother's frequent ministrations" prompt a child to have a "powerful emotional attachment to her." Yet, Kurtz (1992: 77) still emphasizes that the mother's withholding of "empathic attention or emotional mirroring" is vital to push the child away from the mother toward the group (see also Minturn and Lambert 1964: 232; Minturn 1993: 283).
4. Seymour 1971: 145, as cited by Kurtz 1992: 61. See also Seymour 1980: 129, Carstairs [1957] 1967: 64, Luschinsky 1962: 123, Minturn and Hitchcock [1963] 1966: 107-108.
5. Seymour 1975: 47, as cited by Kurtz 1992: 49. See also Kurtz 1992: 42, 49, Minturn and Hitchcock [1963] 1966, Minturn 1993: 285, Carstairs [1957] 1967: 64-67.

6. Other cross-cultural studies similarly conclude that practices like co-sleeping generate a strong sense of interdependence, and limit the awareness of independence and self reliance (Abbott 1992: 40-1).

7. The focus on how a prolonged period of maternal closeness shapes a self image that emphasizes meeting the needs of others is similar to the argument Nancy Chodorow (1978) makes about American women. Chodorow (1978) argues that because American mothers identify with their daughters, they craft a closer bond with their daughters in the earliest years than they do with their sons, who are instead treated as opposite gendered others. Girls consequently come to experience themselves as less separate than boys, and as having more permeable ego boundaries. Consequently, as Carol Gilligan (1982) has demonstrated, American women define themselves more in terms of connections to others than American men do. The similarity between the early experiences of infant Indian boys and infant American girls and the subsequent similarity of their self-conceptions supports my suggestion that infant experiences shapes self-conceptions and ethnopsychology.

Recent feminist thinking focuses on how American women are controlled by being made objects of the male gaze (Mulvey [1975] 1988). I show in chapter 3 that Indian men, like American women, see themselves in a frame. Indian men often say, for instance, that love marriages are "seen with bad eyes," or a "very hateful look." This suggests the similarity between Indian men's and American women's understandings of how social control works. Jadwin (1992) argues that because women are the object of the gaze, mimetism is a female mode of opposing social pressures. Indian men, who often see themselves as always observed, similarly must be innovative mimetists when they work to get around social norms (see chapter 7).

For other parallels between the infant experiences of American girls and north Indian Hindu boys and the self-conceptions that they develop, see Derné 1992a.

8. Even Kakar and Roland (1988:232) recognize the presence of "substitute mothers" (Kakar [1978] 1981: 80) in extended families. Both downplay their significance in their focus on the mother-infant bond.

9. For a fuller statement of the argument in this section see Derné forthcoming b. As I demonstrate there, my argument that structural realities shape emotional paradigms is indebted to the work of Catherine Lutz (1988) and Ann Swidler (forthcoming). In that article, I also consider how American and Ifaluk conceptions of love are consistent with American and Ifaluk social structure.

10. My findings appear consistent with Trawick's ground-breaking work on love in a South Indian Tamil family. Trawick (1990: 83, 94-5) describes how the people she studied believe that the love between spouses, or of a mother for her child must be "contained" and "kept within limits." Trawick (1990: 103) argues that these attempts to limit love between the closest blood relatives protects the joint family. "The great danger to a joint family,"

she says, is "that it would fracture along dividing nuclear units—each pair of spouses with their respective children. Love, which naturally . . . was given to one's own, had to be redirected across those lines. The stronger the love, the stronger the force that had to be exerted against it, to drive it outwards" (Trawick 1990: 103).

BIBLIOGRAPHY

ABBOTT, SUSAN. 1992. "Holding on and Pushing Away: Comparative Perspectives on Eastern Kentucky Child-Rearing Practice." *Ethos* 20:33-65.

ALBERT, M. ELIZABETH. 1988. "In the Interest of the Public Good?: New Questions for Feminism." Pp. 84-96 in *Community in America: The Challenge of Habits of the Heart* (Charles H. Reynolds and Ralph V. Norman, eds.) Berkeley: University of California Press.

ALLEN, MICHAEL. 1982. "Introduction: The Hindu View of Women." Pp. 1-20 in *Women in India and Nepal* (M. Allen and S.N. Mukherjee, eds.) Australia National University Monographs in South Asia.

ALTER, JOSEPH S. 1992. *The Wrestler's Body: Identity and Ideology in North India.* Berkeley: University of California Press.

APPADURAI, ARJUN. 1986. "Is Homo Hierarchicus?" *American Ethnologist* 13: 745-761.

ARCHER, MARGARET S. 1988. *Culture and Agency: The Place of Culture in Social Theory.* New York: Cambridge University Press.

ASTHANA, H.S. 1988. "Personality." Pp. 153-190 in *Psychology in India: The State-of-the-Art*, Vol. 1. *Personality and Mental Processes* (Janak Pandey, ed.) New Delhi: Sage.

AVERILL, JAMES R. 1985. "The Social Construction of Emotion: With Special Reference to Love." Pp. 89-110 in *The Social Construction of the Person* (Kenneth J. Gergen and Keith E. Davis, eds.) New York: Springer-Verlag.

BABB, LAWRENCE A. 1987. *Redemptive Encounters: Three Modern Styles in the Hindu Tradition.* Berkeley: University of California Press.

———. 1983. "Destiny and Responsibility: Karma in Popular Hinduism." Pp. 163-181 in *Karma: An Anthropological Inquiry*

(Charles F. Keyes and E. Valentine Daniel, eds.) Berkeley: University of California Press.

BAILEY, F.G. 1991. "Religion and Religiosity: Ideas and Their Use." *Contributions to Indian Sociology* (n.s.) 25: 211-232.

———. 1983. *The Tactical Uses of Passion: An Essay on Power, Reason and Reality*. Ithaca: Cornell University Press.

BARNETT, STEVE. 1976. "Coconuts and Gold: Relational Identity in a South Indian Caste." *Contributions to Indian Sociology* (n.s.) 10: 133-156.

BASHAM, A.L. 1954. *The Wonder that Was India*. New York: MacMillan.

BASSA, D.M. 1978. "From the Traditional to the Modern: Some Observations on Changes in Indian Child-Rearing and Parental Attitudes With Special Reference to Identity Formation." Pp. 333-344 in *The Child in His Family: Children and Their Parents in a Changing World* vol. 5, (E. James Anthony and Colette Chiland, eds.) New York: John Wiley.

BASU, AMRITA. 1992. *Two Faces of Protest: Contrasting Modes of Women's Activism in India*. Berkeley: University of California Press.

BAYLEY, DAVID H. 1976. *Forces of Order: Policing Modern Japan*. Berkeley: University of California Press.

BEECH, MARY HIGDON. 1982. "The Domestic Realm in the Lives of Hindu Women in Calcutta." Pp. 110-138 in *Separate Worlds: Studies of Purdah in South Asia* (Hanna Papanek and Gail Minault, eds.) Delhi: Chanakya.

BEISEL, NICOLA. 1993. "Morals Versus Art: Censorship, the Politics of Interpretation, and the Victorian Nude." *American Sociological Review* 58:145-162.

BELLAH, ROBERT N., RICHARD MADSEN, WILLIAM M. SULLIVAN, ANN SWIDLER, and STEVEN M. TIPTON. 1991. *The Good Society*. New York: Knopf.

———. 1985. *Habits of the Heart: Individualism and Commitment in American Life*. New York: Harper and Row.

BENNETT, LYNN. 1983. *Dangerous Wives and Sacred Sisters: Social and Symbolic Roles of High Caste Women in Nepal*. New York: Columbia University Press.

BERGER, PETER L., and THOMAS LUCKMANN. 1966. *The Social Construction of Reality: A Treatise in the Sociology of Knowledge*. New York: Doubleday Anchor.

BERGER, PETER L., BRIGITTE BERGER, and HANSFRIED KELLNER. 1973. *The Homeless Mind: Modernization and Consciousness*. New York: Random House.

BERREMAN, GERALD D. 1981. *The Politics of Truth*. New Delhi: South Asian Publishers.

————. 1976. "Social Mobility and Change in India's Caste Society." Pp. 294-322 in *Responses to Change: Society, Culture and Personality* (George A. DeVos, ed.) New York: D. Van Nostrand.

————. 1972. *Hindus of the Himalayas: Ethnography and Change*. Berkeley: University of California Press.

————. 1971. "The Brahmannical View of Caste." *Contributions to Indian Sociology* (n.s.) 5:18-25.

————. 1962. *Behind Many Masks: Ethnography and Impression Management in a Himalayan Village*. Reprinted in Berreman 1972, xvii-lvii.

BÉTEILLE, ANDRÉ. 1991. "The Reproduction of Inequality: Occupation, Caste, and Family." *Contributions to Indian Sociology* (n.s.) 25:3-28.

————. 1986. "Individualism and Equality." *Current Anthropology* 27:121-134.

————. [1979] 1983. "Homo Hierarchicus, Homo Equalis." In Béteille, *The Idea of Natural Inequality*. Delhi: Oxford University Press.

BILLIG, MICHAEL S. 1991. "The Marriage Squeeze on High-Caste Rajasthani Women." *Journal of Asian Studies* 50:341-360.

BINDER, AMY. 1993. "Constructing Racial Rhetoric: Media Depictions of Harm in Heavy Metal and Rap Music." *American Sociological Review* 58:753-767.

BOURDIEU, PIERRE. [1979] 1984. *Distinction: A Social Critique of the Judgement of Taste*. Translated by Richard Nice. Cambridge: Harvard University Press.

————. 1977. *Outline of a Theory of Practice*. Translated by Richard Nice. Cambridge: Cambridge University Press.

BRAITHWAITE, JOHN. 1989. *Crime, Shame and Reintegration*. Cambridge: Cambridge University Press.

BRUBAKER, ROGERS. 1985. "Rethinking Classical Sociological Theory: The Sociological Vision of Pierre Bourdieu." *Theory and Society* 14: 723-744.

CALMAN, LESLIE. 1992. *Toward Empowerment: Women and Movement Politics in India*. Bolder: Westview.

CANCIAN, FRANCESCA M. 1987. *Love in America: Gender and Self-Development*. Cambridge: Cambridge University Press.

CAPLAN, PATRICIA. 1985. *Class & Gender in India: Women and Their Organizations in a South Indian City*. London: Tavistock.

CARBAUGH, DONAL. 1988. *Talking American: Cultural Discourses on DONAHUE*. Norwood, NJ: Ablex.

CARNOY, MARTIN and HENRY M. LEVINE. 1985. *Schooling and Work in the Democratic State*. Stanford: Stanford University Press.

CARSTAIRS, G. MORRIS [1957] 1967. *The Twice Born: A Study of a Community of High-Caste Hindus*. Bloomington: Indiana University Press.

CHADHA, ADITI. 1986. "Eve-Teasing Analysed." *Hindustan Times*, 10 July 1986.

CHAFETZ, JANET SALTZMAN. 1990. *Gender Equity: An Integrated Theory of Stability and Change*. Newbury Park, CA: Sage.

CHODOROW, NANCY. 1978. *The Reproduction of Mothering*. Berkeley: University of California Press.

CLIFFORD, JAMES. 1986. "Introduction: Partial Truths." Pp. 1-26 in *Writing Culture: The Poetics and Politics of Ethnography* (James Clifford, ed.) Berkeley: University of California Press.

COLLIER, JANE FISHBURNE. 1974. "Women in Politics." Pp. 89-96 in *Woman, Culture, and Society* (Michelle Zimbalist Rosaldo and Louise Lamphere, eds.) Stanford: Stanford University Press.

COLLINS, RANDALL. 1990. "Stratification, Emotional Energy, and the Transient Emotions." Pp. 27-57 in *Research Agendas in the Sociology of Emotions* (Theodore D. Kemper, ed.) Albany: SUNY Press.

————. 1988. "The Durkheimian Tradition in Conflict Sociology." Pp.

107-128 in *Durkheimian Sociology: Cultural Studies* (Jeffrey C. Alexander, ed.) Cambridge: Cambridge University Press.

————. 1987. "Interaction Ritual Chains, Power and Property: The Micro-Macro Connection as an Empirically Based Theoretical Problem." Pp. 193-206 in *The Micro-Macro Link* (Jeffrey C. Alexander, Bernhard Giesen, Richard Munch, and Neil J. Smelser, eds.) Berkeley: University of California Press.

————. 1985. *Three Sociological Traditions*. New York: Oxford University Press.

————. 1981. "On the Microfoundation of Macrosociology." *American Journal of Sociology* 86:984-1014.

————. 1975. *Conflict Sociology: Toward an Explanatory Social Science*. New York: Academic Press.

————. 1971. "A Conflict Theory of Sexual Stratification." *Social Problems* 19:3-21.

CONNELL, R.W. 1990. "A Whole New World: Remaking Masculinity in the Context of the Environmental Movement." *Gender & Society* 4:452-478.

————. 1987. *Gender and Power: Society, The Person, and Sexual Politics*. Stanford: Stanford University Press.

D'ANDRADE, ROY G. 1984. "Cultural Meaning Systems." Pp. 88-119 in *Culture Theory: Essays on Mind, Self and Emotion* (Richard A. Shweder and Robert A. Levine, eds.) Cambridge: Cambridge University Press.

DANIEL, E. VALENTINE. 1984. *Fluid Signs: Being a Person the Tamil Way*. Berkeley: University of California Press.

DANIEL, SHERYL. 1983. "The Tool Box Approach of the Tamil to the Issues of Moral Responsibility and Human Destiny." Pp. 27-62 in *Karma: An Anthropological Inquiry* (Charles F. Keyes and E. Valentine Daniel, eds.) Berkeley: University of California Press.

DAS, VEENA. 1976a. "Masks and Faces: An Essay on Punjabi Kinship." *Contributions to Indian Sociology* (n.s.) 10:1-30.

————. 1976b. "Indian Women: Work, Power and Status." Pp. 129-145 in *Indian Women from Purdah to Modernity* (B.R. Nanda, ed.) New Delhi: Vikas.

————. 1988. "Femininity and the Orientation to the Body." Pp. 193-207 in *Socialisation, Education and Women: Explorations in Gender Identity* (K. Chanana, ed.) New Delhi: Orient Longman.

DERNE, STEVE. forthcoming a. "Popular Culture and Emotional Experiences: Rituals of Filmgoing and the Reception of Emotion Culture." *Social Perspectives on Emotion.* Vol. 3. (Carolyn Ellis and Michael G. Flaherty, eds.) Greenwich, CT: JAI Press.

————. forthcoming b. "Structural Realities, Persistent Dilemmas, and the Construction of Emotional Paradigms: Love in Three Cultures." *Social Perspectives on Emotion.* Vol. 2. (William Wentworth and John Ryan, eds.) Greenwich, CT: JAI Press.

————. forthcoming c. "Market Forces at Work: Religious Themes in Commercial Hindi Films." *Media and the Transformations of Religions in South Asia* (Lawrence A. Babb and Susan Wadley, eds.) Philadelphia: University of Pennsylvania Press.

————. 1994a. "Cultural Conceptions of Human Motivation and Their Significance for Culture Theory." Pp. 267-287 in *Sociology of Culture: Emerging Theoretical Perspectives.* (Diana Crane, ed.) Cambridge, MA: Blackwell.

————. 1994b. "Hindu Men Talk About Controlling Women: Cultural Ideas as a Tool of the Powerful." *Sociological Perspectives* 37:203-227.

————. 1994c. "Handling Ambivalence Toward 'Western' Ways: Hindi Films Construct Self, Gender, and Emotion." Forthcoming in the *International Journal of Indian Studies.* Vol. 4.

————. 1994d. "Arranging Marriages: How Fathers' Concerns Limit Women's Educational Achievements." Pp. 83-102 in *Women, Education and Family Structure in India.* (Carol Chapnick Mukhopadhyay and Susan Seymour, eds.) Boulder: Westview.

————. 1993. "Equality and Hierarchy Between Adult Brothers: Culture and Sibling Relations in North Indian Urban Joint Families. Pp. 165-189 in *Siblings in South Asia: Brothers and Sisters in Cultural Context* (Charles Nuckolls, ed.) New York: Guilford.

————. 1992a. "Beyond Institutional and Impulsive Conceptions of Self: Family Structure and the Socially Anchored Real Self." *Ethos* 20:259-288.

————. 1992b. "Commonsense Understandings as Cultural Constraint." *Contributions to Indian Sociology* (n.s.) 26:195-221.

————. 1991. "Purifying Movements and Syncretic Religious Movements: Religious Changes and the 19th Century Munda and Santal Peasant Revolts." *Man in India* 71:139-150.

————. 1990. "The Kshatriya View of Caste: A Discussion of Raheja's *Poison in the Gift.*" *Contributions to Indian Sociology* (n.s.) 24:259-263.

————. 1988. "Culture in Action: Hindu Men's Talk About Women, Marriage and Family." Ph.D. dissertation, Department of Sociology, University of California, Berkeley.

————. 1985. "Religious Movement as Rite of Passage: An Analysis of the Birsa Movement." *Contributions to Indian Sociology* (n.s.) 19:251-268.

DiMAGGIO, PAUL. 1987. "Classification in Art." *American Sociological Review* 52: 440-455.

DISSANAYAKE, WIMAL and MALTI SAHAI. 1992. *Sholay: A Cultural Reading*. New Delhi: Wiley Eastern.

DOUGLAS, MARY, ed. 1982a. *Essays in the Sociology of Perception*. London: Routledge and Kegan Paul.

————. 1982b. "Introduction to Grid/Group Analysis." Pp. 1-8 in Douglas 1982a.

————. 1966. *Purity and Danger: An Analysis of Concepts of Pollution and Taboo*. New York: Praeger.

DUMONT, LOUIS. [1966] 1980. *Homo Hierarchicus: The Caste System and Its Implications*. Translated by Mark Sainsbury, Louis Dumont, and Basia Gulati. Chicago: University of Chicago Press.

DURKHEIM, EMILE. [1893] 1933. *The Division of Labor in Society*. Translated by George Simpson. New York: The Free Press.

————. [1912] 1915. *The Elementary Forms of the Religious Life*. Translated by Joseph Ward Swain. New York: Free Press.

ENTMAN, ROBERT. 1991. "Framing U.S. Coverage of International News: Contrasts in Narratives of the KAL and Iran Air Incidents." *Journal of Communication* 41: 6-27.

ECK, DIANA L. 1983. *Banaras: City of Light*. London: Routledge and Kegan Paul.

EWING, KATHERINE P. 1991. "Can Psychoanalytic Theories Explain the Pakistani Woman?: Intrapsychic Autonomy and Interpersonal Engagement in the Extended Family." *Ethos* 19:131-160.

———. 1990. "The Illusion of Wholeness: Culture, Self, and the Experience of Inconsistency." *Ethos* 18:251-278.

FERNANDEZ, JAMES W. 1965. "Symbolic Consensus in a Fang Reformative Cult." *American Anthropologist* 67:902-929.

FESTINGER, LEON. 1957. *A Theory of Cognitive Dissonance*. Stanford: Stanford University Press.

FINE, GARY ALAN, and KENT SANDSTROM. 1993. "Ideology in Action: A Pragmatic Approach to a Contested Concept." *Sociological Theory* 11:21-38.

GANESH, KAMALA. 1989. "Seclusion of Women and the Structure of Caste." Pp. 75-96 in *Gender and the Household Domain: Social and Cultural Dimensions* (Maithreyi Krishnaraj and Karuna Chanana, eds.) New Delhi: Sage.

GARFINKEL, HAROLD. 1967. *Studies in Ethnomethodology*. Englewood Cliffs, NJ: Prentice-Hall.

GEERTZ, CLIFFORD. 1975. "Common Sense as a Cultural System." *Antioch Review* 33:5-26.

———. [1966] 1973a. "The Impact of the Concept of Culture on the Concept of Man." Pp. 33-54 in *The Interpretation of Cultures*. New York: Basic.

———. [1966] 1973b. "Person, Time, and Conduct in Bali." Pp. 360-411 in *The Interpretation of Cultures*. New York: Basic.

———. [1972] 1973c. "Deep Play: Notes on the Balinese Cockfight. Pp. 412-453 in *The Interpretation of Cultures*. New York: Basic

———. 1973d. "Thick Description: Toward an Interpretive Theory of Culture." Pp. 3-30 in *The Interpretation of Cultures*. New York: Basic

GERGEN, KENNETH J. and KEITH E. DAVIS, eds. 1985. *The Social Construction of the Person*. New York: Springer-Verlag.

GIDDENS, ANTHONY. 1984. *The Constitution of Society: Outline of a Theory of Structuration.* Berkeley: University of California Press.

GILLIGAN, CAROL. 1982. *In a Different Voice: Psychological Theory and Women's Development.* Cambridge: Harvard University Press.

GOFFMAN, ERVING. 1974. *Frame Analysis: An Essay on the Organization of Experience.* New York: Harper and Row.

————. 1971. *Relations in Public: Microstudies of the Public Order.* New York: Harper and Row.

————. 1967. *Interaction Ritual: Essays on Face-To-Face Behavior.* Garden City, New York: Doubleday Anchor.

GORDON, STEVEN L. 1990. "Social Structural Effects on Emotions." Pp. 145-179 in *Research Agendas in the Sociology of Emotions* (Thomas D. Kemper, ed.) Albany: SUNY Press.

GORE, M.S. 1978. "Changes in the Family and the Process of Socialization in India." In *The Child in His Family: Children and Their Parents in a Changing World.* Vol. 5. (E. James Anthony and Colette Chiland, eds.) New York: John Wiley.

————. 1968. *Urbanization and Family Change.* Bombay: Popular Prakashan.

————. 1961. "The Husband-Wife and Mother-Son Relationship." *Sociological Bulletin* 11:91-102.

GOVERNMENT OF INDIA. 1985. *Census of India 1981, Town Directory, Series 22: Uttar Pradesh.* Vol. X-A.

————. 1971a. *1971 Census, District Census Handbook, Series 21: Uttar Pradesh.* Vol. X-A.

————. 1971b. *1971 Census, District Census Handbook, Series 21: Uttar Pradesh.* Vol. X-B

GRAMSCI, ANTONIO. 1971. *Selection from the Prison Notebooks.* New York: International Publishers.

HANSEN, KATHRYN. 1992. *Grounds for Play: The Nautanki Theatre of North India.* Berkeley: University of California Press.

HARAGOPAL, G. and V.S. PRASAD. 1990. "Social Bases of Administrative Culture in India." *Indian Journal of Public Administration* 36: 384-397.

HARDING, VINCENT. 1988. "Toward a Darkly Radiant Vision of America's Truth: A Letter of Concern, An Invitation to Re-Creation." Pp. 67-83 in *Community in America: The Challenge of Habits of the Heart* (Charles H. Reynolds and Ralph V. Norman, eds.) Berkeley: University of California Press.

HARLAN, LINDSEY. 1992. *Religion and Rajput Women: The Ethic of Protection in Contemporary Narratives.* Berkeley: University of California Press.

HARTJEN, CLAYTON A. and S. PRIYADARSINI. 1984. *Delinquency in India: A Comparative Analysis.* New Brunswick: Rutgers University Press.

HARTMANN, HEIDI. 1976. "Capitalism, Patriarchy, and Job Segregation by Sex." *Signs* 1 (Part 2):137-169.

HAWLEY, J.S., and MARK JUERGENSMEYER. 1988. *Songs of the Saints of India.* New York: Oxford University Press.

HEELAS, PAUL. 1981a. "Introduction: Indigenous Psychologies." Pp. 3-18 in Heelas and Lock 1981.

————. 1981b. "The Model Applied: Anthropology and Indigenous Psychologies." Pp. 39-64 in Heelas and Lock 1981.

HEELAS, PAUL, and ANDREW LOCK, eds. 1981. *Indigenous Psychologies: The Anthropology of the Self.* New York: Academic Press.

HELLER, THOMAS, MORTON SOSNA, and DAVID WELLBERY, eds. 1986. *Reconstructing Individualism: Autonomy, Individuals and the Self in Western Thought.* Stanford: Stanford University Press.

HERITAGE, JOHN. 1984. *Garfinkel and Ethnomethodology.* Cambridge: Polity Press.

HERSHMAN, PAUL. 1977. "Virgin and Mother." Pp. 269-292 in *Symbols and Sentiments* (Ioan Lewis, ed.) London: Academic Press.

HEWITT, JOHN. 1989. *Dilemmas of the American Self.* Philadelphia: Temple University Press.

HOCHSCHILD, ARLIE RUSSELL. 1983. *The Managed Heart: Commercialization of Human Feeling.* Berkeley: University of California Press.

HOMANS, GEORGE C. 1964. "Bringing Men Back In." *American Sociological Review* 29:809-818.

IRIGARAY, LUCE. 1985. *This Sex Which is Not One* Translated by Catherine Porter. Ithaca: Cornell University Press.

JACOBSON, DORANNE. 1982. "Purdah and the Hindu Family in Central India." Pp. 81-109 in *Separate Worlds: Studies of Purdah in South Asia* (Hanna Papanek and Gail Minault, eds.) Delhi: Chanakya.

JADWIN, LISA. 1992. "The Seductiveness of Female Duplicity in *Vanity Fair*." *Studies in English Literature*. 32:663-687.

JAIN, MADHU. 1990. "Cinema: Return to Romance." *India Today*, 15 May 1990, pp. 62-69.

JUERGENSMEYER, MARK. 1982. *Religion as Social Vision: The Movement Against Untouchability in 20th Century Punjab*. Berkeley: University of California Press.

KAKAR, SUDHIR. [1982] 1990. *Shamans, Mystics and Doctors: A Psychological Inquiry into India and its Healing Traditions*. Delhi: Oxford University Press. [American edition: New York, Knopf, 1982].

———. 1989. *Intimate Relations: Exploring Indian Sexuality*. New Delhi: Penguin.

———. [1978] 1981. *The Inner World: A Psycho-analytic Study of Childhood and Society in India*. Delhi: Oxford University Press, Second Edition.

KANDIYOTI, DENIZ. 1988. "Bargaining With Patriarchy." *Gender & Society* 2:274-289.

KEESING, ROGER M. 1982. "Introduction." Pp. 2-43 in *Rituals of Manhood: Male Initiation in Papua New Guinea* (Gilbert H. Herdt, ed.) Berkeley: University of California Press.

KHARE, RAVINDRA S. 1984. *The Untouchable as Himself: Ideology, Identity and Pragmatism among the Lucknow Chamars*. New York: Cambridge University Press.

KHARE, VISHNU. 1985. "The *Dinman* Hindi Film Inquiry: A Summary." Pp. 139-148 in *The Hindi film: Agent and Re-agent of Cultural Change* (Beatrix Pfleiderer and Lothar Lutze, eds.) New Delhi: Manohar.

KISHWAR, MADHU. [1984] 1991. "Indian Women: The Continuing Struggle." Pp. 1-49 in *In Search of Answers: Indian Women's Voices from Manushi* (Madhu Kishwar and Ruth Vanita, eds.) New Delhi: Horizon India Books.

――――. [1983] 1991. "Denial of Fundamental Rights to Women." Pp. 191-203 in *In Search of Answers: Indian Women's Voices from Manushi* (Madhu Kishwar and Ruth Vanita, eds.) New Delhi: Horizon India Books.

KOHLI, KUSUM. 1981. "The New Savitri." *Manushi*, no. 9:20.

KOLENDA, PAULINE. 1993. "Sibling Relations and Marriage Practices: A Comparison of North, Central, and South India." Pp. 103-141 in *Siblings in South Asia: Brothers and Sisters in Cultural Context* (Charles Nuckolls, ed.) New York: Guilford.

――――. 1990. "Untouchable Chuhras Through Their Humor: 'Equalizing' Marital Kin Through Teasing, Pretence, and Farce." Pp. 116-153 in Lynch 1990b.

――――. 1987 "Marked Regional Differences in Family Structure in India." Pp. 214-288 in Kolenda, *Regional Differences in Family Structure in India*. Jaipur: Rawat.

――――. 1978. *Caste in Contemporary India: Beyond Organic Solidarity*. Menlo Park: Benjamin/Cummings.

――――. 1967. "Region, Caste, and Family Structure: A Comparative Study of The Indian 'Joint' Family." Pp. 339-396 in *Structure and Change in Indian Society* (Milton Singer and Bernard S. Cohn eds.) Chicago: Aldine.

KUMAR, NITA. 1992. *Friends, Brothers, and Informants: Fieldwork Memoirs of Banāras*. Berkeley: University of California Press.

――――. 1988. *The Artisans of Banāras: Popular Culture and Identity, 1880-1986*. Princeton: Princeton University Press.

――――. 1986. "Open Space and Free Time: Pleasure for the People of Banāras." *Contributions to Indian Sociology* 20:41-60.

KURTZ, STANLEY. 1992. *All the Mothers are One: Hindu India and the Cultural Shaping of Psychoanalysis*. New York: Columbia University Press.

LIDDLE, JOANNA. and RAMA JOSHI. 1986. *Daughters of Independence: Gender, Caste and Class in India*. New Brunswick: Rutgers University Press.

LORENZEN, DAVID N. 1987. "Traditions of Non-Caste Hinduism: The Kabir Panth." *Contributions to Indian Sociology* (n.s.) 21:263-283.

LUSCHINSKY, MILDRED STROOP. 1962. "The Life of Women in a Village of North India: A Study of Role and Status." Ph.D. dissertation, Cornell University. Ann Arbor: University Microfilms.

LUTGENDORF, PHILIP. 1990. *The Life of a Text: Performing the Ramacaritmanas of Tulsidas.* Berkeley: University of California Press.

————. 1987. "The Life of a Text: Tulsi Das' *Ramacaritmanas* in Performance." Ph.D. dissertation, Department of South Asian Languages and Civilizations, University of Chicago.

LUTZ, CATHERINE A. 1988. *Unnatural Emotions: Everyday Sentiments on a Micronesian Atoll and Their Challenge to Western Theory.* Chicago: University of Chicago Press.

LYNCH, OWEN M. 1990a. "The Social Construction of Emotion in India." Pp. 3-36 in Lynch 1990b.

————. 1990b. ed. *Divine Passions: The Social Construction of Emotion in India.* Berkeley: University of California Press.

————. 1990c. "The Mastram: Emotion and Person Among Mathura's Chaubes." Pp. 91-115 in Lynch 1990b.

MAHAR, J. MICHAEL. 1972. "Editor's Preface." *The Untouchables in Contemporary India* (J. Michael Mahar, ed.) Tucson: University of Arizona Press.

MANDELBAUM, DAVID G. 1988. *Women's Seclusion and Men's Honor: Sex Roles in North India, Bangladesh, and Pakistan.* Tucson: University of Arizona Press.

————. 1970. *Society in India.* Berkeley: University of California Press.

MANIMALA. [1983] 1991. "Women in the Bodhgaya Land Struggle." Pp. 121-148 in *In Search of Answers: Indian Women's Voices from Manushi* (Madhu Kishwar and Ruth Vanita, eds.) New Delhi: Horizon India Books.

MANKEKAR, PURNIMA. 1993a. "Television Tales and a Woman's Rage: A Nationalist Recasting of Draupadi's 'Disrobing.'" *Public Culture* 5:469-92.

————. 1993b. "National Texts and Gendered Lives: An Ethnography of Television Viewers in a North Indian City." *American Ethnologist* 20:543-563.

MANUSHI. 1985. "Is It Normal For Women to Commit Suicide: A Manushi Protest Demonstration." *Manushi*. No. 27, pp. 13-19.

————. [1981] 1991. "Why Can't We Report to Each Other: A *Manushi* Editorial." Pp. 219-226 in *In Search of Answers: Indian Women's Voices from Manushi* (Madhu Kishwar and Ruth Vanita, eds.) New Delhi: Horizon India Books.

————. 1981. "Protest Against Film." *Manushi* no. 18:19.

————. 1980. "Anti-Dowry Protests." *Manushi* no. 6:23.

————. [1979] 1991. "Women Against Dowry: A *Manushi* Report." Pp. 178-183 in *In Search of Answers: Indian Women's Voices from Manushi* (Madhu Kishwar and Ruth Vanita, eds.) New Delhi: Horizon India Books.

MARRIOTT, McKIM, ed. 1990. *India Through Hindu Categories*. New Delhi: Sage.

————. 1989. "Constructing an Indian Ethnosociology." *Contributions to Indian Sociology* (n.s.) 23:1-40. Reprinted in Marriott 1990.

————. 1976. "Hindu Transactions: Diversity Without Dualism." Pp. 109-142 in *Transaction and Meaning: Directions in the Anthropology of Exchange and Symbolic Behavior* (Bruce Kapferer, ed.) Philadelphia: Institute for the Study of Human Issues.

MARRIOTT, McKIM, and RONALD B. INDEN. 1977. "Toward an Ethnosociology of South Asian Caste Systems." Pp. 227-238 in *The New Wind: Changing Identities in South Asia* (Kenneth David, ed.) Chicago· Aldine.

MARSELLA, ANTHONY J., GEORGE A. DeVOS, and FRANCIS L.K. HSU, editors. 1985. *Culture and Self: Asian and Western Perspectives*. New York: Tavistock.

MENCHER, JOAN. 1974. "The Caste System Upside Down or the Not-So-Mysterious East." *Current Anthropology* 15:469-493.

MILLER, BARBARA D. 1981. *The Endangered Sex: Neglect of Female Children in Rural North India*. Ithaca: Cornell University Press.

MILLS, C. WRIGHT. [1959] 1963. "The Cultural Apparatus." Pp. 405-422 in *Power Politics and People: The Collected Essays of C. Wright Mills*. New York: Ballantine.

MINES, MATTISON. 1992. "Individuality and Achievement in South Indian History." *Modern Asian Studies* 26:129-156.

————. 1988. "Conceptualizing the Person: Hierarchical Society and Individual Autonomy in India." *American Anthropologist* 90:568-579.

MINES, MATTISON and VIJAYALAKSHMI GOURISHANKAR. 1990. "Leadership and Individuality in South Asia: The Case of the South Indian Big-Man." *Journal of Asian Studies* 49:761-786.

MINTURN, LEIGH. 1993. *Sita's Daughters: Coming Out of Purdah*. New York: Oxford University Press.

MINTURN, LEIGH, and JOHN T. HITCHCOCK. [1963] 1966. *The Rajputs of Khalapur, India*. New York: John Wiley.

MINTURN, LEIGH, and WILLIAM W. LAMBERT. 1964. *Mothers of Six Cultures*. New York: Wiley.

MOFFATT, MICHAEL. 1979. *An Untouchable Community in South Asia: Structure and Consensus*. Princeton, NJ: Princeton University Press.

MUJAHID, ABDUL MALIK. 1989. *Conversion to Islam: Untouchables' Strategy for Protest in India*. Chambersburg, PA: Anima.

MUKHOPADHYAY, CAROL CHAPNICK. 1994. "Family Structure and Indian Women's Participation in Science and Engineering." Pp. 103-132 in *Women, Education and Family Structure in India* (C. Mukhopadhyay and S. Seymour, eds.) Boulder: Westview.

MUKHOPADHYAY, CAROL CHAPNICK and SUSAN SEYMOUR. 1994. "Introduction and Theoretical Overview." Pp. 1-33 in *Women, Education and Family Structure in India* (C. Mukhopadhyay and S. Seymour, eds.) Boulder: Westview.

MULVEY, LAURA. [1975] 1988. "Visual Pleasure and Narrative Cinema." Pp.47-56 in *Feminism and Film Theory* (Constance Penley, ed.) New York: Routledge.

NADER, LAURA. 1974. "Up the Anthropologist: Perspectives Gained from Studying Up." Pp. 284-311 in *Reinventing Anthropology* (Dell Hymes, ed.) New York: Vintage.

NANDY, ASHIS. 1981. "The Popular Hindi Film: Ideology and First Principles." *India International Centre Quarterly* 8, no. 1:89-96.

NARAYAN, R.K. 1962. *The Man-Eater of Malgudi.* Mysore: Indian Thought Publications.

OBEYESEKERE, GANANATH. 1984. *The Cult of the Goddess Pattini.* Chicago: University of Chicago Press.

————. 1981. *Medusa's Hair: An Essay on Personal Symbols and Religious Experience.* Chicago: University of Chicago Press.

OMVEDT, GAIL. 1993. *Reinventing Revolution: New Social Movements and the Socialist Tradition in India.* Armonk, NY: M.E. Sharpe.

————. 1980. *We Will Smash This Prison: Indian Women in Struggle.* London: Zed.

ORTNER, SHERRY B; and HARRIET WHITEHEAD. 1981. "Introduction: Accounting for Sexual Meanings." Pp. 1-27 in *Sexual Meanings: The Cultural Construction of Gender and Sexuality.* (Ortner and Whitehead, eds.) Cambridge: Cambridge University Press.

PANDEY, GYANENDRA. 1990. *The Construction of Communalism in Colonial North India.* Delhi: Oxford University Press.

PAPANEK, HANNA. 1989. "Family Status-Production Work: Women's Contribution to Social Mobility and Class Differentiation." Pp. 97-116 in *Gender and the Household Domain: Social and Cultural Dimensions* (Maithreyi Krishnaraj and Karuna Chanana, eds.) New Delhi: Sage.

————. 1973. "Purdah: Separate Worlds and Symbolic Shelter." *Comparative Studies in Society and History* 15:289-325.

PARSONS, TALCOTT. 1963. "Introduction." Pp. xix-lxvii in Max Weber, *The Sociology of Religion.* Boston: Beacon.

PATHAK, RAHUL. 1994. "The New Generation." *India Today.* January 31, pp. 48-60.

PEACOCK, JAMES L. 1988. "America as a Cultural System." Pp. 37-46 in Reynolds and Norman 1988.

PFLEIDERER, BEATRIX, and LOTHAR LUTZE, eds. 1985. *The Hindi Film: Agent and Re-Agent of Change.* New Delhi: Manohar.

Pioneer [Varanasi]. Women's Body Plans Rally Against Price Hike, 7 March 1986.

QUINN, NAOMI. 1992. "How Love and Marriage Go Together: Culture as a Product of the Interaction between Inner Experience and the Outer World." Annual Meetings of the American Anthropological Association, December, San Francisco.

RAHEJA, GLORIA GOODWIN. 1988. *The Poison in the Gift: Ritual, Prestation, and the Dominant Caste in a North Indian Village.* Chicago: University of Chicago Press.

RAHEJA, GLORIA GOODWIN and ANN GRODZINS GOLD. 1994. *Listen to the Heron's Words: Reimagining Gender and Kinship in North India.* Berkeley: University of California Press.

RAMANUJAM, B.K. 1979. "Toward Maturity: Problems of Identity Seen in the Indian Clinical Setting. Pp. 37-55 in *Identity and Adulthood* (Sudhir Kakar, ed.) Delhi: Oxford University Press.

RAMANUJAN, A.K. 1989. "Is There an Indian Way of Thinking?: An Informal Essay." *Contributions to Indian Sociology* (n.s.) 23: 41-58. Reprinted in Marriott 1990.

RANI, PRABHA. [1983] 1991. "Women and Water Shortage in Tamil Nadu." Pp. 94-103 in *In Search of Answers: Indian Women's Voices from Manushi* (Madhu Kishwar and Ruth Vanita, eds.) New Delhi: Horizon India Books.

RAO, V.V. PRAKASA, and V. NANDINI RAO. 1982. *Marriage, the Family, and Women in India.* New Delhi: Heritage.

RESKIN, BARBARA. 1988. "Bringing the Men Back In: Sex Differentiation and the Devaluation of Women's Work." *Gender & Society* 2:58-81.

REYNOLDS, CHARLES H., and RALPH V. NORMAN, eds. 1988. *Community in America: The Challenge of Habits of the Heart.* Berkeley: University of California Press

RICHARDSON, LAUREL. 1988. "Secrecy and Status: The Social Construction of Forbidden Relationships." *American Sociological Review* 53:2, 209-219.

ROLAND, ALAN. 1988. *In Search of Self in India and Japan: Toward a Cross-Cultural Psychology.* Princeton: Princeton University Press.

ROSALDO, Michelle Z. 1980. *Knowledge and Passion: Ilongot Notions of Self and Social Life*. Cambridge: Cambridge University Press.

RUDOLPH, LLOYD I., and SUSANNE H. RUDOLPH. 1967. *The Modernity of Tradition: Political Development in India*. Chicago: University of Chicago Press.

SCHEFF, THOMAS J. 1990. *Microsociology: Discourse, Emotion, and Social Structure*. Chicago: University of Chicago Press.

SCHNEIDER, DAVID. 1976. "Notes Toward a Theory of Culture." Pp. 197-220 in *Meaning in Anthropology* (Keith Basso and Henry Selby, eds.) Albuquerque: University of New Mexico Press.

SCHUDSON, MICHAEL. 1989. "How Culture Works: Perspectives from Media Studies on the Effects of Symbols." *Theory and Society* 18:153-180.

SCOTT, JAMES C. 1990. *Domination and the Arts of Resistance: Hidden Transcripts*. New Haven: Yale University Press.

SEGHAL, CHARU. 1985. "Handicapped—By Gender or by Men's Attitudes," *Manushi*, no. 29:21-22.

SEYMOUR, SUSAN. 1993. "Sociocultural Contexts: Examining Sibling Roles in South Asia." Pp. 71-101 in *Siblings in South Asia: Brothers and Sisters in Cultural Context* (Charles Nuckolls, ed.) New York: Guilford.

———. 1983. "Household Structure and Status and Expressions of Affect in India." *Ethos* 11:263-277.

———. 1980. "Patterns of Childrearing in a Changing Indian Town." Pp. 121-154 in *The Transformation of a Sacred Town: Bhubaneswar, India* (Susan Seymour, ed.) Boulder: Westview Press.

———. 1976. "Caste/Class and Child-Rearing in a Changing Indian Town." *American Ethnologist* 3:783-796.

———. 1975. "Child Rearing in India: A Case Study in Change and Modernization." Pp. 1-58 in *Socialization and Communication in Primary Groups* (T.R. Williams, ed.) The Hague: Mouton.

———. 1971. "Patterns of Child Rearing in a Changing Indian Town." Ph.D. dissertation, Harvard University.

SHAH, A.M. 1973. *The Household Dimension of the Family in India.* New Delhi: Orient Longman.

SHARMA, K.L. 1991. "You Don't Know What You Are Missing." *Woman's Era* May (Second), 36-37.

SHARMA, URSULA. 1989. "Studying the Household: Individuation and Values." Pp. 35-54 in *Society from the Inside Out: Anthropological Perspectives on the South Asian Household* (John N. Gray and David J. Mearns, ed.) New Delhi: Sage.

————. 1980a. *Women, Work and Property in North-West India.* London: Tavistock.

————. 1980b. "Purdah and Public Space." Pp. 213-239 in *Women in Contemporary India and South Asia* (Alfred de Souza, ed.) New Delhi: Manohar.

————. 1978. "Women and Their Affines: The Veil as Symbol of Separation." *Man* (n.s.) 13:218-233.

SHIKHARE, DILIP. 1986. "Women Demolish Liquor Shops," *Manushi* no. 34:33.

SHWEDER, RICHARD A. 1991. *Thinking Through Cultures: Expeditions in Cultural Psychology.* Cambridge: Harvard University Press.

————. 1990. "Cultural Psychology: What Is It?" In *Cultural Psychology: Essays on Comparative Human Development* (James W. Stigler, Richard A. Shweder and Gilbert Herdt, eds.) Cambridge: Cambridge University Press. As reprinted in Shweder 1991, pp. 73-110.

————. 1985. "Menstrual Pollution, Soul Loss, and the Comparative Study of Emotions." In *Culture and Depression* (Arthur Kleinman and Byron J. Good, eds.) Berkeley: University of California Press. As Reprinted in Shweder 1991, pp. 241-265.

SHWEDER, RICHARD A. and EDMUND J. BOURNE. [1982] 1991. "Does the Concept of the Person Vary Cross-Culturally?" In *Cultural Conceptions of Mental Health and Therapy* (Anthony J. Marsella and Geoffrey M. White, eds.) Kluwer Academic Publishers. As reprinted in Shweder 1991, pp. 113-155.

SHWEDER, RICHARD A. and ROBERT LEVINE, eds. 1984. *Culture Theory.* Cambridge: Cambridge University Press.

SHWEDER, RICHARD A., MANAMOHAN MAHAPATRA, and
    JOAN G. MILLER. 1987. "Culture and Moral Development." Pp.
    1-83 in *The Emergence of Morality in Young Children* (Jerome
    Kagan and Sharon Lamb, eds.) Chicago: University of Chicago
    Press. (Reprinted in Stigler *et al.*, 1990.)

SHWEDER, RICHARD A. and JOAN G. MILLER. 1985. "The Social
    Construction of the Person: How is it Possible?" Pp. 41-69 in *The
    Social Construction of the Person*, (Kenneth J. Gergen and Keith
    E. Davis, eds.) New York: Springer-Verlag. (Reprinted in
    Shweder, 1991.)

SHWEDER, RICHARD A. and NANCY C. MUCH. 1987. "Determi-
    nations of Meaning: Discourse and Moral Socialization." Pp. 197-
    242 in *Moral Development Through Social Interaction*, (William
    W. Kurtines and Jacob Gewirtz, eds.) New York: John Wiley.
    (Reprinted in Shweder, 1991.)

SINGH, R.L. 1955. *Banāras: A Study in Social Geography*. Banāras:
    Nand Kishore and Bros.

SNOW, DAVID A., E. BURKE ROCHFORD Jr., STEVEN K. WOR-
    DEN, and ROBERT D. BENFORD. 1986. "Frame Alignment
    Processes, Micromobilization and Movement Participation."
    American Sociological Review 51:464-481.

SONAL and FLAVIA. 1982. "Reclaiming Women's Compartments,"
    Manushi, November-December 1982, pp. 19-21.

SRINIVAS, M.N. 1984. *Some Reflections on Dowry*. Delhi: Oxford
    University Press.

———. 1969. *Social Change in Modern India*. Berkeley: University of
    California Press.

STACK, CAROL B. 1974. *All Our Kin: Strategies for Survival in a
    Black Community*. New York: Harper and Row.

STANDING, HILARY. 1991. *Dependence and Autonomy: Women's
    Employment and the Family in Calcutta*. New York: Routledge.

STEARNS, PETER N. 1989. *Jealousy: The Evolution of an Emotion in
    American History*. New York: New York University Press.

STIGLER, JAMES W., RICHARD A. SHWEDER, and GILBERT
    HERDT, editors. 1990. *Cultural Psychology: Essays on Compara-
    tive Human Development*. Cambridge: Cambridge University Press.

STROMBERG, PETER G. 1991. "Symbols into Experience: A Case Study in the Generation of Commitment." *Ethos* 19:102-126.

———. 1986. *Symbols of Community: The Cultural System of a Swedish Church.* Tucson: University of Arizona Press.

———. 1985. "The Impression Point: Synthesis of Symbol and Self." *Ethos* 13:56-74.

———. 1981. "Consensus and Variation in the Interpretation of Religious Symbolism: A Swedish Example." *American Ethnologist* 8:544-599.

SWIDLER, ANN. forthcoming. *Talk of Love: How Americans Use Their Culture.* Chicago: University of Chicago Press.

———. 1986. "Culture in Action: Symbols and Strategies." *American Sociological Review* 51:273-286.

———. 1980. "Love and Adulthood in American Culture." Pp. 120-147 in *Themes of Work and Love in Adulthood* (Neil Smelser and Erik Erikson, eds.) Cambridge: Harvard University Press.

THUROW, LESTER. 1980. *The Zero-Sum Society: Distribution and the Possibilities for Economic Change.* New York: Basic.

TRAWICK, MARGARET. 1990. *Notes on Love in a Tamil Family.* Berkeley: University of California Press.

———. 1988. "Spirits and Voices in Tamil Song." *American Ethnologist* 15: 193-215.

TURNER, RALPH. 1976. "The Real Self: From Institution to Impulse." *American Journal of Sociology* 81:989-1016.

TURNER, VICTOR W. 1969. *The Ritual Process: Structure and Anti-Structure.* New York: Aldine.

TYAGI, SANGEETA. 1993. "Counternarrative Strategies: An Analysis of Women's Folk Songs in Northern India." Paper presented at the Annual Meetings of the Eastern Sociological Society, Boston.

VARENNE, HERVE. 1977. *Americans Together: Structured Diversity in a Midwestern Town.* New York: Teachers College Press.

VATUK, SYLVIA. 1990. "'To Be a Burden on Others': Dependency Anxiety Among the Elderly in India." Pp. 64-88 in Lynch 1990b.

———. 1989. "Making New Homes in the City: Urbanization and the

Contemporary Indian Family." Pp. 187-202 in *Contemporary Indian Tradition* (Carla M. Borden, ed.) Washington: Smithsonian Institute Press.

————. 1972. *Kinship and Urbanization: White Collar Migrants in North India*. Berkeley: University of California Press.

WADLEY, SUSAN. 1983. "*Vrats*: Transformers of Destiny." Pp. 147-160 in *Karma: An Anthropological Inquiry* (Charles F. Keyes and E. Valentine Daniel, eds.) Berkeley: University of California Press.

WADLEY, SUSAN and BRUCE W. DERR. 1989. "Eating Sins in Karimpur." *Contributions to Indian Sociology* (n.s.) 23:131-148. Reprinted in Marriott, 1990.

WEBER, MAX. 1949. *The Methodology of the Social Sciences*. Translated by Edward A. Shils and Henry A. Finch. New York: Free Press.

WEIS, LOIS. 1985. *Between Two Worlds: Black Students in an Urban Community College*. Boston: Routledge and Kegan Paul.

WHITE, GEOFFREY, and JOHN KIRKPATRICK, eds. 1985. *Person, Self, and Experience: Exploring Pacific Ethnopsychologies*. Berkeley: University of California Press.

WHITING, BEATRICE B., and JOHN W. M. WHITING. 1975. *Children of Six Cultures: A Psycho-Cultural Analysis*. Cambridge: Harvard University Press.

WHYTE, WILLIAM FOOTE. 1943. *Street Corner Society: The Social Structure of an Italian Slum*. Chicago: University of Chicago Press.

WILLIAMS, CHRISTINE L. and E. JOEL HEIKES. 1993. "The Importance of Researcher's Gender in the In-Depth Interview: Evidence from Two Case Studies of Male Nurses." *Gender & Society* 7:280-291.

ZERUBAVEL, EVIATAR. 1991. *The Fine Line: Making Distinctions in Everyday Life*. New York: Free Press.

ZOLLARS, CHERYL and THEDA SKOCPOL. 1990. "Cultural Myth-making as a Policy Tool: The Social Security Board's Definition of Individualism." Paper presented at the Annual Meetings of the American Sociological Association, Washington, D.C.

INDEX

Aashiqui, 99, 100
advice columns, 102
affect. *See* emotion.
age: of respondents, 5, 182n.9; and family authority, 42-43, 85, 86, 145-146, 194n.2; and focus on the individual, 159; and restrictions on husband-wife interactions 142, 143; and restrictions on women's movements outside the home, 25; and women's household labor, 21-22; as culturally empowering experience, 45-46, 53, 142-146
agency point of view, 64
ahir (caste), 5, 182n.7
alcohol, 70, 71, 77, 108, 113, 153, 172, 185n.22
alliances between families, 114-115
Alter, Joseph, 92
anger, 39, 47, 75, 85
arranged marriages: prevalence of, 45; and collectivist framework for understanding action, 45-46; and male dominance, 19; and men's emotion culture, 170, 189n.23; as dependent on family honor, 114, 120; as driven by honor, 49-50; as driven by tradition, 49-50; as prompted by social fear, 73; attitudes toward, x, 8, 19, 45-46, 52, 68, 78-80, 118, 122, 129, 186n.2; inherent tensions in practice of, 169; groom's input into match, 190n.7; success of guaranteed by family pressure, 52, 79-80; success of guaranteed by parents' experience, 78, 145. *See also* love marriages.

authentic self. *See* real self.
Ayurvedic medicine, 65

Bachchan, Amitabh, 96
Bailey, F. G., 64, 187n.9, 187n.12
Banaras (city), 3, 181nn.4,5
Banaras Hindu University, 43, 122, 176
barat (wedding procession), 127-128
Bellah, Robert N., 55, 187n.9
Benares. *See* Banaras.
Bennett, Lynn, 33, 36, 111
Berger, Peter, viii
Béteille, André, 87
bhabhi-devar relations, 33, 129, 147-148, 195n.4
bhakti, 87
bhaybhit, 188n.11
Bhubaneshwar, 63
birth order: and husband-wife interactions, 142, 146-147
boycotts, 52, 58-59, 99, 114, 139, 172, 194n.14
brahman (caste), 4-5, 181-182nn.6-7
Braithwaite, John, 173
breast-feeding, 161
brothers, relations between, 84-85, 88-89, 94, 133, 165, 170, 186n.4, 194n.2
Bush, George, 173
businesses, 173

Cancian, Francesca, 71
Carstairs, G. Morris, 160
caste: as forming group identity, 47-48, 54; and women's wage labor, 54; in Banaras, 3; in India, 4-5, 181-182n.6; movements protest-